Praise for the documentary *Cowspiracy*

"*Cowspiracy* may be the most important film made to inspire saving the planet."
— Louie Psihoyos, Oscar-winning director of *The Cove*

"A documentary that will rock and inspire the environmental movement."
— Darren Aronofsky, director of *Noah* and *Black Swan*

"★ ★ ★ ★ ★! A fresh take. Few films are brave enough to
tackle a topic this controversial."
— Examiner.com

"[Kip Andersen] pulls no punches and makes no apologies: 'The future of our
planet is being destroyed by this industry.' Hard to argue with the data."
— *The Huffington Post*

"Producers Kip Andersen and Keegan Kuhn have teamed up
to do what *Blackfish* is currently doing to Sea World."
— James McWilliams, journalist and author of *The Modern Savage* and *Just Food*

"*Cowspiracy* really makes one connect the dots. It's an undeniable,
statistical tour-de-force!"
— Shaun Monson, director of *Earthlings*

"I hope that every single person on Earth sees this critical documentary."
— Julieanna Hever, dietician and author of *The Vegiterranean Diet*
and *The Complete Idiot's Guide to Plant-Based Nutrition*

THE
SUSTAINABILITY
SECRET

THE SUSTAINABILITY SECRET

RETHINKING OUR DIET
TO TRANSFORM THE WORLD

By KIP ANDERSEN and KEEGAN KUHN

Introduction by CHRIS HEDGES

EARTH AWARE
EDITIONS
San Rafael, California

EARTH AWARE
EDITIONS

PO Box 3088
San Rafael, CA 94912
www.mandalaeartheditions.com

Find us on Facebook: www.facebook.com/MandalaEarth
Follow us on Twitter: @mandalaearth

Library of Congress Cataloging-in-Publication Data available.

ISBN: 978-1-60887-657-0

PUBLISHER: Raoul Goff
CO-PUBLISHER: Michael Madden
ACQUISITIONS MANAGER: Robbie Schmidt
ART DIRECTOR: Chrissy Kwasnik
DESIGNER: Jon Glick
EXECUTIVE EDITOR: Vanessa Lopez
PROJECT EDITOR: Courtney Andersson
PRODUCTION EDITOR: Rachel Anderson
PRODUCTION MANAGER: Anna Wan

Every effort has been made to correctly attribute all material reproduced in this book and to ensure the accuracy of the information contained in the text. If any error has been made unwittingly, we will be happy to correct it in future editions.

ROOTS of PEACE   REPLANTED PAPER

Insight Editions, in association with Roots of Peace, will plant two trees for each tree used in the manufacturing of this book. Roots of Peace is an internationally renowned humanitarian organization dedicated to eradicating land mines worldwide and converting war-torn lands into productive farms and wildlife habitats. Roots of Peace will plant two million fruit and nut trees in Afghanistan and provide farmers there with the skills and support necessary for sustainable land use.

Manufactured on FSC certified 10% PCW recycled paper and with plant-based inks in the United States by Insight Editions.

11 10 9 8 7 6 5 4 3 2

Dedicated to those who speak up for truth and justice for the planet, for the animals, and for all of humanity working together toward a thriving future.

CONTENTS

ACKNOWLEDGMENTS

We would like to thank: first and foremost, Eunice Wong, for without her incredible talent, her dedication to truth, and her tireless work for justice on every level, this book would not have been possible; our dear friend Greg Anzalone, for his continued support and for his belief in this project; Courtney Andersson, for her patience and understanding with us through this whole process; and Dr. Richard Oppenlander, for his extensive research and advice on the topic.

THE
SUSTAINABILITY
SECRET

INTRODUCTION

I grew up in Schoharie, a small dairy town in upstate New York. I played in the fields and pastures. I have deep respect for the life of dairy farmers. They usually begin work before dawn and are only finished after dusk. They love their farms. And they were often kind and welcoming to us children.

Not once as I was growing up did anyone around me question the consumption of meat and dairy products. We were told we had to drink milk and eat eggs and meat to be strong and healthy. I believed this universal mantra. This was unusual, as I questioned, even at a young age, nearly everything told to me by figures of authority.

I left the United States in 1983 to cover the wars in El Salvador and Nicaragua for five years. I would spend two decades as a foreign correspondent, most of them for the *New York Times*, for whom I was the Middle East Bureau Chief and the Balkan Bureau Chief. During those two decades, the faltering democracy of the United States was effectively snuffed out. We underwent what the Canadian philosopher John Ralston Saul calls a "coup d'état in slow motion." The liberal institutions that once made incremental and piecemeal reform possible, including the liberal wing of the Democratic Party and the press, surrendered to corporate power and corporate money. We devolved into what the political philosopher Sheldon Wolin calls a system of "inverted totalitarianism."

Inverted totalitarianism is different from classical forms of totalitarianism, such as fascism or communism, Wolin writes in *Democracy Incorporated: Managed Democracy and the Specter of Inverted Totalitarianism*. It does not revolve around a demagogue or charismatic leader. Rather, it finds its expression in the anonymity of the corporate state. The corporate forces behind inverted totalitarianism do not, as classical totalitarian movements do, replace decaying structures with a new, revolutionary structure. They purport to honor electoral politics, the Constitution, the three branches of government, and the iconography and language of American patriotism. But internally they seize the levers of power to render the citizen impotent. Politics is empty theater, a form of legalized bribery. Money has replaced the vote. There is no national institution left in the United States, Wolin points out, that can accurately be described as democratic.

Liberals, socialists, trade unionists, independent journalists, and intellectuals, many of whom were once important voices in our society, have been marginalized, silenced, or pushed out of corporate-controlled academia, the media, and corporate-funded political parties. The uniformity of opinion is reinforced by the skillfully orchestrated mass emotions of nationalism and patriotism, which paint all dissidents as "soft" or "unpatriotic."

The civic, patriotic, and political language we use to describe ourselves remains unchanged. We pay fealty to the same national symbols and iconography. We find our collective identity in the same national myths. We continue to deify the founding fathers and our "liberties." But the America we celebrate is a fiction. It does not exist. Our government and judiciary have no real sovereignty. Our press provides diversion, not information. Our wholesale security and surveillance apparatus, which ensures that we are the most watched, photographed, eavesdropped on, and monitored population in human history, keeps us domesticated and fearful.

I have battled this corporate leviathan for more than a decade through public lectures and in books such as *American Fascists: The Christian Right and the War on America*; *Death of the Liberal Class*; *Empire of Illusion: The End of Literacy and the Triumph of Spectacle*; *Days of Destruction, Days of Revolt*, which I wrote with the cartoonist Joe Sacco; and *Wages of Rebellion: The Moral Imperative of Revolt*. I had thought I understood most of the inner workings of corporate power. But I was mistaken. There was one huge hole I had missed.

It was only when my wife, Eunice Wong, took me to see *Cowspiracy*, the documentary by Kip Andersen and Keegan Kuhn, that I fully understood how severe the damage the animal agriculture industry has done to our democracy, as well as to our health and our environment. My attitude toward becoming a vegan before seeing the film was similar to Augustine's attitude toward becoming celibate: "God grant me abstinence, but not yet." For many years I had been "mostly" a vegetarian, although I would occasionally eat fish and at times chicken and meat. I did not even consider avoiding dairy and eggs. Diet seemed a triviality in the face of the surveillance state, the dismantling of our democracy, the endless imperial war, the rise of a global neo-feudalism, and the pressing danger of global warming.

The film documents the cascading, domino-like impact of animal agriculture on the global ecosystem. I realized when I saw it that the animal agriculture industry was one of the most important forces in the corporate strangulation of the common good. And I kicked myself for missing this.

The refusal by major environmental organizations, including Greenpeace, 350.org, and the Sierra Club, to confront the animal agricultural business is a window into how even the activist community has surrendered to corporate power. Politicians, bought off by agro-business money, of course, will not advocate for a diet that can have a massive impact on reversing global warming anymore than they will revoke the subsidies the state provides to the fossil fuel industry. The media, which depends on advertising dollars from the animal agriculture industry, is not going to tell us the truth about what this industry is doing to the planet, anymore than it will challenge the weapons manufacturers that bleed the country of one trillion dollars a year and also advertise. And for those few intrepid souls who dare to speak out, the government—read agro-business lobbyists—has passed draconian ag-gag laws that make it a crime to speak, or show, the truth about animal agriculture.

There are some 70 billion land animals raised and killed for food every year across the planet. There are 7 billion humans on the earth. Animal agriculture is responsible for producing more greenhouse gas emissions annually than what is created by powering all worldwide transportation combined—cars, trucks, trains, ships, and planes. Depending on the study one looks at, livestock and their waste and flatulence account for up to 32 billion tons of carbon dioxide per year, or 51 percent of all worldwide greenhouse gas emissions. Livestock also causes 53 percent of all emissions of nitrous oxide, a greenhouse gas with 298 times the warming potential of carbon dioxide. Crops grown for livestock feed consume 56 percent of the water used in the United States. Livestock consumed 80 percent of the world's yearly soy crop, and most of this soy is grown on cleared lands that were once tropical rain forests. All this is taking place as an estimated 3 million children across the planet die each year from starvation, and as hunger and malnutrition affect an additional 1 billion people. In the United States, 70 percent of the grain we grow goes to feed livestock raised for consumption. Given what lies ahead as global warming ravages the ecosystem, the failure to curb the destruction wrought by the animal agriculture industry, especially as droughts plague huge swaths of the globe, is collective insanity.

The natural resources used to produce even minimal amounts of animal products are staggering—one thousand gallons of water to produce one gallon of milk, for example. Add to this the massive clear-cutting and other destruction of forests—especially in the

Amazon, where the production of livestock has been responsible for up to 91 percent of the loss of the rain forest and savannah, and we find ourselves lethally despoiling the lungs of the earth largely for the benefit of the animal agriculture industry. Our forests, especially our rain forests, absorb carbon dioxide from the atmosphere and exchange it for oxygen. Killing the forests is a death sentence for the planet. Yet land devoted exclusively to raising livestock represents 45 percent of the earth's ice-free land mass. All this does not include the assault on the oceans, where three-quarters of the world's primary fisheries have been overexploited, and vast parts of the seas are in danger of becoming dead zones. Major environmental organizations, the media, schools, and politicians keep this vital information from us. It is kept from us to protect the massive corporate profits flowing into the animal agriculture industry. This is why the public is taught—falsely—that consuming animal protein is a necessity. It is why we are told to recycle and switch to compact fluorescent lightbulbs. It is why we are told to conserve water. It is why we are told to bike or drive a hybrid car. None of these adjustments, all presented as some kind of response to the climate crisis, come close to the immense effects for good we can have on our environment, not to mention our health, by becoming vegan. The truth, and a rational response to a global crisis, has been sacrificed for greed.

Timothy Pachirat, who spent almost six months working undercover in a Nebraska slaughterhouse, writes in his book, *Every Twelve Seconds: Industrialized Slaughter and the Politics of Sight*, "In all political processes where the unacceptable must be rendered acceptable, where the morally and physically disgusting must be made digestible, fabrication departments—literal and allegorical—perform a dual work of construction and manufacture and of framing, forgery, and the invention of legends and lies."

This is true whether it is the culture of war, the corruption of electoral politics, or the broken systems of brutality and environmental devastation that produce our food.

I interviewed Keegan and Kip by phone after seeing *Cowspiracy*.

"Hiding the animals, hiding the farms, hiding the entire issue is a marketing tool that is used by the [animal agriculture] industry," Keegan told me. "Their attitude is, if you can't see it, it's not there. There are upwards of 10 billion farm animals slaughtered every year in the United States. But where are these 10 billion animals? We live in a country with 320 million humans. We see humans everywhere. But where are these billions of animals? They are hidden away in sheds. It allows the industry to carry out these atrocities, whether it's how they treat the animals or how they treat the environment."

We are kept blind. This is by design.

One vegan saves more than 1,100 gallons of water, 30 square feet of forest, 45 pounds of grain, the equivalent of 20 pounds of carbon dioxide, and one animal's life—every day. And becoming a vegan is something we can do immediately. We must refuse, in large and small ways, to be complicit in the devastation of our planet. We have very little time left.

Pachirat recounts in his book an August 5, 2004, story from the *Omaha World-Herald*. An "old-timer" who lived five miles from the Omaha slaughterhouses recalled the wind carrying the stench of almost six and a half million cattle, sheep, and hogs killed each year in South Omaha. The sickly odor permeated the buildings.

"It was the smell of money," the old-timer said. "It was the smell of money."

Chris Hedges
Princeton, New Jersey

PROLOGUE: WAKING UP

My name's Kip. I had a stereotypical U.S. American childhood. My mom was a teacher. My dad was in the military, and I have one sister. I played all the sports growing up, but I especially loved the outdoors and camping. I remember the first time I visited the redwood groves in Northern California. I was about eight years old. I had to crane my neck as far back as it would go to look up at the ancient, colossal trees stretching into the sky, their enormous trunks like cliff faces made of wood. Around me grew enormous ferns that came up to my shoulders. I didn't have the words at the time, but in the presence of those trees my eight-year-old self felt awe, reverence, and an odd little ache in my belly that had to do with their majestic beauty and the fact that I was standing next to a living being that had already lived hundreds or thousands of years. I know now that that wonder and awe wasn't simply for the redwood trees, but for the astonishing planet from which they grew. I left that redwood grove changed, and I never forgot the realization that our planet is a miracle and a gift, to us and to all the creatures who live on it. I became a young man who believed in the goodness all around me. Life was simple. Not a care in the world.

And then Al Gore showed up. Like so many of us, I saw the film *An Inconvenient Truth*, which is about the impacts of global warming, and it scared the emojis out of me. In the film, Gore describes how our Earth is in peril. Climate change stands to affect all life on this planet. Monster storms, raging wildfires, record droughts, melting ice caps, acidification of the oceans, even entire countries going underwater—that could all be caused by the burden of human beings on the Earth. Scientists are warning that unless we take drastic measures to correct our environmental footprint, our time on this planet may be limited to only fifty more years.

I wanted to do everything I could to help. I made up my mind right then and there to change how I lived and to do whatever I possibly could to find a way for all of us to live together, in balance with the planet, sustainably, forever.

I started to do all the things Al told us to do. I became an OCE: Obsessive Compulsive Environmentalist. I separated the trash and recycling. I composted, changed all the incandescent lightbulbs to compact fluorescents, took short showers, turned off the water when I brushed my teeth, turned off lights when leaving a room, and rode my bike instead of driving everywhere. I was doing everything I thought I could to help the planet. But as the years went by, it seemed as if things were getting worse. I had to wonder—with all the continuing ecological crises facing the planet, even if every single one of us adopted these conservation habits, was this really going to be enough to save the world?

Then, with one friend's Facebook post, everything changed. The post sent me to a report online, published by the Food and Agriculture Organization of the United Nations (FAO), stating that raising livestock produces more greenhouse gases than the combined exhaust of the entire transportation sector. This means that the meat and dairy industries produce more greenhouse gases than all cars, trucks, trains, boats, and planes combined. Worldwide. That's 13 percent for the global transportation sector compared to 18 percent for livestock.[1] Cows and other animals produce a substantial amount of methane from their digestive process. Methane gas from livestock has a global warming potential eighty-six times greater than carbon dioxide from vehicles. This makes it a vastly more destructive gas than carbon dioxide on a twenty-year time frame.[2]

Here I'd been riding my bike everywhere to help reduce emissions! It turns out there's a lot more to climate change than just fossil fuels. I started doing more research. The UN, along with other agencies, reported that not only does livestock play a major role in global warming, it is also the leading cause of resource consumption and environmental degradation destroying the planet today.

The more research I did, the more I found that the situation is actually worse than I had thought.

In 2009, Robert Goodland and Jeff Anhang, two environmental advisors to the World Bank Group, released an analysis on human-related greenhouse gases, concluding that animal agriculture was responsible not for 18 percent as the FAO stated but was actually responsible for 51 percent of all greenhouse gases.[3] *Fifty-one percent.* Yet all we hear about is burning fossil fuels.

This difference in the figures is due to factors that the FAO didn't take into account, such as the massive loss of carbon sinks from clear-cutting rain forests for grazing in

Global Greenhouse Gas Emissions (yearly)

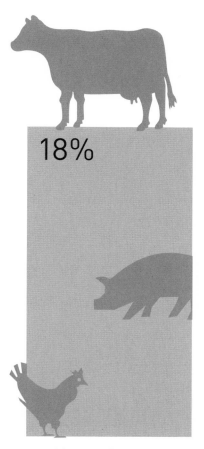

18%

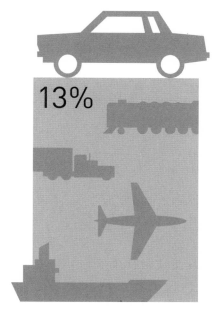

13%

Transportation Sector Emissions   Livestock Emissions

addition to the respiration and waste produced by animals. Goodland and Anhang used the Greenhouse Gas Protocol, the global standard for measuring emissions set by the World Resources Institute and World Business Council on Sustainable Development, to reach the figure of 51 percent. According to their calculations, animal agriculture is the number one contributor to human-caused climate change.

I also found out that raising animals for food consumes a third of all the planet's fresh water,[4] occupies up to 45 percent of the Earth's land,[5] is responsible for up to 91 percent of Amazon destruction,[6] and is a leading cause of species extinction, ocean dead zones, and habitat destruction.[7]

How is it possible I wasn't aware of this? I prided myself on being up-to-date on environmental issues. I thought this information would be plastered everywhere in the environmental community. Why didn't the world's largest environmental groups, who are supposed to be saving our planet, have this as their main focus? I went to the biggest organizations' websites—350.org, Greenpeace, the Sierra Club, the Climate Reality Project, Rainforest Action Network, Amazon Watch—and was shocked to see they had virtually nothing on animal agriculture. Why would they not have this information on there? What was going on?

I had to find out. I teamed up with fellow filmmaker Keegan Kuhn to see if we could get to the bottom of this.

CHAPTER ONE

A JOURNEY TOWARD TRUTH

Greenpeace has done some terrific work over the years. They famously helped get a moratorium on commercial whaling passed. The continent of Antarctica was declared a world park after five years of campaigning. They helped ban the dumping of industrial and radioactive waste in oceans around the world.[1] They've worked with McDonald's, Unilever, and Coca-Cola on reducing their greenhouse gas emissions. They successfully sued the Bush administration to provide more protection for the polar bear, which has become threatened by the melting of Arctic ice caused by global warming.[2] I'll never forget the computer-generated snippet in *An Inconvenient Truth* of a desperate, exhausted polar bear swimming in an endless Arctic Ocean, no ice floes anywhere to rest on. Greenpeace does good stuff. I've supported them for years.

So why was there practically no information on the devastating impacts of animal agriculture on Greenpeace's website, nor on any of the other major environmental organizations' websites? It seemed the main focus for many of these groups was natural gas and oil production. Did they not know what was going on?

We decided to speak with these organizations about why they weren't addressing this issue. We called every single PR person listed on these groups' websites every day for weeks, spending hours on hold. We sent email after email requesting interviews and received silence in return. Days became weeks, and weeks became months, and for some reason, no one wanted to talk to us about this.

I'd had enough. No more emails, no more phone calls. I realized if I wanted answers, I would have to go to the headquarters of these organizations in person.

First stop was Greenpeace headquarters, Mission Street, San Francisco. Keegan and I headed over there on a windy, sunny afternoon. As we entered the small lobby area, the front desk receptionist, seeing our cameras, jumped up from her seat to quickly lock the door to the adjoining main offices, as if we were going to charge right on through.

"We're doing a project on sustainability and animal agriculture," I explained to the woman behind the desk. "And we're seeing if we could talk to David Barre [Communications Director of Greenpeace]."

Seeming nervous, the young woman asked, "Do you have an appointment with him?"

I explained that we had been trying to contact Greenpeace for months and hadn't received any response. We were hoping, we told her, that we could set something up.

She asked us to take a seat. After about ten minutes, they sent out a public relations person. She came out from behind the frosted glass doors of the main office and told us to turn off the camera, refusing to be filmed. We told her what we hoped to discuss with Greenpeace, and she promised finally that someone from their rain forest, ocean, and climate change departments would speak with us. I gave her my email address, and we left feeling like we were making progress.

Okay. Fingers crossed. We decided to try the Sierra Club next, another organization I've been proud to support for years. Their space was large and airy, with tall windows, situated in the financial district of San Francisco. After an awkward exchange with the receptionist and communications rep, we were finally able to line up an interview with Bruce Hamilton, the Deputy Executive Director of the Sierra Club.

When we sat down with Hamilton, he was affable and welcoming.

"What is the leading cause of climate change?" I asked him, getting right to the issue.

"Well, it's basically burning too many fossil fuels," Hamilton said. He had a kind, weathered face with a trim white beard and the look of an outdoorsman—someone who looked like he'd spent a lifetime in wilder places than a San Francisco office building. "Coal, natural gas, oil, tar sands, oil shale. All these new exotic fuels that are kind of hybrids between them. [Those are] basically what is loading up the atmosphere so we have this greenhouse effect where the heat is getting trapped, and the temperatures are soaring at a rate that has never existed in the history of the Earth.

"The world's climate scientists tell us that the highest safe level of emissions would be around 350 parts per million of carbon dioxide and greenhouse gases in the atmosphere," he continued. "We're already at 400. They also tell us that the safest we could hope to do without having perilous implications as far as drought, famine, human conflict, and major species extinction would be about a 2-degree-Celsius increase in temperature. We're rapidly approaching that, and with all the built-in carbon dioxide that's already in the atmosphere, we're easily going to exceed that. On our watch, we are facing the next major extinction of species on the Earth, [something] we haven't seen since the time of the dinosaurs disappearing. When whole countries go underwater because of sea level rise, when whole countries find that there's so much drought that they can't feed their population, and as a result, they need to desperately migrate to or invade another country—we're going to have climate wars in the future," he concluded emphatically.

"And, what about livestock?" I asked. "Animal agriculture?"

Hamilton paused. He looked confused.

"Uh—well, what about it? I mean . . . Do you want to . . ."

His confusion threw me as well.

"We have this research," I tried to explain. "The UN report says livestock accounts for more greenhouse gases than all transportation put together. A recent 2009 World Watch Report states that livestock causes 51 percent of all greenhouse gas emissions."

Hamilton took a drink from his mug.

"Yeah, well. It *is* a big issue," he said, wagging his head side to side, "and we need to address that as well. But, you know, there are just so many different potential sources of methane and carbon emissions." It sounded like he was saying, "Well, we can't deal with *everything*."

"If the number one leading cause of climate change is animal agriculture and meat consumption," I said, "then doesn't that need to be the number one focus? If not, then number two?"

Hamilton closed his eyes briefly.

"Well," he said brightly, "that's your assessment. Our assessment is different." He shrugged and laughed.

That was bizarre. It was too bizarre. Why would a highly educated person such as Hamilton, not to mention a leader of the Sierra Club, avoid addressing one of, if not the, largest sources of global warming?

The next day Greenpeace got back to me by email: "It was great to meet with you yesterday. I have spoken with various people here at Greenpeace about your request, but I'm afraid we're not going to be able to help this time. Thanks again and we wish you the best of luck."

I just couldn't understand why the world's largest environmental organizations were not addressing this issue when their entire mission is to protect the environment.

I was, however, able to connect with a handful of environmental authors and advocates who were willing to address the issue, including why the big environmental organizations might be keeping quiet. I took my trusty old van, Super Blue, out of carbon dioxide retirement and hit the road in search of answers to my questions.

At a local speaking event in California, I met and talked to *New York Times* best-selling writer Michael Pollan, author of *The Omnivore's Dilemma*, who makes his home in the east bay of San Francisco.

"Environmental groups say use less coal, ride your bike," I said. "What about eat less meat?"

Pollan nodded. He's got an intelligent, long face and a bald head and was dressed in a khaki jacket with round wire glasses.

"I think they focus-grouped it and it's a political loser," he said. "Because they're membership organizations, you know. A lot of them. They're looking to maximize the number of people making contributions, and if they get identified as being anti-meat or challenging people on their everyday habits, something that's so dear to people, that it will hurt their fund-raising. I don't know, but that is what I would suspect."

We also met up with Dr. Will Tuttle, author of *The World Peace Diet*, in a Bay Area venue as he traveled the country on his extensive lecturing tour. He agreed with Pollan.

"They do not want to address the primary driving cause of environmental devastation, which is animal agriculture, because they're businesses, and they want to make sure that they have a reliable source of funding," Tuttle said to me.

"It's like when we talk about a dysfunctional family," he went on, "and the father is an alcoholic. That's the one thing no one talks about. Everybody just goes around that, and yet it's the one thing that's causing the devastation in the relationships in the family, and it keeps getting worse because no one wants to talk about it."

Several weeks later, in a park outside of Washington, D.C., we spoke with Demosthenes Maratos, Communications Director of the Sustainability Institute at Molloy College. Maratos, a tall man with a shaved head, black-rimmed glasses, and several small hoops in his ears, was presenting at a conference there.

"If you listen to a majority of the major environmental organizations," Maratos explained in his raspy voice, "they're not telling you to do much besides live your life the way you've been living it, but change a lightbulb from time to time, drive less, use less plastic, recycle more. It's better for their fund-raising and better for their profile to create a victim-and-perpetrator sort of plot line. How could these organizations not know? I mean, the issue is right in front of them. It's unmistakable at this point, and these organizations are falling all over themselves to show the general public that climate change is human caused, and in doing so, [the public] completely fail[s] to see what's right in front of them. That animal agriculture, raising and killing animals for food, is really what's killing the planet."

What Maratos said made a lot of sense. The general public feels that they're doing all they can to help the environment by making small changes in their lives, like driving less, turning off lights, taking shorter showers—the same way I felt when I was biking everywhere. The greenhouse gas we hear the most about from the environmental organizations is carbon dioxide. In the public mind, carbon dioxide emissions are the biggest cause of global warming. And to be sure, according to the Environmental Protection Agency, carbon dioxide makes up 77 percent of global greenhouse gas emissions.[3]

But as I learned recently, methane is 86 times more destructive than carbon dioxide.[4] That's because its global warming power—the ability of methane to trap heat in the atmosphere—is 86 times greater than that of carbon dioxide. Globally, cattle produce 150 billion gallons of methane every day.[5]

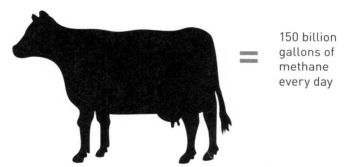

150 billion gallons of methane every day

Again, why wasn't the public being informed about methane emissions? In his office at the University of California, Berkeley, surrounded by books and papers, Kirk R. Smith, Professor of Global Environmental Health, said to me, "I was invited to a meeting with Al Gore some years ago now. [I] made these methane arguments, and he was really [taken aback]. [His argument is that] 'It's hard enough to get people to think about carbon dioxide. Don't confuse them.'"

But there's a very good reason to focus on methane instead of carbon dioxide. Not only is methane more destructive than carbon dioxide, its levels have a much more immediate impact on the environment. "If you reduce the amount of methane emissions," Smith said, "the level in the atmosphere goes down fairly quickly,[6] within decades, as opposed to carbon dioxide. If you reduce the [carbon dioxide] emissions to the atmosphere, you don't really see a signal in the atmosphere for about one hundred years or so."

And if the public is going to be "confused" by information about methane, as Al Gore said to Professor Smith, then what are they going to think about nitrous oxide? Nitrous oxide is a greenhouse gas that has a global warming potential 296 times greater than that of carbon dioxide.[7] It stays in the atmosphere for 150 years.[8] And 65 percent of human-produced nitrous oxide comes from the animal agriculture industry, most of it generated by manure.[9]

"Livestock is one of the most significant contributors to today's most serious environmental problems," senior UN FAO official Henning Steinfeld said in a 2006 UN report. "Urgent action is required to remedy the situation." Steinfeld is the senior author of the FAO report, "Livestock's Long Shadow," which states that, "The environmental costs per unit of livestock production must be cut by one half, just to avoid the level of damage worsening beyond its present level."[10]

And here's a gem from *Time* in December 2013: "There may be no other single human activity that has a bigger impact on the planet than the raising of livestock."[11]

I still wanted to hear directly from the big environmental organizations. What about Natural Resources Defense Council (NRDC)? Unlike on the other big non-governmental organization's websites, I actually found a few things on their website about animal agriculture.

We met with Ann Notthoff, California Advocacy Director of NRDC, in her San Francisco office. She stared at us calmly as we got settled and then continued the discussion we had started in our initial outreach

"The leading cause of environmental degradation is too much pollution and too many engines churning too fast in too many places around the globe," she told us.

"In 2009," I said, "there was a Worldwatch report that stated that livestock causes fifty-one percent of greenhouse gas emissions. Transportation is around thirteen [percent]. Then at the low end for animal agriculture emissions, the UN's analysis was around eighteen percent, which is still more than all transportation. All put together."

Notthoff grimaced and frowned. "Internationally? Or nationally?"

"Around the globe."

"I think energy production," Notthoff said slowly, "and transportation are still major sources, so I think—I guess I'm not going to comment on that, because I'm not familiar with those numbers, so it's—" She began to laugh. "Don't quote me on this, but that's cow farts, that's what I think that is." She laughed again. "I think that's cow farts."

After Notthoff pulled herself together, I asked her about NRDC's position on food, diet, and animal agriculture.

"NRDC absolutely has a big food program," Notthoff says. "Every year, we do the Growing Green Awards and we recognize food innovators. In this last year, one of the awardees was a sustainable pork producer that doesn't use any antibiotics. Also . . . the majority of the antibiotics in the United States is administered to healthy livestock."[12]

After the research I'd done so far, I found it odd that NRDC would give an environmental award to a meat producer—even one who didn't use antibiotics. But I wanted to maintain an open mind and keep learning about the connections between animal agriculture and the environment. Perhaps there really was a way to raise animals for meat that didn't cause such devastation to the planet. I ended up leaving their office more confused than when I went in.

A few days later I wrote back to Greenpeace, begging them to reconsider my request for an interview. This was their second email reply:

"I'm afraid we've explored the options here in terms of helping you and are not going to be able to be involved this time. You mentioned you were also speaking to Oceana. I'm sure they will be able to give you some great quotes about ocean-related issues. Thanks again for thinking of us."

Unbelievable.

I was, however, able to contact Will Anderson, the cofounder of Greenpeace Alaska, author of *This Is Hope: Green Vegans and the New Human Ecology*, and a former member of Greenpeace USA's board of directors, who now speaks openly about the animal agriculture industry. He agreed to talk with us in person.

"Environmental organizations, like other organizations, are not telling you the truth about what the world needs from us as a species," he told me. "It's so frustrating when the information is right before their eyes. It's documented in peer-reviewed papers and journals. It's there for anybody to see, but the environmental organizations are refusing to act. Nowhere do you find in their policies and nowhere do you find in the Greenpeace mission that diet is important, that animal agriculture is the problem."

Anderson, with intense gray eyes and close-cropped hair, spoke with controlled emotion. "They are refusing—like other environmental organizations—to look at the issue. The environmental community is failing us, and they're failing ecosystems. It's so frustrating to see them do this."

The pain and disappointment that Anderson felt over the organization he had founded a chapter of, supported, and believed in, was palpable.

After speaking with Anderson, we left feeling a strange relief that the cofounder of Greenpeace Alaska was seeing the real issue. When you notice something, but everyone around you is saying it's not there, you can't help but start to wonder whether you really saw it.

When big institutions are silent, it's usually individual voices that speak up. We came across the work of Dr. Richard A. Oppenlander, author of *Comfortably Unaware* and *Food Choice and Sustainability*. He has been studying the environmental impact of our food choices since the early 1970s.

We arranged an interview with Oppenlander and asked him about the ecological footprint of animal agriculture.

"So my calculations," he told us as we all sat in his office, "are that, without using any gas or oil or fuel ever again from this day forward, we would still exceed our maximum safe carbon-equivalent greenhouse-gas emissions—565 gigatons—by the year 2030, without the electricity sector or energy sector even factoring in the equation, all simply by raising and eating livestock."[13]

Nearly everyone else we interviewed echoed Oppenlander's sentiments that animal agriculture, more than any other industry, was destroying our planet

Demosthenes Maratos of the Sustainability Institute described the situation in his own words. "Deforestation, land use, water scarcity, the destabilization of communities, world hunger—the list [of effects] doesn't stop. [Animal agriculture] is an environmental disaster that is being ignored by the very people who should be championing [its awareness]."[14]

Dr. Will Tuttle also spoke about deforestation, loss of biodiversity, and land use when we interviewed him during his lecture tour.

"The rain forest is being cut down at the rate of an acre per second," he said. "The driving force behind all of this is animal agriculture, cutting down the forests to graze animals and to grow soybeans—genetically engineered soybeans—to feed to the cows and pigs and chickens and factory-farmed fish. Free-living animals 10,000 years ago made up 99 percent of the biomass. Human beings, we only made up 1 percent of the biomass. Today, only 10,000 years later, which is really just a fraction of time, we human beings and the animals that we own as property make up 98 percent of the biomass. Wild, free-living animals make up only 2 percent. We've basically completely stolen the world—the Earth—from free-living animals to use for ourselves and our cows and pigs and chickens and factory-farmed fish. The oceans have been even more devastated."

Maratos put it pretty simply: "The leading cause of environmental destruction is animal agriculture."

So why do so few people know this?

CHAPTER TWO
WATER: AN ~~INFINITE~~ RESOURCE

I live in California. People usually think of golden beaches and surfers riding blue waves when they think of my state, but in the past few years, the lakes and the reservoirs have been drained, large stretches of land lie parched and cracked under the sun, and grass has turned brown and brittle as straw. A severe historic drought began in 2011. Governor Jerry Brown called it "the worst drought that California has ever seen since records [began] about one-hundred years ago."[1] Some studies indicate that it may be the worst drought in more than one thousand years.[2]

In January 2014, Governor Brown declared a state of emergency after 2013 ended up being the driest year in California's history,[3] surpassed only by 2014[4]—at least until 2015 weighs in. The rivers and reservoirs fell below their record low points, and the snowpack in California's mountains—the state's largest and most important water storage reservoir, which releases water as the snow melts during the summer[5]—was approximately 20 percent of the normal average. Governor Brown called on all the residents of California to be more mindful of their water use and conserve as much water as possible.[6] He then set a voluntary target of 20 percent water use reduction as part of the drought emergency. That target was never reached.[7]

On April 1, 2015, for the first time in the history of California, Governor Brown imposed a 25 percent mandatory water use reduction in cities and towns across the state. This was a few days after the governor signed emergency legislation approving a $1 billion emergency drought package.[8] The water reduction will be enforced with fines if necessary and means that Californians will have to cut back on watering their lawns and washing their cars. They'll have to fix leaky faucets and take shorter showers, and the government will offer rebate programs to replace washing machines, toilets, and dishwashers with water-efficient models.

"The current drought in California is devastating," California Congressman Kevin McCarthy said in the *New York Times*. "Today's order from the governor should not only alarm Californians, but the entire nation should take notice that the most productive agriculture state in the country has entered uncharted territory."[9]

Hold up—what's that about agriculture?

The California agriculture industry is exempted from the mandatory 25 percent reduction in water use, even though, according to the Public Policy Institute of California, roughly nine million acres of farmland in California are irrigated, which is when water is brought from somewhere else and applied to land to grow crops. That irrigation accounts for 80 percent of the state's water usage.[10]

To be sure, the drought has taken its toll on farmers. In 2014, economists estimated that farmers lost about $2.2 billion because of increased water prices and lost crops and that about 17,100 jobs have been sliced from the agriculture sector by the drought.[11]

I spoke with Heather Cooley, the Water Program Co-Director of the Pacific Institute. She received the Environmental Protection Agency (EPA) award for outstanding achievement for her work on agricultural water conservation and efficiency. She testified before the U.S. Congress on the impacts of climate change for agriculture and on innovative approaches to solving water problems in the Sacramento–San Joaquin delta.

Her office was airy, with a large picture window looking out onto tall green trees and lots of beautiful California sun.

"The average Californian uses about 1,500 gallons [of water] per person, per day," Cooley told me. "About half of that is related to the consumption of meat and dairy products. Meat and dairy products are incredibly water-intensive, in part because the animals are using very water-intensive grains. That's what they eat, and so all of the water embedded in the grain and that the animal eats, essentially, is considered part of the virtual water footprint of that product."

I found out that one quarter-pound hamburger requires more than 660 gallons of water to produce.[12] Here I've been taking these short showers, trying to save water and following the government's guidelines, and then I find out that eating just one hamburger is the equivalent of showering for two entire months.

What Cooley told me is confirmed by a 2012 Pacific Institute report, which says that 47 percent of California's water footprint is associated with meat and dairy products. Crops grown for animal feed, due to the sheer number of the crops required, have the greatest water requirement of anything grown in California, greater even than

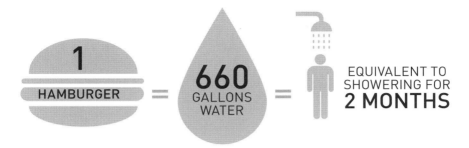

water-intensive almonds and avocados.[13] Household water use, compared to the 47 percent associated with meat and dairy, is about 4 percent.

Similarly, across the United States, domestic water use, which is the subject of so many water reduction campaigns, is only 5 percent of water consumed, versus 55 percent for animal agriculture.[14] That's because it takes upwards of 2,500 gallons of water to produce one pound of beef.[15]

Water Use Comparison

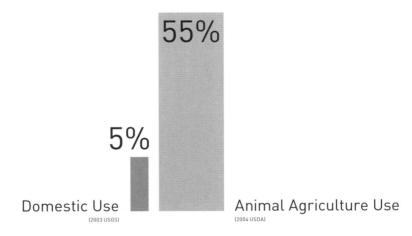

I returned to the websites of the big environmental organizations to see what they had to say about water conservation. The latest hot issue regarding water on these sites was water use and contamination from fracking (hydraulic fracturing). Hydraulic fracturing for natural gas uses an incredible amount of water. A staggering 70 to 140 billion gallons of water are used for fracking every year in the United States,[16] but when I compared this with animal agriculture, raising livestock—just in the United States— consumes at least *34 trillion* gallons of water per year,[17] and it turns out the methane emissions from both industries are nearly equal.[18]

Gallons of Water Used in the United States (per year)

Fracking:
140 billion gallons

Animal Agriculture:
340 trillion gallons

I looked at the government's California Department of Water Resources' "Save Our Water" campaign webpage, which outlines behavior changes to help conserve our water, like using low-flow showerheads, efficient toilets, water-saving appliances, and fixing leaky faucets and sprinkler heads.

But there was nothing about animal agriculture—not on the environmental organizations' websites, not on the government websites.

When I added up all of the government's recommendations, I was saving 47 gallons a day, but that's not even close to the 660 gallons of water for just one burger.

I wanted to see if I could somehow talk with the government about this.

I called up the California Department of Water Resources. "I'm just calling to see if we could schedule an interview."

"Yeah," the man I spoke to said. "That would be good. What does your schedule look like this afternoon or tomorrow afternoon?"

Wow.

"Tomorrow afternoon could be good," I said. That was amazingly easy.

The next day I showed up at the California government offices in Sacramento. I met with Dr. Manucher Alemi and Kamyar Guivetchi. Alemi was the Chief of the Water Use and Efficiency Branch of the California Department of Water Resources, and Guivetchi worked with Statewide Integrated Water Management for the Department of Water Resources.

Water Saved Through Recommended
Water Conservation Practices
vs. Water Cost of a Hamburger (per day)

660
gallons
Cost in gallons
for one 1/4 lb.
hamburger

1 gallon	3 gallons	9 gallons	24 gallons
HE faucets	HE shower	HE toilet	HE appliances

We spoke in a conference room. Alemi, in a short-sleeved, button-down white shirt, with bushy salt-and-pepper eyebrows, a mustache, and dark, thick hair, said, in slightly accented English, "For the environment, there are a lot of things that can be done to save water. You know, using low-flow showerheads, low-flow faucets, efficient toilets, efficient water-using appliances. All those are really good areas that can help quite a lot, but the biggest water savings is from . . . " I fully expected him to say diet, but he went on to say, ". . . outdoors. Checking the sprinkler a lot for leaks and broken sprinklers and things like that, that wastes water. Those are the areas [where] there's a lot of room for conservation."

Guivetchi, bald with graying stubble, a broad face, and wearing a blue-and-white plaid shirt, spoke up. "We have to be mindful of the way we use water. We have to use it as efficiently as possible. We have to protect its quality and we have to be good stewards of the environment, [which] depends on water."

Disappointed that they didn't bring up animal agriculture, I prodded. "It kept on coming up a lot in my research, the subject of animal agriculture?" Neither of the men said anything. "Can you comment on that at all, about how much that plays a role in water consumption and pollution?"

They were both quiet, until Guivetchi sighed very heavily. "I mean, that's not— my area."

I kept trying. "There's one study that found that one pound of beef takes 2,500 gallons of water."

Guivetchi nodded slowly, as though he'd heard the statistic before. "Yeah."

I went on. "One pound of eggs is 477 gallons of water, and one pound of cheese, almost 900 gallons.[19] It takes 1,000 gallons of water to produce one gallon of milk.[20] If it's that simple, why isn't it on California's Save Our Water website? It's kind of like if my neighbor has a giant hose turned full blast until 660 gallons of water are flooding the entire street. I think I would say, 'Hey, turn that off, please.' It's the same as eating a single burger. It seems like it's a huge thing that we could be doing, far more than anything else."

How Many Gallons of Water Does It Take to Make Animal By-products?

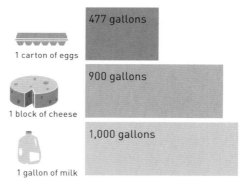

1 carton of eggs — 477 gallons

1 block of cheese — 900 gallons

1 gallon of milk — 1,000 gallons

Guivetchi nodded. "I think that the water footprint of animal husbandry is greater than other activities. There's no ifs, ands, or buts about it."

"That would be really powerful," I said, "rather than waiting till we're in a drought, you know, what do you think about just starting now and—whoever's in charge of Save Our Water, say to them, 'Hey, let's start encouraging people to eat less meat now, because these studies are coming out.'"

Guivetchi nodded again, but with a "I-hate-to-break-this-to-you" look on his face. "I . . . don't think that'll happen."

"Why?"

"I . . . don't think that'll happen," he repeated.

"Why?" I really wanted a concrete answer.

"Because . . . of the way government is set up here."

"That's interesting," I said. "Why, though?"

He shook his head for a long time. "One [aspect] is water management and the other is behavior change."

"Behavior?" I said. "Taking showers, and not watering your lawn, and doing all that. That's behavior."

Guivetchi looked at me for a very long time, nodding very slightly. "Yeah." His voice was so quiet I could barely hear him. The pained look on his face suggested that he knew what I was talking about, but he wasn't allowed, or willing, to address the issue.

Wow. Clearly the government did not want to talk about this issue.

It wouldn't be the last time I heard this from organizations or government officials— that they don't want to dictate people's behavior, implying that's why they're sitting on the sidelines of this issue. But they're happy to talk about turning off the faucet when we brush our teeth, or taking fewer showers, or telling us not to water our lawns because of water shortages. Which is fine. But how about just putting out the information, side by side with our domestic water consumption numbers—washing our cars or watering our lawns—with information about the water that's being used in animal agriculture? Just put it out there. Don't tell people what to do. Let them decide for themselves what the most dangerous threat to environmental protection is and what they can do in their own lives to help the environment. Let people make informed choices.

This same silence was bizarre in the otherwise solid coverage by the *New York Times* of the drought in California. Again and again, the *Times* focused on the water required to grow nuts, fruits, and vegetables, with little or no attention given to the much, much greater amounts of water needed for animal agriculture.

On April 20, 2014, Stephanie Strom wrote in the *New York Times*, "Anywhere between one-third and one-half of the nation's fruits and vegetables are grown in California, meaning Americans are facing higher prices on melons, broccoli, baby greens, almonds and other popular crops."[21]

The *Times* produced a short video that appeared on their website alongside many of its stories on the drought, called "California's Extreme Drought, Explained." The narrator tells us, "California produces 90 percent of the nation's tomatoes, 95 percent of its broccoli, and 99 percent of its almonds . . . California's agricultural output could fall by $3.5 billion dollars this year. Costs across the nation are already up, attributed at least partly to the drought, with more increases expected down the line, as crop yields come in this fall. The price for a single avocado could jump by 28 percent."[22]

Jumping ahead to this year, on March 17, 2015, Adam Nagourney, writing for the *Times*, interviewed Geoffrey C. Galloway, a citrus farmer in the Central Valley. "I'm going to fallow two acres of my land immediately," Galloway told Nagourney. "Depending on how the season goes, we may let another four go."[23]

There was repeated mention of "thirsty crops" four days in a row in the *Times*'s drought coverage in early April, after the 25 percent mandatory water cutback was announced.

On April 4, 2015, the *Times* wrote, ". . . there is also likely to be increased pressure on the farms to move away from certain water-intensive crops—like almonds,"[24] and "Farmers . . . may need to change what they plant. California farmers are already reducing their production of some water-intensive crops . . ."[25]

On April 5, 2015: "The expansion of almonds, walnuts and other water-guzzling tree and vine crops has come under sharp criticism from some urban Californians."[26]

On April 6, 2015: "Even as the worst drought in decades ravages California, and its cities face mandatory cuts in water use, millions of pounds of thirsty crops like oranges, tomatoes, and almonds continue to stream out of the state and onto the nation's grocery shelves."[27]

And on April 7, 2015: "Even today, as almond trees in the Central Valley's Kern County stand dead, farmers elsewhere in the state are planting new acres with this extremely thirsty crop, which sucks as much water in a year as Los Angeles does in three."[28]

This was making it sound like almonds in particular were the bad guys. It turns out that almonds do use about 10 percent of California's water supply each year, which is indeed nuts. But that 10 percent of California's water grows 80 percent of the entire world's supply of almonds.[29] And most Americans don't eat twelve ounces of almonds every day, the way they eat meat and other animal products.[30] The water footprint of meat, dairy, and eggs are vastly greater not only because of the huge amounts of water embedded in their production but also because there is so much consumer demand, keeping the rate of production high.

There's another big California crop that soaks up 15 percent of California's water—alfalfa.[31] "[A] single plant is leading California's water consumption. Unfortunately, it's a plant that's not generally cultivated for humans: alfalfa. Grown on more than a million acres in California, alfalfa sucks up more water than any other crop in the state. And it has one primary destination: cattle." James McWilliams, professor of history at Texas

State University–San Marcos, wrote in an excellent op-ed for the *New York Times* in March 2014 titled "Meat Makes the Planet Thirsty."[32]

Kudos to the *Times* for running the article—but it was on their opinion page. McWilliams wasn't airing his opinions. Apart from that op-ed, I didn't see one mention of "thirsty, water-guzzling" alfalfa in the *Times*. And I was amazed that alfalfa is not even grown for humans to eat—70 percent of the alfalfa grown in California is fed to the country's dairy cows.[33]

Does the other 30 percent of alfalfa go into alfalfa-sprout sandwiches for hungry vegetarians? Nope. If an American dairy cow isn't eating it, there's a good chance California alfalfa is exported to countries like Japan,[34] South Korea, China,[35] the United Arab Emirates, and Saudi Arabia—countries that haven't got enough land or water of their own to grow hay for their animals—the same animals soon to be eaten by their people.[36]

"A hundred billion gallons of water per year is being exported in the form of alfalfa from California," says Professor Robert Glennon from the Rogers College of Law at the University of Arizona in an article for the BBC. "It's a huge amount. It's enough for a year's supply of water for a million families—it's a lot of water, particularly when you're looking at the dreadful drought throughout the Southwest."[37]

California, true to the spirit of American capitalism, exports this enormous amount of water in the midst of an excruciating drought because of the profits to be made.

And Professor Glennon was only talking about the water footprint of exported alfalfa—a much smaller percentage than what is being fed to livestock within our borders. In fact, more than 30 percent of California's water is used to raise animals for food,[38] either directly, as drinking water for the animals and water needed to "process" them—such as hosing down the slaughterhouses, trucks, and other equipment, and for filling scalding tanks and chilling tanks, or indirectly, for feed crops, alfalfa, and pastures.

That's a statistic also found worldwide: 20 to 33 percent of global fresh water use is swallowed up by animal agriculture.[39]

Dr. Richard Oppenlander points out in his book *Food Choice and Sustainability* that if you just considered the amount of water used by livestock for drinking—about 1 to 2 percent of the total water usage in the country—you're still looking at between four to eight billion gallons of water every day, just in the United States. The amount of drinking water needed daily for a dairy cow is 35 to 45 gallons, 20 to 30 gallons for a dry cow, 12 gallons for beef cattle, 5 to 8 gallons for a pig, 15 gallons for every 100 turkeys, and 9 gallons for every 100 chickens.[40] Nearly 10.2 billion land animals were raised and killed for food in the United States in 2010.[41] Worldwide, 70 billion land animals are raised and killed for humans to eat every year.[42] Multiply the amount of livestock drinking water in the United States by 7, and you get the global livestock drinking amount of 28 to 56 billion gallons of water every single day.

I wanted to know, apart from the 660 gallons needed to produce one quarter-pound burger, how much water is required to produce a pound of meat, taking into account drinking, processing, and feed crops. On the next page are conservative figures from the Water Footprint Calculator—most other estimates are much higher.[43][44]

"But what about the protein?!" I can hear the omnivores protesting. More on the protein question later, I promise, but all it takes is forty gallons of water, at most, to grow one pound of high-quality, plant-based protein like lentils, beans, peas, and chickpeas. Beef, by comparison, needs at least forty-five times as much water—1,800 gallons—to produce a single pound.[45]

A report by water expert Arjen Y. Hoekstra, published in the journal *Environmental Research Letters*, puts it simply: "The water footprint (WF) of any animal product is larger than the WF of a crop alternative with equivalent nutritional value."[46]

The enormous water footprint of animal products is often left out when water use is calculated. Dr. Oppenlander frequently uses the following argument in his presentations:

"According to the EPA, the average household of three in our country consumes 50,000 gallons of water in one year for indoor use . . . However, this estimate does not include the water required to bring food to our table, which is by far the most important factor in our water consumption."

Average American Meat Consumption (per year)

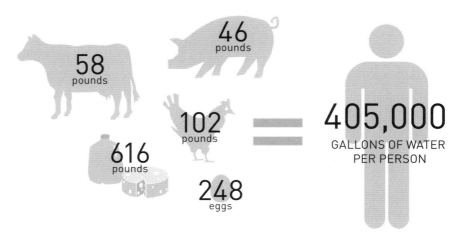

58 pounds

46 pounds

616 pounds

102 pounds

248 eggs

= 405,000 GALLONS OF WATER PER PERSON

How Much Water Does It Take to Make One Pound of . . . ?

2,500 GALLONS = 1 POUND OF BEEF

731 GALLONS = 1 POUND OF SHEEP

576 GALLONS = 1 POUND OF PORK

468 GALLONS = 1 POUND OF CHICKEN

880 GALLONS = 1 GALLON OF MILK

60–120 GALLONS = 1 EGG

22 GALLONS = 1 POUND TOMATOES

24 GALLONS = 1 POUND CABBAGE

30 GALLONS = 1 POUND POTATOES

55 GALLONS = 1 POUND ORANGES

83 GALLONS = 1 POUND APPLES

102 GALLONS = 1 POUND BANANAS

107 GALLONS = 1 POUND OF CORN

154 GALLONS = 1 POUND OF WHEAT BREAD

244 GALLONS = 1 POUND OF TOFU

368 GALLONS = 1 POUND OF GROUNDNUTS

Consider that the average person in the United States consumes 206 pounds of meat in one year, and far more than that in animal by-products. Generally speaking, this breaks down to 405,000 gallons of water per person per year consumed just to support that animal product diet.

As Oppenlander points out, it's a bit of a miscalculation when the EPA is looking at their household of three people in the United States, and they forget to factor in the immense amount of water needed to produce the average American diet. But the EPA should certainly know, and be very worried, about the fact that that single animal-product-consuming American household of three people uses, every year, well over one million gallons of water, not fifty thousand gallons. That's a big difference; 96 percent of that obscene water use is a direct result of choosing to eat animals and their by-products. Why isn't this being addressed when there is a drought or water shortage, as there is in California? What about setting limits on meat and dairy consumption as well as washing your car? It's really the same thing: that steak and that glass of milk are worth enormously more than their own weight in precious water.[47] Why aren't governments of drought-stricken areas, desperate to save water, encouraging their citizens to change their diets?

Oppenlander's argument makes me think of something I read in the *Sacramento Bee*, when Governor Brown announced the 25 percent water reduction for urban California but exempted Big Ag. John Carter, the manager of the Yellowstone to Uintas Connection, a wildlife conservation project in Idaho, told the *Bee* that water use in California should be restricted for agricultural use as well, especially water used to grow feed crops for livestock. "We know why [agriculture has] been exempted," Carter said. "They have political power, and they've been there a long time."[48]

A human newborn baby is 75 percent water. An adult male is 60 percent water, an adult female 55 percent (women have more fatty tissue, which is drier). As we age, we dry out. Elderly people are about half water.

Our brains, hearts, lungs, kidneys, and livers are our wettest tissues (65 to 85 percent), but even our bones—"dry as a bone"—are 31 percent water.[49]

We literally can't live without the stuff. Well, we can live roughly three days without it—some have gone eight to ten days.[50] The point is, it's not a long time.

About 97.5 percent of the water on the planet is salt water. We can't drink it or use it for crops. The other 2.5 percent of the Earth's water is fresh water. Of that 2.5 percent, 69.5 percent is locked up in glaciers, snow, and permafrost, 30.1 percent is in deep aquifers beneath the ground, and 0.4 percent is surface and atmospheric water found in lakes, marshes and wetlands, soil, air, plants, and animals, including ourselves. If you were to fill a medium-sized bucket with water, and then take one drop out of it on the tip of your finger, the bucket would represent all the water on Earth, while the droplet on your finger would be the amount usable by the human species: one hundred-thousandth of the total amount.[51]

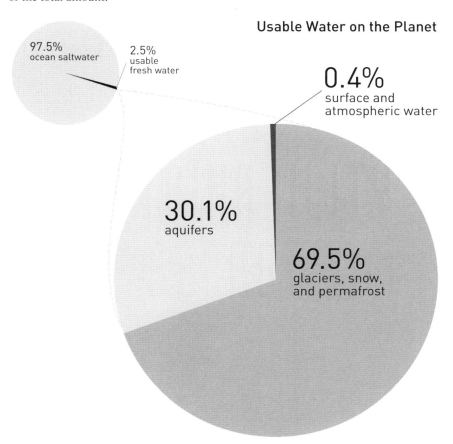

Usable Water on the Planet

97.5%
ocean saltwater

2.5%
usable
fresh water

0.4%
surface and
atmospheric water

30.1%
aquifers

69.5%
glaciers, snow,
and permafrost

The human species is running out of water. By 2025 it's estimated that 5.3 billion people, or two-thirds of the global population, will suffer from water shortages.[52]

And yet, the global population continues to balloon. From 1941 to 2011 the number of human beings on the planet tripled (though fresh water consumption quadrupled),[53] and the United Nations projects that by 2050 there will be 8 to 10.5 billion people on the planet.[54]

While the world's population explodes, the amount of fresh water available to us remains finite. In order to meet the astronomically increasing demands for water, we are using up ancient sources—like aquifers—at astounding rates that will not be renewable in our lifetimes.

Aquifers are enormous underground reservoirs of water stored in porous, water-permeable rock—imagine massive, country-spanning underground sponges. The mighty Ogallala Aquifer in the United States is one of the largest in the world and runs from South Dakota down to Texas, covering about 174,000 square miles beneath Colorado, Kansas, Nebraska, New Mexico, Oklahoma, South Dakota, Texas, and Wyoming.[55] In the United States we rely on aquifers for half our water needs—even more so in times of drought, when surface water goes dry.[56] During normal times, the Ogallala provides 30 percent of this country's groundwater used for irrigation.[57]

The water in the Ogallala Aquifer has been there for at least three million years; it was formed when the southern Rocky Mountains were still gushing lava.[58] Other estimates say the aquifer was formed more than twenty million years ago.[59] There is enough water in the Ogallala, by some calculations, to cover the entire forty-eight contiguous states of the United States in 2 feet of water. That sounds like a lot, and it is. The problem is that the Ogallala water is geologic, or "fossil" water. The aquifer formed millions of years ago and is being replenished very slowly,[60] mostly due to the impermeability of the rock that contains the water and also because of high evaporation rates.[61] Once the water is used up, it is gone for our lifetime. The Ogallala refills at less than half an inch every year, and scientists estimate that it would take six thousand years for the aquifer to refill itself by natural processes.[62]

The water level is now being drawn down for human use at a rate of 3 to 10 feet annually.[63] We are removing the equivalent of eighteen Colorado Rivers from the Ogallala every year.[64] This massive source of groundwater, one of the largest in the world, which took millions of years to form, could be gone as early as 2030.[65]

Where is eighteen Colorado Rivers worth of water going? The huge majority of this extracted groundwater is used for cattle and livestock feed crops.

I find it ironic, and terribly sad, that the Ogallala Aquifer is named after the Oglala Sioux, one of the native Lakota tribes of the Great Plains. The Oglala were almost wiped out as a people to satisfy the American dream of endless expansion, and now, more than a century later, the same thing is happening to the great prehistoric aquifer named after them.

The Ogallala is just one example of what is happening around the world. "Between 50 and 75 percent," Richard Oppenlander writes in *Food Choice and Sustainability*, "of all water withdrawal from the largest aquifers in the world—Ogallala, North China Plain, San Joaquin, Columbia River Basin—can be attributed to livestock and the alfalfa, corn, sorghum, and other crops they eat; their drinking water and the water used to generally service them; processing and packaging animal products; and the slaughtering process."[66]

Many aquifers worldwide are being depleted at rates as high as 250 times their capacity to refill,[67] thanks to advances in technology and the surge in demand for animal meat and products.

"Only within the last half-century have we acquired the ability to use powerful diesel and electric pumps to empty aquifers in a matter of decades . . ." according to *Time* magazine in 1999. "Around the world, as more water is diverted to raising [cattle], pigs and chickens, instead of producing crops for direct consumption, millions of wells are going dry. India, China, North Africa, and the United States are all running freshwater deficits, pumping more from their aquifers than rain can replenish."[68]

And how much would we have to cut back on pumping in order for the aquifers to replenish themselves? A 2013 study from the Proceedings of the National Academy of Sciences (PNAS) of the United States looked at the crucial Kansas portion of the Ogallala. It discovered that 30 percent of the groundwater under Kansas has already been pumped and used. If current depletion rates continue, over the next 50 years, another 39 percent will be gone. At that rate, agriculture in the area will peak in 2040. If water extraction is cut back by 20 percent, the region would not hit peak agriculture production until 2070. But in order for Kansas to farm sustainably and indefinitely and preserve the resources of the Ogallala for many future generations, current aquifer pumping would need to be reduced by 80 percent to bring it back in line with rainwater replenishment.[69]

"This would require a drastic reduction of corn and cattle production," the *Washington Post* stated in response to the PNAS's 80 percent groundwater cutback figure.

"'That ain't gonna happen,'" John Fleck, a journalist who has been tracking water issues out West for many years, notes in the same *Washington Post* article.[70] And of course, the vast majority of the corn production mentioned by the *Post* is grown for cattle and other livestock to eat.

"Society," reads the PNAS report, "has an opportunity now to make changes with tremendous implications for future sustainability and livability."

Speaking of future sustainability and livability, you hear a lot about how global warming is contributing to the disastrous rise in sea levels, which will put cities and islands around the world under water, but not many people think about how the huge amounts of groundwater we pump out are adding to the oceans. Extracted groundwater remains in the greater planetary hydrological cycle, so it's got to go somewhere—and most of it is unable to return to depleted aquifers because of impermeable rock and evaporation. Along the way, a lot of it becomes contaminated when toxins and polluting substances such as animal manure, human sewage, chemicals, pathogens, insecticides, herbicides, petroleum products, industrial waste, fertilizer, and heavy metals are released into the water, making it useless for sustaining human life. Most of the extracted groundwater eventually enters the oceans, where it not only becomes unusable for human life but also contributes to rising sea levels.

"Researchers found that the effect on rising sea levels by pumping of groundwater could be as much as five times larger in scale than the melting of the planet's ice caps in Greenland and Antarctica," Dr. Oppenlander writes in *Food Choice and Sustainability*.

Professor Robert Nicholls, a sea level expert at the University of Southampton in England, says, in Dr. Oppenlander's book, that "sea levels would rise 10 meters or more if all the world's groundwater was pumped out."[71] According to the EPA, if sea levels rose 10 meters, it would flood the homes of 25 percent of the U.S. population.[72]

We seem to be determined to use up all of the world's freshwater, one way or another. In the 1980s there were proposals, once people became aware that the Ogallala might be drained dry, of building a pipeline to send freshwater to the Great Plains and the southwestern United States from the Great Lakes,[73] which contain 84 percent of the surface freshwater in North America and about 21 percent of the world's freshwater supply.[74]

Other proposed solutions have been to desalinate ocean water (an extremely expensive procedure, with the undesirable by-product of concentrated saltwater slurry, which must then be specially treated before returning it to the ocean, where it can sink to the ocean floor and disrupt the marine ecosystem), or to drill even deeper into the earth for water.

"Our civilization," Dr. Oppenlander points out in his book, "displays a curious instinct when confronted with a problem related to overconsumption—we simply find a way to produce more of what it is we are consuming, instead of limiting or stopping that consumption."[75]

How about not eating animal products? That would be a lot easier. It would save a lot of water, and we need freshwater to survive as a species. Do we really need meat, dairy, and eggs?

"When you are discontent, you always want more, more, more," the Dalai Lama said. "But when you practice contentment, you can say to yourself, 'Oh yes—I already have everything that I really need.'"

John Robbins, founder of EarthSave and author of numerous books, including *The Food Revolution* and *Diet for a New America*, uses a terrific analogy comparing our peak water situation to driving a car with no fuel gauge. You keep flooring the accelerator, and the car zooms along fine, as though the tank were full, until suddenly the car stops because you're out of gas. There was no warning at all. But this is where the analogy breaks down. If your car runs out of gas, you have to walk or get another ride, maybe hitchhike. If you're the human species and you've come to the bottom of your global freshwater tank, you've reached the end of the road. There is no other ride.

The snowpack in California in 2015 was at 5 percent of the average. California's snowpack provides about a third of the state's drinking water—which means that 95 percent of one third (or 33 percent) of the drinking water is gone.[76] There doesn't seem to be any end to the drought in sight. It's really scary, and it doesn't just affect California; it affects the entire country—in fact, since we're a closed global system, it affects the whole world.

I can't do much to make California's mandatory water reductions apply to animal agriculture and irrigation of feed crops—an email here, a phone call there.

But here's what I can do directly: take shorter showers with my low-flow shower-head, not wash Super Blue until she becomes Super Brown, fix all my leaky faucets and install aerators, switch to a water-conserving toilet (or just put a large jug of water in the toilet tank to displace the amount of water needed for each flush), collect my used dishwater and laundry water (from my water-efficient front-loader) to water plants, and switch out the outdoor greens with gorgeous desert succulents. But with all this, how much can I really save if all domestic water use is only 5 percent of total water use? More important than all my domestic water use put together is my diet. Wouldn't reducing (or eliminating) my meat and dairy consumption be the place to start?

CHAPTER THREE
HAPPY FARMS: "I LOVE ANIMALS—THAT'S WHY I'M IN THE MEAT BUSINESS"

.

Maybe it makes a difference where animal products come from—what sort of farm they're raised on and how they're produced. I remembered Ann Notthoff telling me about the sustainable pork producer who had won the NRDC's Growing Green award. Perhaps sustainable meat production wasn't the oxymoron I thought it was. I've heard a lot about how much better grass-fed cattle are for the environment and how much more natural it is to let cows graze the way they always have.

I wanted to visit one of these sustainable farms. I found the Markegard Family Grass fed beef farm on the lush, misty California coast. It was beautiful—gentle green hills dotted with wildflowers and peacefully grazing cows and sheep.

I met Erik and Doniga Markegard and their four children, Lea, Larry, Quill, and Quince. They were extremely kind. The Markegards are a good-looking family—all the kids inherited Doniga's blond hair, while Erik has dark, rugged looks. Lea, the oldest child, about eleven, walked ahead of the group, hand in hand with her father. They both wore cowboy hats, plaid shirts, blue jeans, and cowboy boots, and Lea's crimped Rapunzel hair reached past her waist. Larry, the little boy, wore a black cowboy hat and stalked through the bushes alongside the dirt path we were on. I spoke with Doniga Markegard, who also wore a cowboy hat, jeans, and cowboy boots, as she held her daughter Quill (also in cowboy boots) by the hand, and kept hold of a rope that attached her to Quince, the youngest, trailing behind.

"Lea and Larry are usually up at six in the morning milking the cows and slopping the hogs," Doniga told me happily, almost singing. "All together, we graze about 4,500 acres. This is our home ranch. This is 952 acres of that. On average, it's about one cow, or a cow and a calf, every ten acres. We produce annually roughly 80,000 pounds of finished, plate-ready meat."

We walked through the fields, as Lea and Erik gently herded the cows. Flocks of sheep ran before us. A sandy-colored sheepdog trotted by.

I met the pigs—three of them came right up to me. A big brown one sniffed my hand. Their snouts were covered in grain from the trough.

"We keep about ten pigs in a roughly fifty-acre area," Doniga told me, "and we move them around in ten-acre pastures."

Lea sat down on a rusty-brown pig who was lying on his side. The pig didn't seem to mind at all, and Lea rubbed his back affectionately.

"Some people think that pigs are dirty and gross, but I really like them," Lea told me. "They know people, and they'll be friends, and are really nice. They could be like your best friend, or be like a sister. See?" she said, as a black-and-white pig approached her, lifting his snout to be scratched. "They know you, and you get to know them."

Larry, Lea's little brother, was smiling at us and leaning sideways over a pig three times his size, his cheek against the pig's back.

"I shouldn't be bonding," Lea said, sitting on another pig, "but you have to have a nice pig."

"Why shouldn't you bond with them?" I asked.

"Well." Lea laughed and got off the pig, but continued to scratch and pat him. "Because they're going to turn into bacon." She kept her face down, rubbing the pig hard.

"Oh."

I walked back over to Doniga, who was carrying Quince in her arms. A few more pigs milled in front of us.

"These pigs are about seven months old now," Doniga said.

"That's it? Wow." Still just babies, I thought to myself. They were already hefty animals, weighing at least one hundred pounds.

"These bigger ones are getting ready to be killed. Those two smaller ones there"— she pointed at two pigs in the shade with Lea and Larry—"they could grow up a few more months."

I had no idea animals were slaughtered at such a young age. It seemed incredibly sad. All I could think about was how traumatic it must be for Lea, having the pigs she loved killed every seven months. They seemed like a big part of her life and, as she said, her family. I remained silent, though I wanted to reach out to give her a big hug. I wanted to tell her how sorry I was, knowing what she would have to go through again in a few weeks. And yet her parents, Erik and Doniga, were kind and caring parents. I wondered how they explained the killing of the animals to their children.

Erik is a sixth-generation cattle rancher, who raised rodeo bulls before he started selling grass-fed beef.[1] Doniga spent years in her youth in the western Washington wilderness learning from wildlife trackers, naturalists, and Native American spiritual elders. She also plays a role in agriculture advocacy and policy, helping to shape legislation affecting family farms.[2]

Doniga, Erik, and I sat in the tall grass of one of their green pastures to talk some more. The blue sky was enormous.

"I love animals," Doniga said, "That's why I'm in the meat business." She smiled.

"It's what more of society needs to see," Erik said. "That that packaged piece of meat is a living animal." He laughed. "A living and breathing creature that—yeah. It's hard. It's hard. But like what Doniga said earlier." Erik paused, seeming to search for words. "We do it because we love them," he said emphatically.

The products the Markegards offer include harder-to-find items like beef cheeks (the facial cheeks of a cow), beef liver, pork feet, pork belly skin, pork back fat, and lamb neck bones.[3]

I ask the Markegards about land use. I'd read that some grass-fed farms can produce a cow on as little as two to two-and-a-half acres per cow, while other farms can go all the way up to thirty acres per animal, or even more.[4]

"Yeah," Erik said. "We have a ranch in South Dakota that's fifty acres [per cow]." He laughed broadly.

"Fifty acres," I echoed.

"Yeah." He laughed again. "It's about fifty acres."

"Why is that?" I asked.

"Same thing," Erik said. "It was farmed and robbed of all the nitrogen. You know. The land was abused."

"It's also seasonal, right?" Doniga said.

"It's also seasonal," Erik confirmed.

"Is it possible," I asked, "is it practical for the whole world to have grass-fed cattle? In Brazil, say, where . . . was it eighty percent of the rain forest was destroyed for cattle? What are your thoughts on that?"

"They shouldn't be eating beef," Erik says decisively. Doniga looks over her shoulder at her husband and smiles, nodding. "If their environment wasn't designed to raise beef, then they shouldn't be eating it."

"Yeah," agrees Doniga.

"How do you offset the carbon footprint of livestock?" I ask. This is my big question—is there a way to sustainably raise animals for food?

"Uh—" Doniga seems at a loss for words. "We . . . don't feel like livestock have a carbon footprint," she says finally, with a smile.

THE SUSTAINABILITY OF GRASS-FED FARMS

I left there feeling confused. Confused by my emotions, about the paradox of a "happy farm" where all the animals are raised to be killed, or the sadness I felt imagining Lea crying in a few short weeks, when the pigs, who were "like your best friend, or like a sister" to her, were sent to slaughter. As far as grass-fed beef not having a carbon footprint, it actually sounded like it could make sense—until I added up the numbers on land use and population.

Stay with me here, we're going to get a bit technical. The average American eats at least 209 pounds of meat a year.[5] The Markegard model of raising animals requires 4,500 acres to produce 80,000 pounds of grass-fed meat. If all 209 pounds of meat were grass-fed beef, only 382 people could be fed by the Markegards' land. In terms of land use, taking the 4,500 acres that the Markegards graze, dividing it by the 382 people gives us 11.7 acres per person. So it takes 11.7 acres of land to raise enough grass-fed meat for one American, for one year. Multiply 11.7 acres by 314 million Americans, and that comes out to 3.7 billion acres of grazing land needed to feed the United States their annual meat, if it were all grass-fed.

Grass-fed Cattle Land Use

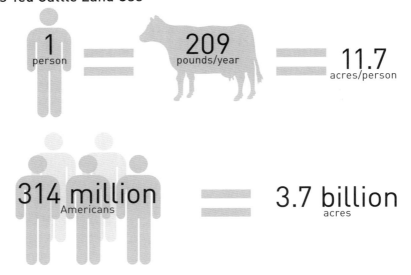

Grain-fed
Cattle Land
Requirement

Grass-fed Cattle
Land Requirement

Unfortunately, there are only 1.9 billion acres of land in the lower forty-eight states of the United States of America. Total.

Currently, nearly half of all the land in the United States is already dedicated to animal agriculture.[6] If we were to switch over to grass-fed beef, it would require clearing every square inch of the United States, up into Canada, all of Central America, and well into South America. This is just to feed the demand for meat of the United States, not to mention the rest of the world.

Additionally, that figure doesn't even take into consideration the fact that much of the land in the United States isn't suited for grazing livestock. We would have to convert all mountain ranges to grassland, clear ancient forests and national parks, and demolish every city just to make room to graze cows.

Apart from land use, it turns out that "sustainable" grass-fed meat takes an even heavier toll on the environment than factory farms.

If all cows in the United States were fed on grass and forage without "growth enhancing technology" (growth hormones), they would be a lot leaner, and we would need many more animals to produce the same amount of meat. I encountered the work of Dr. Jude Capper during my research. Capper is an adjunct professor of dairy sciences at Washington State University, and she calculates that to produce 26.1 billion pounds of grass-fed beef—the amount of beef consumed in the United States in 2001[7]—the country would need an additional 50.2 million cows.[8]

Animals raised in pasture also require more water than feedlot-raised animals, because they're physically active and spend time outside in the sun.[9] Capper estimates that supplying the country with all grass-fed beef would increase water use by 468 billion gallons—which is equivalent to the yearly water use by 53.1 million households in the United States.[10]

"There's a perception that grass-fed animals are frolicking in the sunshine, kicking their heels up full of joy and pleasure," Capper said in an article on Examiner.com. "What we actually found was, from the land-use basis, from the energy [and] water [use]—and particularly, based on the carbon footprints—grass-fed is far worse than corn-fed."[11]

Dr. Capper clearly has some interest in promoting the industrial agriculture sector—she was associated with American Farmers for the Advancement and Conservation of Technology (AFACT),[12] an advocacy front group formed with significant support from Monsanto, the giant chemical company that, among other things, manufactures recombinant bovine somatotropin (rBST), the synthetic growth hormone injected into dairy cows to increase their milk production. AFACT was created to defend the dairy industry's use of rBST and help win over consumers who were concerned about growth hormones in their milk.[13]

So I was more than a little wary about taking Capper's comments at face value. But after some digging, I found that her statements are corroborated by the research out there. Western Watersheds Project, James McWilliams, Demosthenes Maratos, and Jeff Anhang (all those we've interviewed or researched so far)—they and many other experts agree: grass-fed beef *is* far worse, environmentally, than corn-fed.

"It takes twenty-three months for a grass-fed animal to grow . . . to the size and age that it's slaughtered," Demosthenes Maratos had told me when I interviewed him, "whereas a grain-fed [animal] takes fifteen months. So that's an additional eight months of water use, land use, feed, [and] waste. In terms of a carbon footprint, that's a huge difference."

There are areas in the United States where it takes one hundred acres to support one grass-fed cow. As Erik Markegard pointed out, the Markegards have a ranch where it takes fifty acres to sustain a single cow—and they can keep animals at that ranch for only part of the year because the land is so depleted. Think about it. One single cow taking up fifty to one hundred acres. It's unsustainable.

And don't forget about the 50.2 million extra cows we would need to make up the gap between leaner, grass-fed animal and fatter, grain-fed, feedlot-raised animals. Those extra eight months of resources would be needed for all of them.

The environmental impacts don't end there. Grass-fed cows emit 60 to 400 percent more methane than cows raised in factory farms[14] due to their different diets.

And remember, methane is eighty-six times more destructive than carbon dioxide.[15] The astounding figure of 400 percent more methane from grass-fed cows comes from Jeff Anhang, an environmental specialist with the World Bank's IFC Environment and Social Development Department[16] and one of the co-authors of the WorldWatch Institute report, "Livestock and Climate Change," citing animal agriculture as the source of 51 percent of human-caused greenhouse gas emissions.

On top of all this are the effects of animal agriculture on animal habitats and our natural landscapes. Western Watersheds Project (WWP) is a non-profit environmental conservation group working to preserve and restore western watersheds and wildlife, "with a primary focus on the negative impacts of livestock grazing on 250 million acres of western public lands, including harm to ecological, biological, cultural, historic, archeological, and scenic resources, wilderness values, roadless areas, Wilderness Study Areas, and designated Wilderness."[17]

WWP asserts that livestock grazing has "by far the biggest impact [on] the American landscape,"[18] beyond urban sprawl or any other use of land.

The Center for Biological Diversity (CBD), a non-profit environmental group based in Tucson, Arizona, works to protect endangered species and habitats. The organization released a study on the negative impacts of livestock grazing in California's East Bay area. The CBD's sources included "over 150 scientific, peer-reviewed research papers and articles detailing the detrimental environmental impacts of livestock grazing in the western United States, and . . . a survey of over 140 peer-reviewed studies on the biological and physical effects of livestock on western rivers, streams, and riparian areas." The CBD researchers searched specifically and systematically for peer-reviewed experimental studies that showed the positive environmental impacts of grazing but could find none.[19]

The CBD study found that cattle grazing damaged water quality by increasing levels of bacteria, protozoa, sediment load, and water temperature, while decreasing the levels of oxygen in the water. Algae growth increased, although there was a decline in the growth and diversity of higher plants. The biomass of trees, shrubs, and overhanging vegetation all decreased. Erosion, bare ground, and stream-bank instability increased.[20]

Of course, this imbalance in the ecosystem causes a chain reaction that has a significant impact on native animal, fish, insect, and plant species. Cattle grazing destroys the conditions necessary for the survival of red-legged frogs, California tiger salamanders, ground squirrel colonies, Western toads, the Alameda whipsnake (a threatened species), the giant garter snake, the Western yellow-billed cuckoo, the foothill yellow-legged frog, California horned and legless lizards, vernal pool shrimp, steelhead trout, tule elk, endangered and threatened butterflies, and endangered, threatened, or sensitive plant species like the Mt. Diablo fairy lantern and the Oakland star-tulip, among many others. Cattle also trample and eat young California oak trees if ranchers do not cut down the trees first. More than 300 species of vertebrates and 5,000 invertebrates directly or indirectly require oaks to survive.[21]

Maybe it's just me, but melancholy leaks through the academic language of the CBD report: "This grassland community evolved with fire and native ungulate browsers such as elk, deer, and antelope. It should be noted that cattle grazing does not mimic the browsing patterns of those native ungulates. The native grassland community of California was considered one of the most diverse, beautiful, and productive grassland ecosystems in the world."

THE SUSTAINABILITY OF DAIRIES

I had to come to terms with the fact there was no way to sustainably, humanely, and "naturally" raise enough grass-fed, pastured animals to meet the world's current demand for meat.

I had my doubts on dairy as well, so I went to talk with a premier organic dairy company to see what they would say.

I drove over to Clover Stornetta Dairy in northern California. Clover Stornetta announces on their website that they lead the nation in sustainable, high-quality dairy farming that makes a difference in the way we eat, drink, and live. Their milk does not contain rBST, and all their farms and the milk they produce are held to safety standards that far surpass state and federal standards. "Our local California family farms in Sonoma and Marin Counties are committed to the sustainability of their land, welfare of their cows and produce the highest quality milk pool in the country," reads the website.[22]

It sounded good.

I spoke with their president and CEO, Marcus Benedetti. He is a tall man with short dark hair, and was dressed casually in jeans and a white checked shirt. A large map of California hung in his office, and there were many artfully framed family pictures on the wall behind his computer screen—baby pictures, kids riding horses and swimming.

I asked Benedetti if he thought dairy is a sustainable product for the world's population. He was very straightforward.

"It requires a lot of inputs to produce milk," he said. "The feed, the water, the land. It does. It may not be practical to expect that there can be enough dairy production produced in a sustainable way to feed the entire world. I just don't think that that's necessarily a given. I think it's maybe too much to expect that the world can be fed with dairy in a sustainable way. I don't know the answer, but common sense would say that's a long shot."

I was shocked to hear such an honest answer. If this is what the dairy's CEO would say, I wondered what the farmer would claim.

I spent a little time looking through their marketing material. A big-screen TV mounted on the wall in the office lobby showed a smiling woman in sunglasses posing with Clo the Cow, Clover's cartoon mascot with a smiling mouthful of teeth and a flowered smock. Clo the Cow, forever smiling, was all over their glossy promotional materials, urging consumers to "MOOve up to Clover Milk."

It seemed their farms were an oasis for cows. A short video called "Welcome to Clover Country" told me that all of Clover's farms are certified by the American Humane Association.

"We like to give them the opportunity whenever we can, environmentally," says one of Clover's farmers on the video, "to let them out of the barns and let them roam around." I had to laugh at the accompanying clip showing a band of black-and-white cows, walking placidly toward the beach. Beach day for the cows!

Robin Ganzert, the president and CEO of the American Humane Association, appears in the video, standing in front of shelves full of Clover products. "Clover farms," she says, "utilize the best practices and the best standards and serve as a model paving the way for the humane treatment of cows."

I headed out to one of the farms. It was not what I expected.

The land was brown and parched, and cows stood with their heads lowered behind mud-crusted metal enclosures.

I went inside the barn to see the cows being milked. It was claustrophobic, with a low ceiling, lit entirely by fluorescents. There was a narrow walkway between two aisles of cows packed tightly next to one another, fenced in by metal racks. They faced away from the walkway, making their udders easily accessible. Each cow was hooked up to a milking machine, with long lengths of thick yellow tubes running out of the milking machines and seemingly up to the ceiling, sometimes looping around. I felt like I was surrounded by two walls of machinery, metal, and tubes, with glimpses of shadowy cow legs and udders behind the machinery. If this was the best of the best, I thought to myself, I can't imagine what the rest of the country's dairy farms must be like.

This farm was the Bivalve Organic Dairy, one of Clover's family farms. John Taylor, the co-owner of Bivalve, interrupted his work to talk with me. Taylor was a big man wearing a green Cal Poly hoodie sweatshirt and a baseball cap.

"Typically, a cow will eat 140 to 150 pounds of feed a day," Taylor told me.

"140 to 150 pounds?" I echoed. It sounded like an enormous amount.

"140 to 150 pounds of feed a day," he said with a nod. "Then, she's also going to drink between thirty and forty gallons of water. We probably go through about twenty tons a week."

"Twenty tons . . . !?!"

"Twenty tons of grain per week," he spelled it out for me patiently. "Primarily for our milking cows, so about 250 cows."

Dairy Cow Resource Consumption (daily)

1 dairy cow = 145 pounds of feed & 35 gallons of water

"The biggest part of sustainability to me, the number one thing on the list, should be profitability," Taylor said to me after we walked back out into the sun. "So how the process completely works, from start to finish, is the cow needs to have a baby in order to give milk, so she'll have her baby. That baby is going to stay with the mother for at least two days. The babies will go off to our calf-raising facility, so they have an individual hutch that they'll be raised in. Since we're a dairy, it's only the girl cows that give us milk, so the boys on typical dairies, they're sold off to beef-raising facilities, but we do keep approximately half, and we raise them for two years and sell them as organic grass-fed beef."

"So do all dairy cows eventually go to the beef industry?" I asked Taylor.

"Mm-hmm." He nodded again.

I suddenly remembered seeing Taylor and his family in the "Welcome to Clover Country" video. There was a shot of him sitting with his wife on some bales of hay, holding his little girl in his lap, speaking to the camera about their farm and their pride in being associated with Clover. Later, the three of them walked back from the milking barn, the little girl in rubber boots with a pink flower in her hair.

I took a look at the calf-raising facility. The calves were surprisingly delicate, very thin, with spindly legs, oversized ears, and big, shiny, dark eyes. Each calf had its own molded plastic shed, sort of a calf-sized, pale-gray doghouse. A wire enclosure extending from the shed gave the baby cow a dirt "yard" slightly longer and wider than its own body. These little Monopoly-like houses were lined up in a long row, side by side.

"At some point in time," Taylor went on, "she's really going to drop off [in milk production], so you have to make a business decision at that point. Are you going to keep investing in her to give milk, or are you going to sell her off again to another dairy or into the beef industry?"

I watched as, in the distance, four farm workers pushed a cow into the long bucket of a yellow CAT compact track loader, using her tethered hind legs to roll her onto her back.

I could hear the cow's guttural *moo*, very high-pitched and drawn out. The cow's eyes were wide and blinking. Her udder, which still looked full, was almost hanging over the lip of the bucket as she lay partly on her side, partly on her back. Her front legs were folded up against her belly, and a rope attached somewhere to her head was tightly lashed around a cross bar of the construction vehicle, forcing her neck to twist as though she were looking over her shoulder. When she was securely in place, the four men backed off. The track loader hoisted the cow several feet off the ground in the bucket and drove up the dirt road. I soon lost sight of them.

A double column of black-and-white cows, fenced in by metal and wire, moved along with their heads lowered. The sun was really hot. As the cows passed, I saw that their bellies and udders were strangely bumpy.

"There's very few places on this planet that have this type of environment," Taylor said, "but the demand on dairy-based protein in the world is only going to increase, and there's not enough land on the planet to do this type of dairying around the world. It's just, the environment is not going to be that way. The land's not there."

"So I guess on a global scale," I said, "the conclusion would be dairy is not sustainable."

Taylor paused in thought. "Unless we start digging up houses and putting pastures back." He laughed briefly and nodded. "The only way to start digging up houses and development is to have fewer people. We all know that population is going to continue to grow, so that means more commercial dairying, I'm sure."

"Either that, or somehow lower demand by the people," I said.

"Yeah, or some other product is going to take its place. We see there are all sorts of soy milks and almond milks and a lot of other products that are coming out, and different blends, where you take juices and proteins. I think you'll see a lot more of that."

I really appreciated the candidness and honesty of John Taylor and Marcus Benedetti. They were right. How could cows' milk be sustainable? One gallon of milk takes upwards of 1,000 gallons of water to produce,[23] and 19 percent of animal agriculture's yearly world-wide water footprint is related to dairy cattle. That's 19 percent of 2,422 billion cubic meters of water.[24]

To produce milk, a dairy cow drinks an enormous amount of water—milk from a Holstein cow, the most common dairy breed in the United States, is about 87 percent water, after all.[25] John Taylor's cows drink between 30 to 40 gallons a day, and he has 250 cows. So on Taylor's farm, using the figure of 35 gallons daily per cow, it takes 8,750 gallons of water every single day just for the cows to drink.

And then dairy cows have to eat. Because the continuous production of milk puts such metabolic demands on their bodies, they eat a tremendous amount. Dairy cows produce about 6 to 7 gallons of milk daily.[26] Divide 140 pounds of feed a day by 7 gallons of milk—it takes 20 pounds of feed to produce one gallon of milk. The feed of dairy cows in the United States is mainly alfalfa hay, grass hay, corn, soy, canola, and other grains.[27] And as I learned when I was finding out about water use, all those crops are water-intensive, especially alfalfa. Remember, 70 percent of the alfalfa grown in California goes to feed dairy cows,[28] and alfalfa is the most water-intensive crop of all those grown in the state.[29] This is a state that provides the nation with almost half of its fruits, vegetables, and nuts,[30] but alfalfa, grown mostly for dairy cows, trumps them all in terms of water use.

And that's not the end of it. There's also the water used for cleaning and maintenance, including automatic manure "flushing" systems that use up to 150 gallons per cow a day.[31] Dairy cows in factory farms across the country produce more than two billion pounds of manure nitrogen every year that are "flushed" off the farm, which then leads to issues like dead zones in the oceans and contaminated water supplies.[32]

In the United States alone, in 2012, there were 9 million dairy cows, on 100,000 farms.[33] Multiply all that water use and feed by 9 million cows. It's staggering.

And what about the greenhouse gases related just to the dairy sector? The FAO released a report called *Greenhouse Gas Emissions from the Dairy Sector: A Life Cycle Assessment* that estimates 4 percent of all greenhouse gas emissions caused by humans is contributed by the dairy industry. About 52 percent of that is methane.[34] The FAO estimates that another 27 percent of dairy-related greenhouse gases is nitrous oxide,[35] which has a global warming potential 296 times greater than carbon dioxide.[36] It's also important to remember that the FAO uses very conservative figures.

Amazingly, among all animal products, cheese is ranked third highest in greenhouse gas emissions by the Environmental Working Group, coming in after lamb and beef.[37]

All right. I love cheese; I love ice cream, chocolate milk, milk shakes, yogurt—and did I mention I reeeeally love cheese? But I had to confront reality. Dairy is not sustainable. Grass-fed, pasture-raised animals are not sustainable. Which leads me straight to where I did not want to go.

Factory farms. Agribusiness. Industrialized meat production.

Could this possibly be the answer to feeding a growing population's demands for animal protein? Like everyone else, I've heard vaguely about the horrors of factory farms, how animals are abused and crowded together in filthy conditions. But could that be the necessary price to pay for the efficient production of meat, using "growth enhancement technology" to raise larger, fewer animals, to feed more people with a minimal impact on the environment?

I felt a little sick about it, but I had to at least look into the issue.

So I did.

CHAPTER FOUR

FACTORY FARMS: STANDARD INDUSTRY PRACTICE

This chapter contains graphic and disturbing information. I'd normally say skip something if it's going to bother you, but I encourage you to learn where most of the world's meat comes from. Stay with me if you can.

Where can I begin with factory farms? Maybe here: "No one fired a pistol to mark the start of the race to the bottom," Jonathan Safran Foer writes in *Eating Animals*. "The earth just tilted and everyone slid into the hole."[1]

The official term for "factory farm" is "concentrated animal feeding operation" (CAFO). The very definition of a CAFO, by the Environmental Protection Agency, stipulates that it is, apart from the enormous numbers of animals it confines within a small space, a "significant contributor of pollutants."[2] By the EPA definition, there is no such thing as a factory farm that is good for the environment.

But they certainly seem to be efficient. Only 2 percent of American livestock farms—obviously the largest, most industrialized operations—raise 40 percent of all the animals raised for food in the country.[3] In fact, more than 99 percent of farmed animals in the United States are raised on factory farms.[4] And over nine billion land animals in the United States alone are killed every year for human consumption.[5]

CAFOs make up roughly 15 percent[6] of the 450,000 animal feeding operations (AFOs) in the United States.[7] An AFO is defined by the Environmental Protection Agency as "agricultural operations where animals are kept and raised in confined situations. AFOs congregate animals, feed, manure and urine, dead animals, and production operations on a small land area. Feed is brought to the animals rather than the animals grazing or otherwise seeking feed in pastures, fields, or on rangeland."[8]

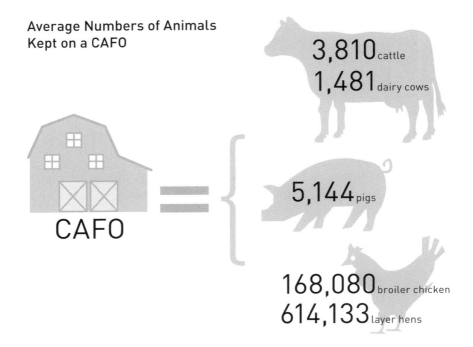

**Average Numbers of Animals
Kept on a CAFO**

3,810 cattle
1,481 dairy cows

5,144 pigs

168,080 broiler chicken
614,133 layer hens

The staggering numbers of animals held in a facility, as well as the amount of pol-lution created by the way manure is released into the water supply, are what transform an AFO into a CAFO. The average numbers of animals, from 2007, kept on a single American CAFO are 3,810 cattle; 1,481 dairy cows; 5,144 pigs; 168,080 broiler chick-ens (raised for flesh); and 614,133 layer hens (raised for eggs).[9]

Keep in mind these numbers are just averages. It is not unusual for a single chicken farm to confine more than one million birds.[10] Sometimes a chicken farm is deemed a CAFO depending on whether a liquid manure handling system is used.[11]

A liquid manure handling system is as attractive as it sounds. The urine and fecal matter of the animals is mixed with water and then stored either under the farm or in massive open air "lagoons"[12] that are sometimes as big as several football fields.[13]

The Pew Commission on Industrial Farm Animal Production found that:

> Decomposing manure produces at least 160 different gases, of which hydrogen sulfide . . . ammonia, carbon dioxide, methane, and carbon monoxide are the most pervasive. . . . Possibly the most dangerous gas . . . is hydrogen sulfide. It can be released rapidly when the liquid manure slurry is agitated, an operation commonly performed to suspend solids so that pits can be emptied by pumping.

During agitation, hydrogen sulfide levels can soar within seconds from the usual ambient levels of less than 5 ppm to lethal levels of over 500 ppm. Animals and workers have died or become seriously ill in swine industrial farm animal production (IFAP) facilities when hydrogen sulfide has risen from agitated manure in pits under the building.[14]

These vast cesspools full of raw feces and urine often rupture or leak, causing huge amounts of toxic contamination to soil and water supplies, which are already being depleted to feed the animals on these farms. An EPA report states that livestock manure has polluted 35,000 miles of rivers in 22 states and that groundwater in 17 states has been significantly contaminated.[15] North Carolina State University released a study in 1995 that estimated up to 55 percent of the fecal lagoons from hog farms in that state were leaking.[16] The same year, an 8-acre lagoon in North Carolina ruptured, causing the worst fecal spill on record,[17] sending 25 million gallons of manure into the New River, killing 10 million fish.[18] In 1999, Hurricane Floyd caused most of North Carolina's manure lagoons to flood over into rivers and the entire flood-prone area.[19] A lagoon at a western New York dairy collapsed in 2005, spilling 3 million gallons of liquefied manure into the Black River, killing more than 250,000 fish.[20] In 2011, 200,000 gallons of manure were spilled into a creek from a hog farm in Illinois, killing more than 110,000 fish.[21]

Needless to say, these rivers and waterways also became toxic to humans. Livestock manure often carries deadly pathogens like E. coli, Salmonella, Cryptosporidium, and fecal coliform, which can be ten to one hundred times more concentrated than in human feces—not to mention the antibiotics, steroids, growth hormones, and other chemical additives.[22] There are more than forty diseases that can be transferred to human beings from manure.[23]

And it's the raw stuff—there are no treatment facilities for animal feces.[24]

The manure is often kept for months before being shipped to farms as fertilizer, requiring the use of large tankers and trucks, which of course require fossil fuels to run and emit greenhouse gases.[25] But with the enormous amounts of manure being produced, there is much more than can be used or repurposed. In the fifteen years between 1982 and 1997, there was a 64 percent increase in the amount of manure in the United States that could not be absorbed into the soil as fertilizer.[26] There is only so much manure that can be applied to soil before the soil is saturated and cannot take any more. The excess liquefied manure eventually enters groundwater by runoff or leaching, while the farmers look the other way.[27]

Of course, there is more—degraded air quality from the toxic gases and particulates released from CAFOs causes asthma—especially in children—bronchitis, lung disease, and even cardiac arrest. The odors are so bad that people living close to CAFOs will keep their windows closed even on hot days without air conditioning, or refuse to let their children out to play or even go to school. Insect swarms plague communities surrounding CAFOs—most frequently houseflies, stable flies, and mosquitoes, as they are drawn to the manure, decaying organic material, and stagnant water. There is even such a thing as CAFO-related post-traumatic stress disorder—and I'm talking about the *humans* living close to factory farms.[28]

LIFE IN A CAFO

But the animals have it much, much worse. No examination of CAFOs, no matter how brief, is complete without looking at the treatment of its inmates. It would be, to borrow an analogy I've heard frequently, like analyzing the carbon footprint of the trains to Auschwitz without mentioning what happened behind the gates.

"The life of an animal in a factory farm is characterized by acute deprivation, stress, and disease," states the Humane Farming Association. "Hundreds of millions of animals are forced to live in cages or crates just barely larger than their own bodies. While one species may be caged alone without any social contact, another species may be crowded so tightly together that they fall prey to stress-induced cannibalism. Cannibalism is particularly prevalent in the cramped confinement of hogs and laying hens. Unable to groom, stretch their legs, or even turn around, the victims of factory farms exist in a relentless state of distress."[29]

Chickens raised for meat—"broilers"—are typically crowded together with 20,000 other birds in a single, enormous shed, often without windows. There are so many chickens covering the floor that workers who collect the dead birds have to shuffle their feet to keep from crushing the other chickens.[30]

Broiler chickens produce about half a pound of excrement for every pound of weight they gain. This waste—produced by the tens of thousands of chickens in one building—often remains on the ground under the chickens for their entire seven-week lives and will sometimes not even be cleaned out before the next flock is brought in.[31] As the birds are young and excitable, they often kick up enormous amounts of their own feces, dust, and bacteria into the air. This is before their inbred genetics and growth hormones take over and they grow to obese proportions, barely able to move. These birds often live their entire short lives standing and sitting in their own feces, suffering from breast blisters and painful ammonia burns to their eyes, which can blind them.[32]

In farm language, when the chicken manure is mixed with the absorbent substrate on the floor of the poultry shed, it becomes a "cake."[33] This tasty "cake" is frequently baked during hot weather, and the chemicals that are released by the heat, combined with a lack of cooling ventilation, can be lethal. A heat wave in 1995 killed more than four million broiler chickens in the United States.[34]

Because of these filthy conditions, broilers are fed almost four times the amount of antibiotics as are consumed by human beings or cattle.[35] Serious diseases are rampant.

"Scientific studies and government records," Jonathan Safran Foer writes in *Eating Animals*, "suggest that virtually all (upwards of 95 percent of) chickens become infected with E. coli (an indicator of fecal contamination) and between 39 and 75 percent of [chicken meat] in retail stores are still infected. Around 8 percent of birds become infected with salmonella. . . . 70 to 90 percent are infected with another potentially deadly pathogen, campylobacter. Chlorine baths are commonly used to remove slime, odor, and bacteria."[36]

In the 1950s, broilers were killed at the age of sixteen weeks. That time dropped to twelve weeks in 1970, and now, in 2015, they are killed at seven weeks.[37] This is thanks to the miracle of genetic manipulation and breeding, along with growth stimulants like sulfa drugs and antibiotics to control the flourishing diseases created by close confinement of so many birds.

The University of Arkansas Division of Agriculture puts it this way: "If you grew as fast as a chicken, you'd weigh 349 pounds at age 2."[38]

Roughly 90 percent of broilers have trouble walking due to their accelerated growth and resulting leg problems.[39] About 6 percent are so crippled that if chickens were covered under the laws banning the use of cows or pigs unable to stand or walk on their own as food,[40] they could not be sold as meat.[41]

The birds start to die of heart attacks and other diseases caused by their unnaturally fast growth at around seven weeks, which is another reason they are rushed to slaughter so young.[42] Farmers call the premature heart attacks "flip-over disease."[43]

"Everyone's saying buy fresh, buy local," said Frank Reese, a poultry farmer, in *Eating Animals*. He raises turkeys, but his words apply to chickens as well. "It's a sham. It's all the same kind of bird, and the suffering is in their genes. When the mass-produced turkey of today was designed, they killed thousands of turkeys in their experiments. Should it be shorter legs or shorter keel bone? Should it be like this or like [that]? In nature, sometimes human babies are born with deformities. You don't aim to reproduce that generation after generation. But that's what they did with turkeys."[44]

Chickens are naturally social and intelligent animals. The extreme crowding, confinement, and filthy conditions of CAFOs thwart all their natural impulses and cause them severe stress, leading to abnormal behaviors like feather-pulling, head-picking, and cannibalism. Agro-businesses could have dealt with this problem easily by allowing the chickens more room and foraging options—but that would have cost money. A more business-savvy solution was simply to cut off their beaks.

Baby chicks are now routinely debeaked, usually in the first week of life, by an electric debeaker, which slices off approximately half their beaks with a hot blade. The machine operator can debeak twelve to fifteen chicks every minute. An alternative is to use a sharp knife.[45]

The beaks of chickens contain more nerve endings than our fingertips.[46] The Brambell Committee, a group of veterinarians and other animal experts, wrote a report exploring animal welfare in concentrated animal farming operations in 1965. "There is no physiological basis," the committee wrote, "for the [farming industry's] assertion that the operation is similar to the clipping of human finger nails. Between the horn and bone [of the beak] is a thin layer of highly sensitive soft tissue, resembling the quick of the human nail. The hot knife blade used in debeaking cuts through this complex horn, bone, and sensitive tissue causing severe pain."[47]

A bird's beak is also its primary instrument of exploration. Debeaking is like cutting off a person's fingers and thumb as a form of crowd control, to prevent them from making fists or grabbing one another. In addition to the beak, the toes of the chickens are clipped, and the combs and leg spurs of the males are cut off.[48]

Pigs in factory farms, like chickens, are subjected to amputations without anesthetic. And like debeaking chickens, these amputations are preemptive "solutions" to the aggressive and unnatural behavior that arises when pigs—also highly intelligent, gregarious animals—are kept in close, continual confinement with one another with no stimulation.

Baby pigs routinely have their tails cut off with wire clippers (docking) to prevent tail biting, and their teeth are clipped for the same reason.[49] Pieces of their ears are cut out (notching) for identification purposes.[50] Male piglets are castrated without anesthetic because customers don't like the taste and smell of uncastrated male pigs.[51]

A 2013 investigative piece in *Rolling Stone* included undercover video footage of this treatment. One particularly horrific clip shows a man holding a male piglet upside down by the hind legs, belly facing the camera, its splayed legs stretching the skin of its underside taut. The man uses a red-handled scalpel, while still holding the pig, to make two neat parallel incisions between the legs, which instantly gape and bleed. Another man digs his latex-gloved thumb and forefinger into the incisions and tears out the piglet's testicles, yanking on the dark spermatic cord until it rips.[52]

The piglet screams and screams.

Piglets that are not big enough to be profitable are killed by "thumping"—taking the animal by the hind legs and bashing its head against the concrete floor.[53] It is also known as PACing—pounding against concrete.

Gail Eisnitz, in her book, *Slaughterhouse*, interviewed a worker on a Missouri farm, who told her, "We've thumped as many as 120 in one day. We just swing them, thump them, then toss them aside. Then, after you've thumped ten, twelve, fourteen of them, you take them to the chute room and stack them up for the dead truck. And if you go in the chute room and some are still alive, then you have to thump them all over again. There've been times I've walked in that room and they'd be running around with an eyeball hanging down the side of their face, just bleeding like crazy, or their jaw would be broken."[54]

The mother sows, kept perpetually pregnant, are housed in gestation crates—metal confinement units that measure 2 feet by 7 feet.[55] They are so small that the pigs cannot turn around or lie down comfortably. They are able to take one or two steps forward and back.[56] As the pregnant animals get bigger, they have so little room they cannot even lay on their sides.[57] The floors are slatted concrete, the standard flooring in industrial pig farms. This cuts cleaning costs, as the urine and feces fall through the slats into excrement collection piles beneath the animals. There is no straw or any other bedding to provide comfort, since that too would fall through the slats.[58] Thick ammonia fumes rise through the slats from the cesspits below.[59]

"A recent examination of 6,000 slaughtered pigs revealed 71 percent suffered from pneumonia," Erik Marcus writes in *Vegan: The New Ethics of Eating*. Maybe this has something to do with the dense, cloud-like air filled with toxins, dust, and gases that the pigs breathe day and night.[60]

The sows live in gestation crates suspended over vast piles of their own excrement for their entire four-month pregnancies. In fact, pigs in industrial operations often live in crates their entire lives.[61] When they are about to give birth, the sows are moved to farrowing crates for birthing and nursing. The farrowing crates keep them confined on their sides, providing the piglets access to their teats. The sow still cannot turn around. After a few weeks of nursing her young, the piglets are taken away and the sow is returned to the gestation crate for another pregnancy.[62]

"So our animals can't turn around for the two and a half years that they are in the stalls producing piglets," Dave Warner, the spokesman for the National Pork Producers Council, said in a 2012 *National Journal* interview. "I don't know who asked the sow if she wanted to turn around."[63]

They did ask the pork producers, who prefer to cram as many animals as possible into a small space to maximize profits.[64] It cuts feed costs if those animals are essentially immobilized—and who wants to waste expensive feed on providing pigs with the energy to run, walk, or, indeed, turn around? Researchers found that by cutting down on floor space given to piglets from 0.22 to 0.14 square meters, feed costs dropped by 10 percent.[65] Good news, right?

Beef cattle have it better than chickens and pigs. They are the only factory-farmed animals that are still raised outdoors for the most part.[66] They are still branded, de-horned—cattle horns are filled with sensitive nerves and blood vessels[67]—and castrated, almost always with no anesthetic, usually at the age of a few weeks.[68] The cows graze on rangeland for the first six months to a year of their lives,[69] and then are packed shoulder to shoulder into trucks or trains, sometimes for more than eighteen hours, to be sent to feedlots, which are CAFOs for cattle.[70]

Feedlots are massive open-air fenced areas. There is no grass—in fact, the very absence of vegetation is part of the definition of a CAFO. Cattle are sent here to be "finished." The phrase makes me think of the "finishing schools" where young upper-class girls were taught the necessary social graces.

The cattle in feedlots, however, are not learning French or how to host a charity ball. They are there to eat. They are fenced in by the thousands and fed a high-calorie diet—rather than the low-calorie, high-fiber plant diet their stomachs are suited for—that will add hundreds of profitable pounds to each animal's regular weight.[71]

The composition of this diet varies greatly. Farmers strive for the cheapest feed with the highest protein and calorie content. The feed is generally grain based, but grain is expensive, and one steer can eat about 4,500 pounds of food in a feedlot in the weeks before being sent to the slaughterhouse.[72] So there are some other things mixed into the feed.

Rendering plants use giant grinders to pulverize "the entire bodies of cows and other farm animals known to be diseased," writes Howard Lyman in *Mad Cowboy*. "Rendering is a $2.4-billion-a-year industry, processing 40 billion pounds of dead animals [per] year. There is simply no such thing in America as an animal too ravaged by disease, too cancerous, or too putrid to be welcomed by the all-embracing arms of the renderer."

Roadkill and euthanized pets are also sent to the renderer. "When this gruesome mix is ground and steam-cooked," Lyman continues, "the lighter, fatty material floating to the top gets refined for use in such products as cosmetics. . . . The heavier protein material is dried and pulverized into a brown powder—about a quarter of which consists of fecal material. The powder is used as an additive to almost all pet food as well as to livestock feed. Farmers call it 'protein concentrate.'"

This "protein concentrate," which contains the remains of countless cows and other animals, was fed back to cattle. After the mad cow scare in the late 1990s, the FDA issued a ban on feeding rendered parts of cud-chewing animals back to cud-chewing animals.

That ban, questionably enforced, still permits cows to be fed dead horses, pigs, dogs, cats, turkeys, chickens, and the blood and feces of other cows and chickens. Roughly 75 percent of the country's beef cattle are fed this "enriched" feed. It is also routine practice to use animal feces in cattle feed. It's a convenient way of getting rid of at least a little bit of the 1.6 million tons of livestock excrement produced every year.

"If you are a meat eater," Howard Lyman writes in *Mad Cowboy*, "understand that this is the food of your food."[73]

After a few months gorging in a feedlot and packing on the weight, the cattle are "finished" and sent to slaughter.

ON TO THE SLAUGHTERHOUSE

Gail Eisnitz, in her book *Slaughterhouse*, interviewed many slaughterhouse workers, including "stickers" (who slit the animals' throats), "knockers" (who stun the animals by firing a steel bolt into their brains), and "head-skinners" ('nuff said).

The slaughterhouse experience begins for the animals with the transport. Regardless of species, they are crammed into trucks or trains, given no food or water on journeys that may last days and hundreds of miles,[74] and often have to endure extreme temperatures without shelter. From a businessman's standpoint, this makes a lot of sense—why spend money providing protection and comfort to animals who are on their way to die, right?

Animals often arrive frozen to the sides of trailers—sometimes still alive. A worker who disposed of DOA (dead on arrival) hogs tells Eisnitz:

> Well, when they come off the truck, they're solid as a block of ice. Sometimes they'd be so froze that you'd have to take a hot water hose to thaw them apart before you were able to chain saw them. Then you take an ax-chopper or a chain saw and split the backbone in three places so it won't wreck the [grinder]. . . . I found two frozen live hogs in that pile. What I'm saying is they were frozen, but they were still alive . . . like a block of ice. Breathing real slow . . . I took my ax-chopper and chopped them to death. Hit them in the head. One bang and that was it. The whole thing made me sick.[75]

Birds are treated in the much same way. Ninety-nine percent of all land animals that are slaughtered for food are farmed birds,[76] primarily chickens. When the chickens are unloaded at the slaughterhouse, the ones that survived the transport are shackled upside down by their ankles onto a metal conveyor belt, something like a dry cleaner's conveyor rack. The birds' bones are frequently already broken from their journey, and many more will be broken in the shackling process.[77] The conveyor belt moves fast—more than two hundred chickens go by in one minute.[78]

The screeching of the chickens is interrupted as they are plunged under water and dragged through an electrified water bath. This is intended to paralyze them but does not keep them from feeling pain.[79] Voltage is kept low on purpose; higher voltages increase heart attacks and broken bones, which damages the saleable merchandise and therefore the profits. Many of the chickens regain—or never lost—consciousness before the next station, which is the automated throat slitter, a circular saw blade whirring at high speed. If the process goes the way it's designed, the bird's throat is cut open and its blood drains out of the severed carotid arteries before the bird is dropped into a scalding tank of boiling water, which prepares the body for feather removal.[80]

It often doesn't work the way it's designed. Chickens are plunged conscious into the scalding tank "all the time," according to a worker who spoke with Jonathan Safran Foer in his book *Eating Animals*. Government estimates, obtained through the Freedom of Information Act, report that approximately four million birds each year are scalded alive.[81]

Contamination is a serious problem throughout the processing system. The scalding tank contains feces from the skin and feathers, which get absorbed through the pores of the chickens, opened up by the boiling water. Defeathering machines pound the feathers off the bodies and beat feces and bacteria into their skin. The automated high-speed blades that eviscerate the chickens often rip open their intestines, spraying fecal matter into their body cavities. And the water in the chill tanks, the giant commercial vats where the bodies are communally cooled, "has been aptly named 'fecal soup' for all the filth and bacteria floating around," Tom Devine of the Government Accountability Project told Eisnitz in *Slaughterhouse*. The carcasses soak up this pathogenic water during the chilling process, to the great advantage of the poultry company's sales—the additional weight gain in "fecal soup" adds more than $1 billion dollars to their business every year.[82] This is legal and is stated prominently, if vaguely, on the chicken label: "may contain up to *x* percent retained water," or "up to *x* percent absorbed water." It isn't unusual for those numbers to be between 8 and 12 percent.[83]

When cattle arrive at the slaughterhouse, they are sent through a dark chute into a "knocking box" that restrains them while the knocker uses a captive bolt gun to shoot a steel bolt into the cattle's brain before retracting it. Sometimes, stun guns instead of bolt guns are used. Done properly, this stuns or instantly kills the animal. Next, a shackler inserts one of the cattle's hind legs into a chain, which then hoists it up onto a moving conveyor system overhead. Hanging from one leg, the animal, which weighs at least several hundred pounds, more often more than a thousand, is transported to the sticker, who slits its throat. It then moves along the bleed rail for several minutes, before moving on to the head-skinners, the first leggers,[84] and the rest of the 121 kill-floor jobs[85]—including rumpers, knuckle droppers, navel boners, splitter top/bottom butt, and feed-kill chain[86]—that will complete the job of skinning, eviscerating, sawing in two, and cutting the cow into chunks.

Things go wrong.

The many slaughterhouse workers interviewed by Eisnitz, who worked different kill-floor jobs in different plants, all tell the same horrific story. Cows that are stunned often regain consciousness and are bellowing while they are skinned, while their legs are amputated, and while they are run through an electrical shock system used to improve meat and texture. This whole process takes roughly ten minutes, during which the animal is frequently completely conscious.[87] When the head-skinners slice into a conscious animal's head, it will start kicking wildly (if it isn't already). The solution, for the safety of the workers, is to shove a knife into the back of the animal's head to sever the spinal cord. The cow is then paralyzed but not unconscious. The animal is able to feel her head being skinned and her limbs dismembered.[88]

An official with the United Food and Commercial Workers Union local in South Dakota tells Eisnitz, "I've seen live animals shackled, hoisted, stuck, and skinned. Too many to count. Too many to remember. It's just a process that's continuously there."[89] A knocker told Eisnitz that 25 to 30 percent of the cows are shackled and hung while conscious.[90]

The process and problems are similar for pigs.

Like the cattle stunners, the pig stunners often fail to render the pigs unconscious. Sometimes more than one pig comes into the restrainer at the same time, and the second pig is completely untouched by the stunner. These unstunned pigs are still sent down the line to the hog stickers. It is a dangerous position for these men, tasked with the job of killing a fully conscious pig. The men often retaliate against the pig's panic with brutality, sometimes driving their knives up to the hilt into the eyes of the pigs.[91]

Jonathan Safran Foer, who investigated several slaughterhouses for his book *Eating Animals*, describes seeing a pig processed after being stuck ("bleeding like a stuck pig") and lowered into the scalder for dehairing:

"It comes out looking a lot less piglike than when it went in—shinier, almost plastic—and is then lowered onto a table where two workers, one with a blowtorch, the other with a scraping device, get to removing any remaining hair.

"The pig is then hung up again," Foer continues, "and someone . . . cuts it lengthwise down the middle with a power saw. One expects—or I expected—to see the belly cut open and so on, but to see the face cut in half, the nose split down its middle, and the halves of the head peeled open like a book is shocking."[92]

Eisnitz spoke with more than two dozen Latino workers at a plant in southeast Washington State. "They all signed sworn affidavits describing how, for decades, they had been forced to skin and dismember *hundreds of thousands of fully conscious, live cows* at the beef plant owned by the largest meat producer in the world."

There are inspectors, but they rarely are able to see anything.

"The way the plants are set up," an inspector from Indiana told Eisnitz, "we aren't in a position to see what's going on. In a lot of plants, the slaughter area is walled off from the rest of the kill floor. Yes, we should be monitoring slaughter. But how can you monitor something like that if you're not allowed to leave your station to see what's going on?"[93]

The Humane Slaughter Act (HSA) was passed in 1958 by Congress. One of its primary stipulations is that all animals must be unconscious after a single application of a stunning mechanism *before* being shackled and hoisted. The USDA, which is closely connected to the meat industry and which opposed the HSA, is the federal agency assigned to enforce the HSA, but the HSA has no general enforcement provision.[94] The law does not apply to birds,[95] which make up 99 percent of all land animals killed for food. It also, strangely, does not apply to pigs that arrive frozen but alive at the slaughterhouse,[96] or to any animals killed in non-inspected slaughterhouses.[97]

The U.S. Animal Welfare Act is a federal law that regulates the treatment of animals and protects them from deliberate cruelty, extreme crowding, and other abuse. Farm animals are specifically excluded from protection under this law.[98]

The USDA is also responsible for health inspections at slaughterhouses, making sure that the meat producers don't cut corners in hygiene in order to make a little more profit. I found this strange, since the USDA is also instructed by Congress to facilitate sales of agricultural products, including meat. I'd say that's a pretty problematic conflict of interest. And this is public health we're talking about.

When Ronald Reagan became president, he took the opportunity to place three leaders of animal agriculture in positions of power within the USDA: John Block, a corporate hog producer from Illinois, was appointed the secretary of agriculture; Richard Lyng, the president of the American Meat Institute, was assistant secretary and later secretary; and C. W. McMillan, the vice-president of the National Cattlemen's Beef Association and a former meatpacking executive, was the assistant secretary for marketing and inspection services. This trend of the agricultural industry running the USDA has continued to the present day.[99]

Donna Bazemore, a former slaughterhouse worker for Perdue, in sworn testimony to Congress on the sanitary conditions of chicken-processing plants, said:

> The floors are covered with grease, fat, sand, and roaches. Bugs are up and down the sides of the walls. . . . There is so much fecal contamination on the floor from chickens that it kept getting into one worker's boots and burned his feet so badly his toenails had to be amputated. . . . The waste is not always from the chickens. The company won't allow workers to leave the line when they have to go to the bathroom. . . . Sometimes they have to relieve themselves on the floor. . . . After they are hung, sometimes the chickens fall off into the drain that runs down the middle of the line. This is where roaches, intestines, diseased parts, fecal contamination, and blood are washed down. Workers get sick to their stomachs into the drain. The drain is a lot less sanitary than anybody's toilet. That doesn't seem to matter, though. The Perdue supervisors told us to take the fallen chickens out of the drain and send them back down the line."[100]

Conditions for workers, as you can imagine, are not good. Workers at a slaughterhouse can make about 10,000 knife cuts during an eight-hour shift. They regularly develop carpal tunnel syndrome, painful back problems, shoulder problems, and fingers frozen into a curl, a condition that frequently requires multiple surgeries.[101]

Other worker injuries are more dramatic. This is a short list of accident reports filed by the Occupational Safety and Health Administration in meatpacking plants:

- Employee Hospitalized for Neck Laceration from Flying Blade
- Employee's Finger Amputated in Sausage Extruder
- Employee's Eye Injured When Struck by Hanging Hook
- Employee Killed When Arm Caught in Meat Grinder
- Employee Decapitated by Chain of Hide Puller Machine
- Employee Killed When Head Crushed in Hide Fleshing Machine
- Caught and Killed by Gut-Cooker Machine[102]

"The contamination they were working in was slightly deeper than their ankles," one inspector wrote, in Eisnitz's *Slaughterhouse*, about a plant where the drain was stopped up. "This contamination consisted of blood, approximately eight tails, approximately twenty snouts, hide pieces, stomach contents and approximately one hundred portions of the ears."[103]

Animals immobilized in crates their entire lives. Cutting off the beaks of chicks with hot blades. Castration without anesthetic. Cutting off tails and pieces of ears without anesthetic. Bashing piglets headfirst onto concrete floors. This is standard industry practice and is protected as such. It doesn't matter how inhumane such practices are. As long as they are considered "normal agricultural practices," they do not violate state anticruelty laws. Many, if not all, of these practices are also standard on "organic," "free-range," and "humane" farms.

So the question for the animal agriculture industry becomes not, "Is it cruel?" or "Is it necessary?" but "Is it normal?" Brutality is legalized because, as the cool kids say in high school, everybody's doing it.

Let me step back from the revolting pollution, genetic disfiguration, and horrific treatment of animals. Let me take a breath, and ask my original question again:

Can the industrial production of meat feed the world in a sustainable way?

Factory farms are considered the most "efficient" producers of meat, using fewer resources like land and water than farms in which the animals are not severely over-crowded. And yet the very definition of a CAFO by the Environmental Protection Agency is an operation that is a "significant contributor of pollutants."[104] Nowhere in that definition does the concept of sustainability fit in. Environmental destruction is the cost of efficient, cheap meat production. And concentrated animal feeding operations justify, more than anything else I can imagine, this passage from Isaac Bashevis Singer:

> As often as Herman had witnessed the slaughter of animals and fish, he always had the same thought: in their behaviour towards creatures, all men were Nazis. The smugness with which man could do with other species as he pleased exemplified the most extreme racist theories, the principle that might is right.[105]

CHAPTER FIVE

OCEANS: THE CIRCULATORY SYSTEM OF OUR PLANET

One word kept coming back to me from all that I had learned about CAFOs and factory farming: *waste*. The waste of water, waste of food, and waste of life. But also the waste products. Manure. Fecal matter. Dung. Excrement. I was a little traumatized thinking of this massive, nonstop torrent of fecal matter and its effect on our planet and our health.

Every year, 1.37 billion tons of solid animal waste is produced in the United States—130 times more than the amount produced by humans; 5 tons of animal excrement is produced for every person.[1] That's 116,000 pounds of farm animal excrement produced every second in the United States alone.[2] It's enough waste per year to cover every square foot of San Francisco, New York City, Tokyo, Paris, New Delhi, Berlin, Hong Kong, London, Rio de Janeiro, Delaware, Bali, Costa Rica, and Denmark—combined.[3]

Where does this brown tide eventually end up? In the water. Our creeks, streams, lakes, rivers, and, finally, our oceans.

When we interviewed Dr. Richard Oppenlander at his home, he talked extensively about the destruction of our oceans by the animal agriculture industry. "Livestock operations on land have created more than 500 nitrogen-flooded dead zones around the world in our oceans,"[4] he told me, "compris[ing] more than 95,000 square miles of ocean completely devoid of life. Any meaningful discussion about the state of our oceans has to always begin by frank discussions about land-based animal agriculture, which is not what our conservation groups—Oceana being the largest one in the world [and] the most influential, as well as others—that's not what's at the apex of their discussions."

130 x
more waste

In fact, in a report for CNN by Nancy Rabalais, executive director of the Louisiana Universities Marine Consortium, "the number of dead zones throughout the world has been increasing in the last several decades and currently totals over 550." A dead zone the size of Connecticut—more than 5,000 square miles—floats off the coasts of Louisiana and Texas, in the Gulf of Mexico. It is the world's second-largest dead zone caused by humans. The largest is in the Baltic Sea.[5]

It's not only sewage and manure that run into the oceans from animal agriculture. There are also herbicides, pesticides, fungicides, chemical fertilizer, as well as the residues of antibiotics, growth hormones, steroids, and other feed additives. The glut of phosphorous and nitrogen in animal excrement causes algal blooms, including red tides,[6] and population explosions in single-celled, potentially toxic microorganisms such as *Pfiesteria piscicida* ("piscicida" means "fish-killer"). Contact with this contaminated water has killed billions of fish and causes skin lesions and sores, narcosis, severe headaches, acute loss of short-term memory, and impaired liver and kidney function in humans.[7]

I went on my favorite ocean protection organization's website, Surfrider Foundation, to see what they were doing about this. Mostly what I found were campaigns about plastic bags and trash, but nothing about animal agriculture.

After unsuccessfully scouring their website, I decided to visit Dr. Chad Nelsen, Surfrider's Environmental Director. He had a thick cap of curly brown hair and sideburns and spoke with the distinctive drawl of a Southern Californian.

"What is the number one coastal water-quality-issue/polluter?" I asked him, diving right into the issue.

He seemed a little surprised at the question. "Yeah, a lot of it . . . It's actually, we call it the toxic cocktail, because it is this sort of diffuse source—so it's heavy metals from tires and brakes and cars. It is herbicides and pesticides. It's really just kind of picking up everything we leave on the ground and collecting it together and pushing it out into the ocean. So it's hard to target one thing."

"When doing our research," I said, "this particular issue on runoff, as we're interviewing more and more people, keeps coming up, with animal agriculture as the number one water polluter—considerably more than any other."

"Yeah, that's interesting," Nelsen said. "I think it depends on the regions that you focus on. Like, the urban areas, which is sort of where we are here in Southern California, we don't see that because there's not a lot of agricultural farms, but if you look in the mid-Atlantic—Maryland, Virginia, North Carolina, that region—I know there's a lot of poultry farms, and a lot of hog farms, and it's a huge waste issue."

After I got home, I looked up the number of farms in Southern California. It's hard to tell how many agricultural operations there are in any particular area since many of them are hidden away, as I'd learned when I was researching factory farms, or they're so physically nondescript that they could be anything. But according to Factory Farm Map, a project of Food & Water Watch, a non-profit public interest organization, Southern California is almost entirely blanketed in red, indicating an "extreme density level" of CAFOs.[8] Yet Dr. Nelsen had told me there were hardly any farms in this area, going so far as to say that for that reason, animal agriculture wasn't really contributing to the destruction of the oceans, at least in our neck of the woods. Dr. Nelsen was Surfrider's Environmental Director; it seemed odd that he would be so wrong. It made me wonder what other erroneous information was being put forward by these organizations.

I wanted to find out if another conservation organization would be more accurate in their assessments of the state of our oceans. I decided to speak with Lisa Agabian of Sea Shepherd Conservation Society.

"The oceans are under siege like never before," she said to me. "Ocean acidification, overfishing, pollution, you name it. Marine environments are in trouble. If we don't wake up and do something about it, we're going to see fishless oceans by the year 2048.[9] That's the prediction from scientists."

"What about the sustainable fishing methods that are coming up?" I asked her.

"I think we came up with this term, 'sustainable fishing,' to make ourselves feel good about eating fish and continuing to take fish out of the oceans, when in fact it's Sea Shepherd's position that there is no such thing as sustainable fishing," Agabian said. "We're fishing our oceans to death. We're fishing species into extinction. We are three short years or less from bluefin tuna going extinct. The cod in New England, the whole fisheries there are in collapse. Pretty much every major fishery is in collapse. We're at a point where we can't sustain what we're taking out of the ocean.

"I think that really the only way to have fisheries come back is to stop eating fish, and that is Sea Shepherd's position as well," Agabian continued. "People look at the oceans, and they think of them as this infinite resource in terms of fish, and that's just not the case. We're fishing species smaller and smaller. In some cases they're taking babies out of fish. We've seen in some areas where hammerhead [sharks], they're taking the babies out of the womb. They're taking the fins off the babies too. We can't sustain this. It takes a shark seven years to reach maturity and they're getting smaller and smaller. Shark species are being finned into extinction—we are finning and killing one hundred million sharks a year.

"Our founder Captain [Paul] Watson likes to say, 'If the oceans die, we die.' That's not a tag line. That's the truth."

"What's the single biggest industry driving ocean devastation today, from plastic bags to runoff to commercial fishing?" I asked Agabian.

"The single biggest industry that is decimating the oceans is industrialized fishing," Agabian answered. "We're taking out tons upon tons of fish with trawlers, with nets, with long lines, with purse nets. As I said, people think it's an infinite resource. They think that they can just keep taking and that the oceans will recover, there's more for the taking for all of us, but there's so many people on the planet now that that's just not possible. We

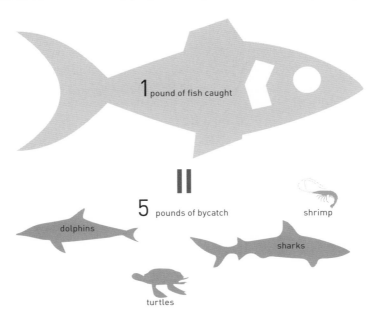

1 pound of fish caught

=

5 pounds of bycatch   shrimp

dolphins

sharks

turtles

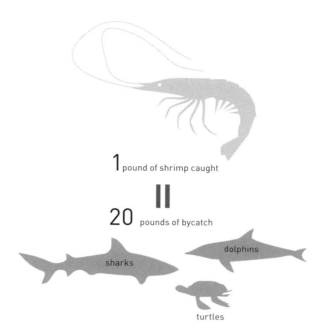

1 pound of shrimp caught

=

20 pounds of bycatch

sharks

dolphins

turtles

need to think about what we're doing to our oceans and we need to think about how we can give them a chance to recover."

"Do you think fish have feelings?" I asked.

"I believe all animals have feelings," Agabian said. "I believe all animals feel pain. I believe that when you take a fish out of the ocean and it suffocates, it absolutely suffers. Yes, I do think that."

Susan Hartland, Administrative Director of Sea Shepherd, knocked on the door and joined us.

"We're at over twenty-eight billion animals that were pulled out of the ocean last year,"[10] Hartland said. "Those are only the numbers we're aware of. There's a lot of bycatch that's not officially counted."

Today, in order to feed the global annual demand for ninety million tons of fish, fishing is done primarily with massive fish nets. For every single pound of fish caught, there is up to five pounds of untargeted species trapped,[11] such as dolphins, whales, sea turtles, and sharks, known as bycatch or bykill.

If we were to imagine this same sort of practice happening on the African savannah, targeting gazelle, but in the process scooping up every single lion, giraffe, ostrich, and elephant, nobody would stand for it. Yet this is what is happening in our oceans every single day.

Even worse, for every single pound of shrimp sold and eaten by humans, for example, there is another twenty pounds or more of other marine animals and fish that are caught and killed as bycatch.[12] It is the fishing industry's equivalent of collateral damage.

Scientists estimate that as many as 650,000 whales, dolphins, and seals are killed as bycatch every year by fishing vessels,[13] not to mention all the other "incidental" species caught. And of course, as with everything in interconnected ecosystems, there is an environmental cost.

"We've got giant trawlers that are out there these days fishing in the Southern Ocean for krill," Hartland said. "It's the bottom of the food chain. If we continue at our current rate, there's going to be nothing left in our lifetime.

"I don't think there's any such thing as sustainable fishing," she said, echoing Agabian. "We're fishing with these giant trawlers with miles and miles and miles of fishing nets and long lines and we're bottom trawling. We're literally scraping up the bottom of the oceans. We've got seven billion people on the planet. There's no such thing as sustainable."

In "Consider the Fishes,"[14] Paul Watson, the founder of Sea Shepherd, considers the many ways in which the oceans are being attacked:

> The trawlers literally leave no stone unturned. Bottom draggers plow the benthonic depths taking ground-fish, mollusks, crustaceans, and damaging vegetation and structure. Mid-water draggers stalk those fish that dwell between the bottom and the surface. Surface trawlers maul the upper reaches of the seas. Those species of the deep that do survive the tri-level assaults must then run the gauntlet of longliner fleets, gill netters, purse seine netters, and crab and lobster pots.
>
> The very foundation of the food chain is being shattered as large Japanese small-mesh plankton trawlers haul in krill by the hundreds of millions of tons. The krill, shrimp-like zooplankton, are then converted into a protein base to use as animal feed. The more krill exploited means less food available for fish and whales.
>
> The global carnage inflicted on the world's fish species ranges from the horrendous waste and slaughter of the huge floating factory operations to the cumulative damage caused by millions of people fishing with rods, small nets and traps, and combing the shorelines for crabs and shellfish.

I was stunned to learn about the incredible waste and mismanagement involved in industrial fishing. But surely, I asked Hartland and Agabian, there had to be some kind of international regulations? Hartland's answer was grim.

"These fish industries, there's nobody governing them," Susan Hartland said. "There's nobody monitoring what they're catching and how much fish. The bycatch is considered just that. They're just throwaway fish. They're creating markets because there's so much of it. There's a lot of fishing that goes on that's not monitored nor managed, a lot of illegal fishing, a lot of poaching sharks. If you can imagine how many of them are tangled right now in miles and miles and miles of ghost nets that are still continuing to kill, that are fished illegally, that are being poached for shark fin and shark cartilage markets, we really don't have an accurate number of what's being overfished and exploited from our oceans. They're not ever given a chance to recover. They can't recover. They don't multiply that quickly. They don't come back. We're not giving them an opportunity. Once they're gone, they're gone."

"What are ghost nets?" I asked.

"Ghost nets [are] from industrial fishing; they leave them out there—nets that [will] remain out there for years, just floating around killing. When I was onboard Sea Shepherd's boat, the *Steve Irwin*, we brought the ship from Australia up to New York and I wouldn't have believed it—you see them at night. It's just miles of fishnets."

Over the past twenty-five years, more than five hundred miles of nonbiodegradable fishing nets have been released into our oceans. They continue to catch innumerable numbers of sea creatures, and since the nets are never collected and cleared, the bodies of the dead animals and fish accumulate into a congealed organic mass.[15]

"They come undone from the buoys or from their markers," Hartland continued, "so the fishermen can't recover them or they just don't. These nets just keep floating throughout the ocean . . . catching everything that comes in their way."

What Hartland said next blew my mind.

"The highest consumer of fish [on land] is livestock. Pigs," she said. "We're over-fishing to feed our livestock. Pigs and all of these factory-farmed animals are the highest consumers, along with cats [through pet food]."

It turns out that pigs and chickens eat six times the amount of seafood that people in the United States eat, and twice the amount eaten by people in Japan![16]

Wild fish are also fed in massive amounts to farmed fish. In 2002, thirty million tons of the global fish catch was used to make fishmeal and fish oil to feed to animals raised for human consumption. About 46 percent of that fishmeal and fish oil was fed to fish raised in fish farms.[17]

Which raises an important question: is aquaculture (the fancy term for fish farming) a sustainable alternative to ocean fishing? I would hope so: global aquaculture now accounts for about half of the world's supply of fish consumed by humans.[18]

It turns out it takes between two and six pounds of wild-caught fish to produce one pound of farmed fish, due to the amount of wild fish fed to farmed fish.[19] That's hardly an efficient or sustainable conversion ratio. And then there's the pollution caused by fish farms.

"People think if they're eating fish from fish farms or factories, or if there's aquaculture where they're actually raising the fish, that there's no impact or that it's better for the environment, and the truth is it's not," Hartland said. "[Fish] farms are incredibly toxic, not only to the area around them but to the humans that work them, and to the wild stocks that live around the farms and swim through them, and to the fish themselves."

Fish farms, like other factory farms, are cesspools of contamination and disease. In *The World Peace Diet*, Dr. Will Tuttle explores the living conditions on these farms:

> Trout, catfish, tilapia, and other freshwater fish are forced to live in horrendously overcrowded concrete troughs. I talked with an investigator who visited a fish farm in Illinois, housed inside an enormous metal shed. When she went in, the air was so putrid she could hardly breathe. The huge shallow pond inside was completely black and at first she couldn't see any fish. Then she realized the water was utterly full of fish, severely crowded together, and the blackness of the water was due to the concentration of their feces. . . . People order this at local restaurants, ironically believing they're getting their healthy omega-3s. . . . Obviously, fish farmed in commercial aquaculture operations accumulate toxins from the water through gill breathing, and large amounts of antibiotics are used, not only to unnaturally spur growth but also to control the disease that is an ever-present threat in such unhygienic conditions. . . . Saltwater fish farming also involves inhumane and unhealthy overcrowding of the fish, usually in offshore pens. These operations cause an enormous amount of water pollution, forcing thousands of fish to live in highly concentrated areas, with feces, antibiotics, pesticides, and toxic chemicals—such as the pigments that turn farmed salmon flesh from dull gray to appetizing pink—all flowing right into the surrounding ocean waters. Scotland's caged salmon, for example, create an amount of untreated waste equivalent to that from eight million people, far more than Scotland's human population.[20]

Scientists have warned that Scottish farmed salmon is so contaminated with toxic chemicals it should be eaten no more than three times a year.[21] (My question is, why would you knowingly eat something contaminated with toxic chemicals three times a year?) And canthaxanthin, one of the more commonly used dyes to make farmed salmon a more salmon-y pink, has been linked to human eye defects and retinal damage. Yet artificial coloring in farmed salmon has more than tripled since 1982.[22]

Fish farms also spread disease to surrounding wild populations, often devastating them. Parasitic sea lice, for example, overwhelm farmed salmon due to their severe overcrowding. Despite extensive pesticide and antibiotic use, the lice, "who spread in clouds in the surrounding water," flourish and cover up to nineteen miles around the fish farms, infesting and devastating the wild salmon in surrounding waters.[23] Fish farming, despite all this, has nearly tripled between 1995 and 2007.[24]

"Why do you think some of the biggest environmental groups aren't talking about the impacts of industrial fishing and eating fish?" I asked Susan Hartland.

"I can't speak for them," Hartland said, "but my opinion would be it's an uncomfortable subject. It makes people have to think about their impact. There's a market for it. That's why there's overfishing, that's why there's factory farming, that's why there's trawlers and trinket markets and shark fin soup, because there's some market for it, because we as consumers are purchasing these products. To say, 'Look, this has to stop. We are killing our oceans. We are killing ourselves. We're killing all the animals in it. We're creating an imbalance in our environment'—people don't want to hear it because that makes them feel like they have to stop doing something and a lot of people don't want to.

"These organizations don't want to tell people what to do," she said, "but we're at a point where we all have to be cognizant and take action, or there is going to be nothing left in a generation or two generations."

I was heartened, despite the bleak picture painted by Hartland and Agabian, that a major organization such as Sea Shepherd was looking squarely at reality and trying to spread the word about it. The first step in dealing with any problem is acknowledging it, right?

I went on the world's largest ocean conservation group's website, Oceana, to see what they were doing about this. On their site, along with the TED talk by their CEO, Andy Sharpless, I was astounded to read they actually recommend eating fish as one of the best ways to help fish. With the world's fish population in near collapse, this seems like saying the best way to help endangered pandas is to eat them.

I couldn't understand how Oceana could say we could eventually get to a point where we could remove one hundred million tons of fish per year from the ocean, and that it could somehow be sustainable and good for our oceans.

I went to visit Dr. Geoff Shester, Oceana's California Program Director, in Monterey. We spoke in his office, where he had large, full-color photographs of vibrant sea creatures like anemone and reef fish, as well as a shore fisherman in silhouette, beautifully framed and matted hanging on the wall.

"According to the United Nations Food and Agriculture Organization," Dr. Shester said, "roughly three-quarters of all the fisheries out there are either fully exploited or over-exploited,[25] so there's really not a whole lot of fish stocks out there that you might consider at healthy levels for the ecosystem."

"Watching Andy [Sharpless]'s TED Talk about feeding the world," I said to Shester, "in 1988, fish catch peaked at eighty-five million tons. How is it possible that we can sustainably catch one hundred million tons by 2050, regardless if it's in a farm or if it's in the ocean? For every pound of farmed fish you're taking out, you're essentially taking out five pounds of wild fish. No matter whether it's in a pond, or it's in the ocean. How can that be sustainable?"

Shester lifted his eyebrows and rolled his eyes up toward the ceiling for a very long time.

"The ultimate question, right," he finally said, "is that there is a tremendous amount of natural production that is basically coming out of the oceans all the time, so we have a massive amount of upwelling from our ocean conveyor belt that's bringing up ancient, thousand-year-old nutrients, and our ecosystems are turning that into fish. Yes, they're eating each other and you're losing some of that production every step up in the food chain, but you get more each year. You can fish and take some out, and next year there will be more.

"If we do that right without ultimately hitting the fundamental driver," Shester went on, "it's sort of like living off the interest, right? As long as you don't bring your principal down, right? If you're investing in something, as long as you're not hitting into that principal and your principal remains high, you could potentially live off the interest forever. That's the basic idea with fish."

I had to interrupt. "With our population right now," I said, "what we're doing—the fishery is now 75 percent depleted. It's a good analogy with money. We're not living off interest. We're in extreme debt." Shester had a strange smile on his face. He was nodding as though I was telling a joke, and he soon started laughing. "If our population," I went on, a little disturbed by his laughter, "which is trying to live as a family on the same amount of money, but our numbers are increasing 35 percent to nine billion people by 2050 . . ."

"Right," Shester jumped in.

"Isn't it just, hey, we got to stop spending money?" I continued.

"Yeah."

"We need to stop eating fish," I said.

"Well, if you could bring the principal back," Shester said brightly.

I left that interview feeling like my head was on backward. Now, I'm no math genius, but there is no way you're going to make more money by spending money as fast as you can, especially since we're not spending our "money" on any wise investments designed to bring back our principal, or original investment. We're just throwing that money away. It was astounding to me to hear an "ocean conservationist" advocating the removal of millions of tons of wild animals from the ocean. The world's oceans are not a bottomless, infinitely renewable pit, and they did not evolve to be preyed on and depleted by an essentially alien, terrestrial species such as *homo sapiens*.

Dr. Oppenlander seemed to have a much clearer view of the state of our oceans. "Fishing of any type is depleting not only one particular species," Oppenlander said to us during his interview. "You get into this serial depletion, where one fish species will be minimized and the fishing industry for that fishery will move on to the next species. It's called serial depletion. It's aptly named. . . . They're losing the fish species [and] they're also destroying habitat.

"The enormous cod industry, which most people know about in the northern Atlantic—cod used to be the highest-demand fish worldwide—was shut down in 2003," he went on. "In 1992, cod had been overfished to 1 percent of their original numbers. A moratorium on fishing in the area was imposed. But the cod population never recovered. They will likely never recover in our lifetime—or ever—because the habitat has actually changed substantially now. The entire ecosystem has changed in those areas."[26]

Cod was used in McDonald's Filet-O-Fish for years before the cod population was destroyed. Then the New Zealand hoki moved up to become Mickey D's fish sandwich, until hoki numbers also dwindled dramatically.[27] The depletion that occurred in the past fifteen years appears to be irreversible, says Dr. Oppenlander. The hoki hasn't come back, either.

A more hopeful situation is seen off the south coast of Cuba, in the Jardines de la Reina area. Industrial fishing there has been banned since 1980, and since that time, resident fish species have grown by up to 50 percent.[28]

"Most of the species that are nearing extinction are being ravaged and haven't recovered on the watch of Oceana," Oppenlander said to me, "or on the watch of Marine Stewardship Council, or very much on the watch of Monterey Bay Aquarium's Seafood Watch, which, as I mention in one of my lectures, is aptly named because that's what they're doing. They're sort of watching this happen instead of aggressively halting it."

"Why are they doing that?" I asked. I could still see Dr. Shester's strange smile.

"All of them have the single motive of economics," Oppenlander said. "If you [look at] the Marine Stewardship Council [MSC], they have 130 to 150 certified fisheries right now, and each one had to pay between $20,000 and more than $100,000 to a third-party certifier to become certified. All the certifiers are essentially independently contracted by these fisheries. The potential for bias is clear. In their history, since 1997 to now, MSC has not denied or declined one fishery from being certified sustainable. Not one.[29]

"World Wildlife Fund [WWF] and Unilever were the initial founding corporate entities of the Marine Stewardship Council," continued Oppenlander. "WWF has partnered with companies such as McDonald's.[30] Unilever is one of the major extractors of ocean wildlife.[31] You see the conflict of interest."

I did indeed see the conflict of interest. How could an organization like Marine Stewardship Council, which is supposed to certify "sustainable" fisheries and protect the oceans from overfishing in the name of profit, do its job when its two corporate founders are both heavily invested in getting the public to buy fish? The public relies on organizations like MSC to guide us toward more sustainable choices. But nobody is telling us about the long reach of the corporations behind these organizations.

"About a year and a half ago, Ted Danson was speaking on behalf of Oceana at Climate One at the Commonwealth Club," Oppenlander continued. "He said, and this is word for word, 'And this [work by Oceana] is about people being able to fish and eat fish forever. This is not to save the fishes. This is to save the fishermen.'[32]

"Tuna is a good example," Oppenlander went on. "I feel it's representative of every single thing that we're doing wrong by certifying something as sustainable, or with the way we are putting the fate of our oceans into the hands of these organizations. These organizations are the ones that are responsible, essentially, for allowing bluefin tuna to be fished. The vote was made [in 2013] just a year and a half ago, to not grant an endangered status to them. At that time their numbers had dropped by 92 percent. Now it's 96 percent. Ninety-six percent of all bluefin tuna that are in our oceans have perished as a species, and yet they're still labeled as sustainably caught with a longline [longline fishing extends a line from the boat, 25 to more than 100 miles long, with thousands of barbs and hooks].

"The bluefin tuna vote was influenced by the fact that they allowed the fishermen to complete questionnaires that asked questions such as, 'Have you seen the bluefin species being diminished in any way over the last ten years of your fishing?' There's five thousand commercial bluefin tuna fishing vessels just in the United States. Of course they're not going to say the bluefin tuna population is down, if they get a vote.'"

When the population of one fish species is affected by fishing, there is a cascading effect that moves throughout marine ecosystems, affecting the predators and prey of that one species. For millions of years, sharks, for example, have played a critical role in balancing the oceans' ecosystems.[33] Today, only 10 percent of all large predator fish, such as tuna, sharks, swordfish, cod, marlin, skates, flounder, and halibut, remain in the ocean.[34]

"Cutting the fins off of sharks and then casting them overboard to die, just for this ridiculous notion of eating shark fin soup, is a terrible enough atrocity on its own," Dr. Oppenlander said to me. "But for me, what trumps that is our perspective. All those people in organizations trying to create change and ban shark fin soup, they're the same ones that eat fish. Between forty and fifty million sharks each year are killed in fishing lines and fishing nets and as by-kill.[35] Then their fins might be cut off or not cut off, but they're caught initially as bykill. It's from fishing. It's from fishing in a 'sustainable manner'—in many cases—for fish that are labeled 'sustainable' by, for instance, Oceana and the sustainable-certified organizations.

"My thought is, why would we want to stop at banning shark fin soup if you're concerned about sharks, which all these organizations are, and most of the public at large is now? If we were really concerned about sharks, we would ban fishing."

The loss of large predatory fish has serious consequences. A new study produced for the European Parliament's Committee on Fisheries found that the depletion of top-predator fish coincides with the proliferation of algae blooms.[36] The author of the study, Britas Klemens Eriksson from the Department of Marine Benthic Ecology and Evolution, Centre for Ecological and Evolutionary Studies of the University of Groningen in the Netherlands, believes that the loss of top predators leads to a population explosion in smaller predatory fish like anchovies and sprat, which prey on invertebrate herbivores like snails and crustaceans that feed on algae. With the marked decrease in the numbers of algal-eating species, algae blooms out of control.[37]

So what? Well, algae is frequently made up of phytoplankton (also known as microalgae).[38] Another study, published in the international journal *Climate Dynamics* examined the global impact of solar radiation and heat absorbed by phytoplankton, which float in the top layers of the ocean. The study found that "the absorption of solar radiation by phytoplankton increases radiative heating in the near-surface ocean and raises sea surface temperature (SST) by overall ~ 0.5°C. The resulting increase in evaporation enhances specific atmospheric humidity by 2 to 5 percent, thereby increasing the Earth's greenhouse effect and the atmospheric temperatures."[39]

It's a lot like paving the oceans with blacktop.

"If we want to manage algal blooms effectively, we need to start by taking an ecosystem perspective . . . we have to restore depleted fish communities," Eriksson said in an article for *Nature: International Weekly Journal of Science*.[40]

"The oceans have balanced themselves naturally for a few hundred million years," Oppenlander said to me. "Then around the early 1800s to mid-1800s, we came and decided that we would start extracting as many fish as we wanted without any calculation. The oceans are one big mitigator: 90 percent of all excess heat that's been generated into our climate since the mid-1960s has been stored in our oceans,[41] causing warming and loss of sea life. And nearly 50 percent of all excessive greenhouse gases that humans produce have been absorbed by our oceans, which has caused a 30 percent drop in pH levels, causing acidification [of the oceans], which makes it very difficult for a number of species to survive."[42]

"What is the sustainable number of fish we can kill per year for food?" I asked. "What is the number?"

"The sustainable number of fish we can take out of our oceans right now is zero," Oppenlander answered bluntly. "We shouldn't be catching any fish, killing, harvesting, or extracting. There shouldn't be one fish taken out of our oceans.

"Sustainability needs to be projected through generations," he continued. "It's a generational thing. There's only one way to help our oceans and this is to stop all extraction, completely. Just leave them alone. Actually let them heal on their own. We complete an immediate restoration of all oceanic ecosystems back to a natural life. Our oceans are actually one global ocean, and they are the circulatory system of our planet. They produce over half the world's oxygen, absorb 70 percent of carbon dioxide, and 80 percent of life on Earth is found under the waves. One hundred percent of life on Earth depends on the health of our oceans. The health of our oceans is dependent upon fish and the infinite numbers of ecosystems that are at play there. If anybody was really concerned, they would stop eating seafood completely and then hope in the next one hundred to two hundred years, well beyond our lifetime, that the oceans will restore themselves."

A few days after interviewing Dr. Oppenlander, I stood looking out at the Pacific from San Francisco's Ocean Beach. It was a cold, gray day. I thought of when the Europeans first approached the coast of North America in their ships, and the fish were so teeming and thick in the water that the crews worried the ships would be beached on their gleaming bodies.[43] I thought of how scientists are predicting that if things do not change, there will be fishless oceans by 2048—thirty-three years from now. And I thought of a quote by the twelfth-century philosopher and nun, Hildegard von Bingen:

"Glance at the sun. See the moon and the stars. Gaze at the beauty of the Earth's greenings. Now, think."

CHAPTER SIX

RAIN FORESTS AND BIODIVERSITY: SAWING OFF THE BRANCH WE STAND ON

"We're in the middle of the largest mass extinction of species in sixty-five million years,"[1] Dr. Will Tuttle told me during an interview. There have been five previous mass extinctions. Scientists believe that each of these five extinctions was caused by events such as large meteors or asteroids colliding with the earth, volcanic eruptions, or massive glaciation.[2] The mass extinction Dr. Tuttle is talking about—the sixth one, the one we're in the middle of—is different. As a plaque in the Hall of Biodiversity in the American Museum of Natural History on Manhattan's Upper West Side explains, "Right now we are in the midst of the Sixth Extinction, this time caused solely by humanity's transformation of the ecological landscape."[3]

Not only is the sixth extinction caused by how human beings are altering the earth, but as we destroy our planet's interconnected biological systems by slashing the rain forests, contaminating and draining our finite freshwater supply, depleting the oceans of life, and pumping greenhouse gases into the atmosphere, we are rapidly and thoroughly annihilating our own species' chances of survival.

On another sign in the Hall of Biodiversity is a quote from Stanford ecologist Paul Ehrlich:[4]

> IN PUSHING OTHER SPECIES TO EXTINCTION, HUMANITY IS
> BUSY SAWING OFF THE LIMB ON WHICH IT PERCHES.

The biodiversity found in the tropical rain forests is staggering—in fact, rain forests contain the greatest biodiversity on earth.[5] The typical temperature ranges from 68 to 93 degrees Fahrenheit, an annual rainfall of more than 100 inches, and an average humidity of 77 to 88 percent combine to provide flourishing and generous conditions

Where Plants Active Against Cancer Cells Come From

1,000 from general areas

2,000 from the rain forest (less than 5% of land surface)

for all forms of life.[6] Today, rain forests cover less than 2 percent of the globe—fifty years ago they covered 15 percent[7]—but they contain almost half of all plant and animal life on land.[8] A 2-acre area in a tropical rain forest could contain more than 750 varieties of trees.[9] By comparison, within the enormous boreal forest of Canada, which covers almost a billion acres and comprises approximately 25 percent of the planet's remaining intact forests, there are roughly twenty species of trees.[10]

"Concerned researchers of the loss of species agree that the primary cause of species loss . . . that we're witnessing is due to over-grazing and habitat loss from livestock production on land and by over-fishing—which I call fishing—in our oceans,"[11] Dr. Oppenlander told us. "Ninety-one percent of the loss of the rain forest in the Amazon area thus far . . . has been destroyed . . . due to raising [or feeding] livestock."[12]

More than an acre and a half of rain forest is cleared every second.[13] That is essentially one to two entire football fields cleared every single second, which means that every year we lose an area more than twice as large as the state of Florida. If this rate of destruction continues, we will lose half of our remaining rain forests by 2025 and by the year 2060 there will be no rain forests left on earth.[14]

Percentage of Rain Forest Explored

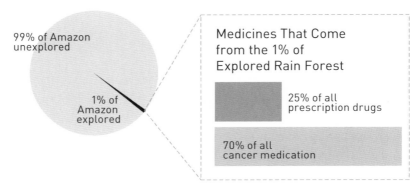

99% of Amazon unexplored

1% of Amazon explored

Medicines That Come from the 1% of Explored Rain Forest

25% of all prescription drugs

70% of all cancer medication

From the destruction of the rain forests, experts estimate that more than 100 species of animals, plants, and insects are lost every day[15]—this adds up to 50,000 species made extinct every year.[16] With the permanent loss of these species also comes the loss of potential cures for countless diseases. There are 3,000 plants identified by the U.S. National Cancer Institute as active against cancer cells. More than 2,000 of these 3,000 plants come from the rain forest.[17] Additionally, 25 percent of prescription drugs and more than 70 percent of all cancer treatment medications are derived from the rain forest[18]—but less than 1 percent of tropical rain forest species have been evaluated for their medical benefits.[19] That means that every single second, as the razing of the rain forests continues, we potentially lose the cure for cancer, Alzheimer's, or any number of currently "incurable" diseases and conditions.

Nor is it only the biodiversity of plants, animals, and insects that is decimated by the obliteration of the rain forests. More than six million indigenous people once lived in the Amazon forests. There are now, because of the loss of the forests, less than a quarter of a million.[20]

Survival International, a human rights organization that works to preserve the rights of indigenous tribal peoples and uncontacted tribes, states that there are an seventy-seven isolated indigenous groups living in Brazil's Amazon rain forest—more than anywhere else in the world.[21]

José Carlos Meirelles worked for FUNAI—the National Indian Foundation, Brazil's government agency dealing with indigenous peoples—for forty years. In early 2011, the BBC interviewed Meirelles during the very first aerial filming of an uncontacted community living in the Amazon rain forest on the border between Brazil and Peru. The BBC was permitted to film the group from a kilometer away, using a stabilized zoom lens, to reduce disturbance. A short, hauntingly poignant video of the aerial footage made by the BBC shows Meirelles in the small plane, looking out over the lush canopy of the rain forest. As the plane dips lower, thatched straw roofs appear between the green of the trees, resembling little Iroquois longhouses. Small groups of nearly naked, brown human forms appear. Despite the "minimized disturbance" of the zoom lens, the figures are frequently motionless and looking upward, straight into the camera, sometimes pointing.

The plane circles around and around the village. Meirelles's words are heard in voiceover, with English subtitles on the screen: "Their future doesn't depend on them. It depends on us—[on] our conscience. . . . It's important for humanity [that] these people exist. They remind us it's possible to live in a different way. They're the last free people on the planet."[22]

GREENHOUSE GASES: THE BIG PICTURE

More than 20 percent of the planet's oxygen is produced by the rain forests.[23] Some figures are as high as 40 percent.[24] The rain forests truly are the lungs of the earth, not something we want to be without. In addition to helping us breathe, they also regulate the globe's temperatures and weather patterns and function as a planetary thermostat.

We hear a lot about greenhouse gas emissions, primarily carbon dioxide, and how these emissions are causing global warming. But we rarely look at other elements on our planet that affect the balance of these gases—such as our forests.

Rain forests are constantly absorbing carbon dioxide from the atmosphere and replacing it with oxygen. Cutting down the rain forests to provide ranch land and crop land for the meat industry means that we are cutting away both the earth's oxygen-producing capacity and its ability to absorb tons of global-warming carbon dioxide.[25]

Not only that, but when rain forests are destroyed, an enormous amount of carbon dioxide is released from the vegetation into the atmosphere.[26] When we cut down the rain forests, we're essentially removing the planet's filtration system while continuing to spew toxins and contaminants into the air, and then we wonder why the air quality is getting worse and worse. We're annihilating the planet's ability to heal itself.

Cattle grazing and clearing land to grow crops for livestock are responsible for as much as 80 percent of all rain forest loss worldwide. Remember that quarter-pound burger that takes more than 660 gallons of water to produce? That same burger—just one burger—would also require fifty-five square feet of cleared rain forest. And it's not just beef. Cleared rain forest land is used to grow crops such as soybeans to feed chickens, turkeys, and pigs, as well as cows.[27] In the single crop season of 2004–5, more than 2.9 million acres of rain forest were razed to the ground, mostly to grow feed for the chickens of Kentucky Fried Chicken.[28]

It takes, on average, eight years of livestock grazing and crop growing for rain forest land to become depleted.[29] Around the world, almost a third of all land—not just rain forest land—is becoming desertified, or turned from arable land to desert.[30] Desertification, according to the United Nations, is caused by human activities such as unsustainable farming, mining, over-grazing, and clear-cutting—and, of course, climate change. "The issue of desertification is not new though—it played a significant role in human history," the UN states, "contributing to the collapse of several large empires and the displacement of local populations. But today, the pace of arable land degradation is estimated at 30 to 35 times the historical rate."

During the Rio Earth Summit in 1992, desertification was identified as one of the largest obstacles, along with climate change and the loss of biodiversity, to sustainable development.[31]

🐄 🐄 🐄

Allan Savory, a Zimbabwean ecologist, gave a wildly popular TED talk in February 2013 on the issue of desertification. At the time of this writing, Savory's talk was viewed almost three million times. Savory claims that the best way to reverse desertification is to actually graze more large hoofed animals—400 percent more, to be exact—on a timed, rotational basis. That, incidentally, means we would also get to eat more animals.

"What are we going to do?" Savory asks in his speech. "There is only one option, I'll repeat to you, only one option left to climatologists and scientists, and that is to do the unthinkable, and to use livestock, bunched and moving, as a proxy for former herds and predators, and mimic nature. There is no other alternative left to mankind."[32]

This is the same man who, during the 1950s, working as a research officer for the game department of what is now Zimbabwe, came up with a theory that elephants were the cause of desertification there. His solution was convincing the government to kill 40,000 elephants.

Yet, after fourteen years of relentless slaughter, the conditions only got worse. His theory was wrong. The culling finally ended, but not until tens of thousands of elephants were killed.

The idea that the solution to desertification—one of the primary causes of which is, according to the UN, over-grazing—is to graze 400 percent *more* animals reminded me of Oceana saying that the best way to help fish is to eat fish. People loved it; Savory received a standing ovation for his TED talk. We can reverse not only desertification, but climate change too, and actually eat even more meat, all while feeling good about it!

Savory's startling claims, accompanied by dramatic before and after photos in his TED talk, led many academic papers to be published in response, testing his theories by both experiment and comparative studies. "The conclusion, overwhelmingly," as reported in the *Guardian*, "is that [Savory's] statements are not supported by empirical evidence and experimental work, and that in crucial respects his techniques do more harm than good."[33]

The international journal *Agricultural Systems*, in their March 2014 issue, printed a piece about Savory's method of intensive rotational grazing (IRG) and his assertion that it regenerates grasslands:

The vast majority of experimental evidence does not support claims of enhanced ecological benefits in IRG compared to other grazing strategies, including the capacity to increase storage of soil organic carbon. . . . IRG has been rigorously evaluated, primarily in the United States, by numerous investigators at multiple locations and in a wide range of precipitation zones over a period of several decades. Collectively, these experimental results clearly indicate that IRG does not increase plant or animal production, or improve plant community composition, or benefit soil surface hydrology compared to other grazing strategies.[34]

The *International Journal of Biodiversity* concluded in April 2014 that Savory's claims were unfounded on every point. These were a few of their conclusions rebutting several of Savory's key arguments:

Contrary to the assumption that grasses will senesce and die if not grazed by livestock, studies of numerous relict sites, long-term rested sites, and paired grazed and ungrazed sites have demonstrated that native plant communities, particularly bunchgrasses, are sustained by rest from livestock grazing. . . . No benefits of hoof action were found. To the contrary, hoof action by livestock has been documented to destroy biological crusts, a key component in soil protection and nutrient cycling, thereby increasing erosion rates and reducing fertility, while increasing soil compaction and reducing water infiltration.[35]

These are the same biological crusts that Savory, in his TED talk, calls "the cancer of desertification."

Savory also asserts his livestock grazing method could potentially reverse global warming by sequestering large amounts of carbon in grassland soil.[36]

According to Dr. Sylvia Fallon of the National Resources Defense Council, however, carbon sequestration resulting from the interaction between grazing animals and grasslands is most effective when these animals spend their whole lifespan living, and then dying, on the land, their bodies decomposing and returning their biological material and waste to the soil with little to no interference from human beings.[37] But this is not part of Savory's plan.

"It is unclear," James McWilliams writes on Slate.com, "given that Savory has identified this type of arrangement as his ecological model, how marketing cattle for food would be consistent with these requirements. Cows live up to twenty years of age, but in most grass-fed systems, they are removed when they reach slaughter weight at fifteen months. Cheating the nutrient cycle at the heart of land regeneration by removing the manure-makers and grass hedgers when only 10 percent of their ecological 'value' has been exploited undermines the entire idea of efficiency that Savory spent his TED talk promoting."[38]

And the *International Journal of Biodiversity* points out that livestock are a major source of greenhouse gas emissions. They also eat and trample vegetation and cause soil erosion, which in turn releases carbon that was previously stored in the plants and soil. This has all been shown by studies in grazed and ungrazed regions.

And perhaps the most damning statement from the *International Journal of Biodiversity*: "Studies supporting HM [holistic management, one of the terms for Savory's method] have generally come from the Savory Institute or anecdotal accounts of HM practitioners. Leading range scientists have refuted the system and indicated that its adoption by land-management agencies is based on these anecdotes and unproven principles rather than scientific evidence."[39]

What Savory fails to mention is the immense connection between desertification and deforestation. "[Desertification]," Dr. Robert Oppenlander writes in *Food Choice and Sustainability*,[40] "is actually a manifestation or side effect of something else—deforestation, which is a by-product of our choice of foods."

PRIME REAL ESTATE: AMERICAN RANGELANDS

In the end it always seems to come down to money. It turns out the cattle industry is having a similar effect on wildlife in the United States as it is having in the rain forests. Land must be provided for grazing. And so wild species that live on that land must be dealt with.

The federal government, using contracted low-flying helicopters, herds thousands of wild horses into corrals every year, removing them from public lands and freeing the land for profitable use by commercial interests.[41]

"The government has been rounding up horses en masse," Deniz Bolbol of the American Wild Horse Preservation Campaign told me as I interviewed her outside on a sunny day, "and we now have more wild horses and burros in government holding facilities than we have free on the range.[42]

"Basically, you have ranchers who get to graze on our public lands for a fraction of the going rate, so they're getting this huge tax subsidy that is about one fifteenth of the going rate. What the Bureau of Land Management has to do is say, 'How much forage and water is on the land?' And then they divvy it up. They give so much to the cows, so much to wildlife and so much to the wild horses and burros. What we see is the lion's share of the forage and water going to the livestock industry. Then they scapegoat the horses and burros and say, 'Oh, there's too many horses and burros. Let's remove them.'

"Wild horses and burros are just one of the victims of the mismanagement of our public lands for livestock . . . we also see predator killing going on," Bolbol continued.

"We know wolves are now being targeted by ranchers. The USDA has aircraft, and all they do is aerial gunning of predators,[43] so all a rancher does is call up and say, 'I've got coyote here.' [The USDA aircraft will] come over and they'll shoot the coyote or they'll shoot the mountain lion or they'll shoot the bobcat. This is all for ranching."

"At what level of government do these actions come from—is it federal?" I asked.

"It starts at the local level with the Bureau of Land Management, but then it goes all the way to Congress," Bolbol said. "We see Congress sitting there willing to allow this type of mismanagement of our public lands to continue.

"I've seen so many pieces of land, I've looked at so many environmental assessments from the Bureau of Land Management where they say the rangelands are not meeting standards. They say straight up, 'Livestock grazing is a cause for not meeting range standards,' and yet they will continue to allow livestock grazing.

"If anyone cares about wild horses and wildlife and public lands and the environment, you can't ignore the impact—the negative impact—that livestock grazing is having on our public lands."

In our interview, Will Anderson, one of the founders of Greenpeace Alaska, echoed Deniz Bolbol's words.

"It is the insistence of and lobbying power of the animal agriculture industry," Anderson said, "that continues to see wolves killed, continues to see an insistence that predators be maintained at a low level that does not benefit ecosystems. Ranchers are at the very core of making sure that cougars are treed by hounds and that wolf packs are run down and that hunting seasons are opened up year-round.

"In Washington State," Anderson continued, "after cattle were found to be attacked by wolves on public lands where they were grazing under permit, the state decided to kill the entire "wedge" pack of wolves.[44] Those wolves were not introduced. They had in-migrated from Canada, but they're no longer there."

Finding out what was happening to the wolves really jolted me. Wildlife, and in particular the plight of wolves, always had a special resonance for me. There are an estimated 5,000 wolves left in the lower 48 states. Genetic data suggests that before the Europeans arrived, the wolf population in the same area was 400,000.[45]

Wolves, much like sharks and other large predatory fish, have a ripple effect on the entire ecosystem around them. In Yellowstone Park, for example, where a lot of wolf research is conducted, they found that when wolves were absent, the moose population exploded and destroyed the woody vegetative habitats needed by birds. Several bird species disappeared from the park because of it. And in the absence of wolves, coyotes hunted pronghorns almost to extinction. It was only when wolves were brought back to Yellowstone and began controlling the coyote population that the pronghorns began to recover.

Wolves feed a wide variety of other species, such as bald eagles, golden eagles, grizzly bears, cougars, lynx, ravens, wolverines, and many others, who nourish themselves with the leftovers from wolf dinners. Wolves also help reduce the amount of disease spread by animals like deer and elk, both by hunting diseased animals and by discouraging the congregation of large groups of animals, which also helps prevent the transmission of disease.[46]

For all these reasons and many others, it is incredibly shortsighted to destroy wildlife and disrupt balanced ecosystems in the name of profit and agro-business.

I gave money to the Sierra Club countless times in order to "save the wolves," but not once did I ever stop to think why they needed to be saved. I looked back at my own ignorant self, upset that I never asked why, and upset that the Sierra Club never told me.

I went to see Lindsey Allen, the executive director of Rainforest Action Network (RAN) in San Francisco. Her long brown hair was parted in the middle, and she wore a denim jacket with a bandana around her neck. Allen joined RAN in 2010 and worked with Greenpeace, targeting "destructive cattle sector expansion into the Amazon rain forest."[47]

She seemed like a good person to talk to.

"What is the leading cause, the absolute leading cause, of rain forest destruction?" I asked her.

She smiled and leaned back in her chair. "Human intervention into rain forests is the leading cause. And so, it's either for logging or it's for agro-business. And that's when you're looking at the top global drivers. It will vary a bit by the rain forest that you're talking about, but the way we're choosing to use these natural resources on a large industrial scale is the leading driver."

I had noticed on RAN's website that they had a massive campaign against oil drilling, so I asked Allen, "In terms of rain forest destruction, is it more fossil fuels or is it more animal agriculture?" I asked.

"I don't know why we would ever do one or the other." She sounded a little sharp.

"I'm just wondering, which is worse?"

Allen paused, then shook her head. "I don't necessarily know."

When I went on Rainforest Action Network's website after the interview with Allen, I couldn't believe I didn't see anything about cattle, but I did see they had a large campaign against palm oil. Palm oil plantations are causing tremendous deforestation in the

Indonesian Rain Forest Deforestation Due to Palm Oil vs. Cattle Grazing (to date)

Indonesian rain forest. It is estimated that palm oil is responsible for 26 million acres being cleared to date.[48] Comparatively, livestock and their feed crops are responsible for 136 million acres of rain forest lost to date.[49]

Instead of talking about animal agriculture, RAN focused on palm, pulp and paper, coal, and tar sands. How could they not have the leading cause of rain forest destruction? Why focus on fossil fuels and not cattle?

In March 2015, when I went back to the website of Rainforest Action Network, I was beyond thrilled to see an international campaign called "Meatout": "part of a growing global movement that draws attention to the increasingly clear connection between industrial meat production and climate change, environmental degradation and animal abuse."[50] Finally! Farm Animal Rights Movement was organizing an international day of action that "encourages the public to eat wholesome, nutritious plant-based foods for just one day."[51]

Hold on—one day? It reminded me of what Dr. Oppenlander said to me about meatless Mondays:

"When you go meatless on Monday, if you ascribe to that campaign, you're essentially contributing to climate change, pollution, depletion of our planet's resources, and [harming] your own health on only six days of the week instead of seven. You're creating a false sense of justification for what you're doing on those other six days of the week. So in other words, we really shouldn't be resting on our laurels of what [we] do right only one seventh of the time."

It's like a smoker diagnosed with lung cancer ascribing to "smokeless Sundays."

The demand for meat and dairy is rising around the world. Between 1990 and 2012, meat production worldwide increased almost 70 percent. Dairy production increased 39 percent. The production of eggs increased a whopping 93 percent.[52] Meatless Mondays and Meatout aren't going to make a big enough impact—they aren't solutions. They're Band-Aids. This increased demand for animal products is inextricably linked to the destruction of the rain forests, not to mention all the other issues.

The research on the connections between environmental devastation and industrial meat production has been available for a long time, even if the public wasn't aware of it. Could Lindsey Allen, the executive director of Rainforest Action Network, one of the world's largest rain forest protection groups, really not know what was going on? I couldn't believe that, not when the information is readily available with a quick Google search. It should have been her job to know. She had worked on targeting cattle grazing in the Amazon—she *had* to know something about it. This was perhaps the most frustrating interview for me in the entire making of *Cowspiracy*. Under her evasiveness, I felt deep down that she knew all the answers. She knew what I was asking. But she evaded the most glaring truth about rain forest destruction. Why?

I immediately went to Amazon Watch in Oakland to see if they would say what the leading cause of rain forest destruction is.

I was able to speak with Leila Salazar Lopez, the program director of Amazon Watch, who had spent more than fifteen years working on international campaigns to protect the world's rain forests, particularly in Indonesia and the Amazon. A self-described "proud Chicana,"[53] she had striking bone structure, freckles, and dark lipstick.

"The most biologically and culturally diverse place on the planet is under massive attack right now. The Amazon rain forest itself could be gone in the next ten years," Lopez told us.

"What is the leading cause of rain forest destruction?" I asked her, as I had asked Allen.

"The leading cause of destruction, I would say . . ." Lopez paused, seeming to search for words. "Well, just to put it in the context of what Amazon Watch works on, there's many, many 'drivers of deforestation,' as we call them. Many different reasons and ways that rain forests are destroyed. The ones that cause the most damage and are the most widespread are mega-projects such as oil and gas pipelines, mining projects, mega-dam projects . . ."

Here, dear reader, I have to admit I tuned out, as the stream of words and lack of clear answers flowed over me. I felt like I was going in circles with all these groups, as if I were stuck in some strange cowspiracy twilight zone where no one could talk about cows. I couldn't believe these organizations just wouldn't say what the leading cause of rain forest destruction truly is. I had to ask one more time.

"But what is the absolute primary, leading cause of rain forest destruction?"

"It's hard to say what is a leading cause of deforestation of the Amazon because they're all destructive," Lopez said. "Oil and gas. Mining. Dams. Agriculture. But in terms of land use, in terms of the amount of land that is destroyed . . . When we talk about a comparison between all those different causes of deforestation—what is causing the most trees to fall, for example—I think it would definitely be agriculture. Unfortunately, one of the biggest causes of deforestation—definitely in the Brazilian Amazon—is agribusiness. Cattle, cattle grazing, and soy production in particular."

"This is what's really going on," I said.

Lopez propped her chin in her hand and nodded.

Her entire demeanor changed. It was as if a weight had been dropped from her. She looked me straight in the eyes. I realized while conducting all these interviews that an amazing simplicity and directness emerge when someone is speaking the truth.

"Why do you think Greenpeace, or no one, is really saying the whole story?" I asked Lopez.

"The whole story about the main cause of deforestation?

"Yeah."

Lopez looked down at her desk and shook her head. "I think you've brought up some really good points about why isn't anybody doing anything about this? I think in Brazil, in particular, when we look at what happened after the Forest Code was passed and people who were standing up against the lobbyists and the special interests—the cattle industry, the agribusiness industry—what was happening to them? A lot of people who were speaking out got killed. You look at José Cláudio Ribeiro da Silva. There are people who are putting themselves out there and saying cattle ranching is destroying the Amazon. . . . Look at Dorothy Stang, you know, the nun who lived out in Pará, who was killed." Lopez widened her eyes. "A lot of people just keep their mouth shut because they don't want to be the next one with a bullet to their head."

CHAPTER SEVEN
ACTIVISTS, GOVERNMENTS, AND CORPORATIONS: SHUTTING DOWN A MOVEMENT

Sister Dorothy Mae Stang, the woman mentioned by Leila Salazar Lopez from Amazon Watch, was a nun born in Dayton, Ohio. She was a teacher in Chicago, Illinois, and Phoenix, Arizona, before she went to Brazil in 1966. There, living in the heart of the Brazilian rain forest, she helped poor farmers and their families create financial independence and stability by farming small plots and extracting small-scale products from the forest in a sustainable manner.

The rich and untapped resources of the rain forest, however, attracted those who were less interested in helping the poor and more interested in making a profit. Logging operations, cattle ranchers, land speculators, and massive agribusinesses began to appear. These were often illegal operations that victimized the local farmers while they devastated the rain forest that the farmers depended on.[1]

Dorothy Stang saw firsthand the destruction of the Amazon rain forest, as well as the ruin and wreckage it brought to the farmers she sought to help. She also understood that the welfare of the rain forest was vitally connected to the welfare of the entire planet. And she saw how the politicians of Brazil turned a blind eye to the devastation, both of the land and of the rural poor who lived on it.

Stang's life work became the protection and preservation of the Amazon rain forest. She was frequently photographed wearing a white T-shirt with green block letters reading, "A MORTE DA FLORESTA É O FIM DA NOSSA VIDA"—Portuguese for "THE DEATH OF THE FOREST IS THE END OF OUR LIFE." With her cap of white hair, glasses, sloping shoulders, and small round face, she looked more like a sweet grandmother than a radical activist.

Stang spoke out openly against the destruction of the rain forest from cattle ranching, loggers, speculators, and agribusinesses for three decades. She received death threats and hate mail.[2] In the late 1990s, when she was in her sixites, her name appeared on a death list, targeted by the region's powerful ranchers, loggers, and agribusinesses.[3]

"I don't want to flee," she said, "nor do I want to abandon the battle of these farmers who live without any protection in the forest. They have the sacrosanct right to aspire to a better life, on land where they can live and work with dignity while respecting the environment."[4]

The state of Pará, in northern Brazil, where Stang lived, was infamous for violence and murders in disputes over land, as well as labor conditions resembling slavery.[5] One third of the annual deaths in the area are contract killings of environmentalists, farmers, and human rights advocates for opposing the razing and burning of the rain forest for cattle grazing, logging, and crop production used mainly to feed livestock.[6] The nun had asked the Brazilian government repeatedly at every level—city, state, and nationally—to provide protection for the local peasants. She was turned down every time.

Early on February 12, 2005, Dorothy Stang was walking on a rural dirt road on her way to meet local farmers. Another farmer was late, walking a short distance behind her. He was able to see everything that happened in the next few minutes.[7] Two men appeared and blocked Stang's way.

"Do you have a weapon?" they asked her.

"Yes," she replied. She pulled out her old Bible. Stang read to the men out loud. "Blessed are the poor in spirit, for theirs is the Kingdom of Heaven. Blessed are the meek, for they will inherit the earth. Blessed are those who hunger and thirst for righteousness, for they will be filled. . . . God bless you, my sons," she said.[8]

One of the men shot Dorothy Stang in the abdomen. Stang, 73 years old, fell facedown. The same man shot her again in the back, and then four times in the head.

Her body lay on the dirt path all day, her arms curled beneath her. Witnesses were afraid they would be shot if they retrieved it. The white cap from her head lay next to her. It rained until the clothes on her body were soaked.[9]

"In the midst of all this violence," Sister Dorothy Stang wrote to her family and friends on her sixtieth birthday, "there are many small communities that have learned the secret of life: sharing, solidarity, confidence, equality, pardon, working together . . . Thus life is productive and transforming in the midst of all this."[10]

In the past twenty years, more than 1,200 people—including human rights activists, environmentalists, small farmers, priests, and judges—have been murdered for trying to protect the rain forest, according to the Catholic Land Pastoral, which tracks rural violence in Brazil. These murders are ordered primarily by ranchers, loggers, and powerful farmers.[11]

A Brazilian rancher, Vitalmiro Bastos de Moura, was charged with ordering Dorothy Stang's murder. He was sentenced in 2013 to thirty years in jail. Another rancher, Regivaldo Galvao, was also convicted for ordering the murder, and was sentenced to thirty years in jail in 2010. He was released in 2012 by the Supreme Court of Brazil, "saying he had the right to remain free pending the outcome of his appeal."[12] The man who confessed to firing the six shots that killed Stang was released from prison after serving less than nine years of his twenty-seven-year sentence. A state judge ruled that he would be permitted to serve the remainder of his time under house arrest.[13]

A 2013 report by the investigative nonprofit Global Witness, *Deadly Environment*, shows a distinct and dramatic escalation in the number of known killings worldwide of environmentalists between 2002 and 2013. At least 908 people were murdered during this time for defending the environment. Of these killings, less than 10 percent were taken to court and only 1 percent resulted in convictions.[14] The convictions in the killing of Sister Dorothy Stang occurred only after intense international and national scrutiny.[15] And in Brazil, more environmental and land-rights activists have been killed than the rest of the world combined. On average, one environmental activist has been killed in Brazil every week since 2002, the beginning of the Global Witness study.[16]

In November 2010, José Cláudio Ribeiro da Silva, the leading rain forest activist mentioned by Leila Salazar Lopez in her interview with us at Amazon Watch, gave a TEDx speech: "I could be here today talking to you and in one month you will get the news that I disappeared. I will protect the forest at all costs. That is why I could get a bullet in my head at any moment. . . . But my fear does not silence me. As long as I have the strength to walk I will denounce all of those who damage the forest."

Six months later, on May 24, 2011, da Silva, 52, and his wife, Maria do Espírito Santo, 51, another rain forest activist, were gunned down.[17]

A simple marble-slab memorial now stands where da Silva and do Espírito Santo were killed. It is inscribed with words spoken by da Silva six months before his death: "They want to do the same thing to me they did to Chico Mendes and Sister Dorothy." Two bullets—vandalism—fracture the marble slab.[18]

"The number one domestic terrorism threat [in the United States] is the ecoterrorism, animal-rights movement." That was a statement in 2004 from John Lewis, the top FBI official in charge of domestic terrorism and a deputy assistant director.[19] And it's not just the FBI that sees the environmental and animal rights movement as a dire threat. The Department of Homeland Security also lists the the Earth Liberation Front (ELF) and the Animal Liberation Front (ALF) as leading hazards to national security, all while overlooking violence from the right wing.[20]

Guess what the total number of fatalities and injuries from the ecoterrorism, animal-rights movement (the *number one* domestic terrorism threat in the United States) is? Exactly zero.[21] Violent attacks from right-wing extremists, such as Christian funda-mentalists, white supremacists, anti-abortion activists, and anti-LGBTQ groups, which result in both injuries and deaths, have increased 400 percent between 1990 and 2011,[22] according to a report by the Combating Terrorism Center of West Point. The report includes information on 4,420 violent incidents in the United States that are classified as right-wing violence or hate crimes that occurred from 1990 to 2011. There were 670 deaths and 3,053 injuries.[23] Approximately 65 percent of those attacks were carried out against ethnic and religious minorities, 14 percent against LGBTQ groups or individu-als, and another 6 percent were related to abortion.[24] The West Point report also docu-ments a sharp spike in the number of victims of right-wing violence between 2007 and 2011, with approximately 190 injuries and 30 fatalities annually.[25]

The Earth Liberation Front and the Animal Liberation Front, the two groups responsible for the largest number of "ecoterrorist" attacks in the United States, each stress three things in their codes of conduct:[26]

◆ To inflict economic damage (by property destruction or releasing animals) on corporations exploiting the environment and animals,
◆ To educate the public, and
◆ To "take all necessary precautions against harming life"—human and nonhuman.

Independent journalist Will Potter went to the Foundation for Biomedical Research (FBR) to confirm the extent of violence committed by environmental and animal rights activists. Potter reasoned that if anyone would have an incentive to emphasize the vio-lence, injuries, and deaths caused by "ecoterrorists," it would be the Foundation for Biomedical Research.

The FBR's website says they are "the nation's oldest and largest organization ded-icated to improving human and veterinary health by promoting public understanding and support for humane and responsible animal research. FBR is the leading voice of scientific reason and medical progress in the ongoing, sometimes violent debate that surrounds animal research." The FBR also has an "Illegal Incidents Report," which monitors and records the criminal activities of "ecoterrorists."

Potter located the FBR's "Top 20 List of Illegal Actions by Animal and Eco-Terrorists 1996–2006," which ranked the most significant crimes in order of severity. These are the top three:

1. Arson at a housing development in San Diego. Injuries: 0
2. Bombing at the Chiron Corporation in California. Injuries: 0
3. Bombing at the Shaklee corporation in California. Injuries: 0

"[Animal] and environmental rights extremists," however, from January 1990 to June 2004, said John Lewis of the FBI, "have claimed credit for more than 1,200 [attacks], resulting in millions of dollars of damages and monetary loss."[27]

Those millions of dollars of damages and monetary loss are, perhaps, the real issue at stake.

The prosecution of Daniel McGowan was made famous by the 2011 Oscar-nominated documentary, *If A Tree Falls: A Story of the Earth Liberation Front*. Daniel McGowan is an environmentalist born in Brooklyn, New York, who was arrested as part of the largest federal roundup of environmental activists in this country's history, triggered by a former Earth Liberation Front member turned informant. McGowan was sentenced to seven years in prison for participating with the Earth Liberation Front in two counts of arson in 2001, protesting the extensive logging of old-growth forests in the Pacific Northwest. No one was hurt in any of the actions.[28] The judge imposed a terrorism enhancement on McGowan's case, labeling him as a successful government terror prosecution for the rest of his life.[29]

The Earth Liberation Front mandates that their protest actions not harm any life—human or nonhuman. An ELF video says, "Take initiative, form your own cell, and do what needs to be done to protect all life on this planet."[30]

Lauren Regan, part of McGowan's legal team and executive director of the Civil Liberties Defense Center based in Eugene, Oregon, which provides legal protection to environmental and social justice activists against corporate and governmental assaults on civil liberties, speaks in the documentary, *If A Tree Falls: A Story of the Earth Liberation Front*:

> The word "terrorism," to me, is about killing humans. It's about ending innocent life; and that is the antithesis of what these people did. Concern for life was a very big part of the plan and implementation of these actions, and is why no one was ever harmed or injured in them; 1,200 incidents are being accredited to the ALF and the ELF in this country, and not a single injury or death. Those statistics don't happen by accident.

Bill Barton, of the Native Forest Council, also speaks in the documentary. "The industry tends to call environmentalists radical," Barton says. "The reality is that 95 percent
of the standing native forest in the United States has been cut down. It's not radical to
try and save the last remaining 5 percent. What's radical is logging 95 percent."

McGowan was released in 2013. He owes almost two million dollars in resti-
tution and is expected to pay it. He was incarcerated for five and a half years, and
ten months into his term he was transferred to a special secretive prison known as
a Communications Management Unit (CMU), built to hold terrorists, and which
severely restricts contact with the outside world. The CMU population is primarily
made up of Muslims and political activist prisoners.[31] The American Civil Liberties
Union has filed a lawsuit challenging the legality of CMUs, which are known by some
prisoners as "little Guantánamo."[32]

ANIMAL ENTERPRISE TERRORISM ACT (AETA) AND THE AMERICAN LEGISLATIVE EXCHANGE COUNCIL (ALEC)

In 2006, the Animal Enterprise Terrorism Act (AETA) was passed by Congress and
signed into law by George W. Bush. Groups representing powerful agricultural, pharmaceutical, and fur industries such as the National Cattlemen's Beef Association, the
National Association for Biomedical Research, United Egg Producers, Fur Commission
USA, GlaxoSmithKline, Pfizer, and Wyeth,[33] as well as the Animal Enterprise Protection
Coalition (AEPC), the American Legislative Exchange Council (ALEC) and the Center
for Consumer Freedom (CCF, funded strongly by the fast-food industry)[34] lobbied heavily to push the law through Congress.

"Under [AETA's] terms," as reported in *The Guardian*, "anyone who damages the
property or the profit line of an animal business and who uses 'interstate commerce'
such as a cellphone or the internet to carry out the action can be convicted of terrorism
even though no violence is involved."[35]

The AETA criminalizes a wide range of First Amendment activities, including protests, boycotts, undercover investigations and whistle-blowing, and picketing,
and is phrased in vague, unclear language. "So in effect," according to the Center for
Constitutional Rights, "the AETA silences the peaceful and lawful protest activities
of animal and environmental advocates." Once the bill had passed the Senate (pushed
through in the middle of the night, hours before the Congressional recess for the
November elections[36]) and was on the House side, Representative Dennis Kucinich
raised the concern that the broad label of "terrorist" would chill free speech and that the
bill created a special class of crimes for a particular kind of protest. Just as it did with

the Senate, however, the bill was rushed through the House late at night with very little notice and a mere handful of members present to vote.[37]

The legal history of the AETA primarily involves animal activists, but it is vital to remember that all the instances of animal activism presented here can be effortlessly interchanged with environmental activism. In the words of Rachel Meeropol, an attorney from the Center for Constitutional Rights, "Activists from any social movements could be subject to prosecution as terrorists if their advocacy, if their lawful protest, affects the bottom line of a business."[38]

The predecessor to AETA, the Animal Enterprise Protection Act (AEPA), which passed in 1992, was used to indict and convict a group of seven animal rights activists, the SHAC 7 (the acronym stands for Stop Huntingdon Animal Cruelty). The official charge was "conspiracy," although in fact they were indicted, convicted, and sent to prison for four to six years each for running a legal, aboveground website opposing animal experimentation.[39]

A small number of people have been prosecuted under the AETA. It was first used in 2008 to charge four activists in California as terrorists for writing in chalk on the sidewalk, handing out leaflets, and chanting outside the homes of biomedical researchers. It took two years for the U.S. District Court to dismiss the case.[40] In 2014, Kevin Olliff and Tyler Lang were indicted under the AETA for freeing mink from fur farms and spray painting "Liberation is Love" on a barn. They each face federal charges that could lead to ten years in prison.[41]

Will Potter, however, contends that prosecution in court is not the true function of the bill. Its effectiveness is in demonizing and suppressing opposition to corporations. "When you start altering your legal actions," writes Potter in *Herbivore* magazine, "and scaling back your nonviolent activism because you're afraid of this legislation, then the law has already accomplished what its supporters intended."

The federal AETA bill is mirrored by what have come to be known as "ag-gag" bills on the state level. Mark Bittman first coined the term in the *New York Times*: "ag" as in agriculture, "gag" as in to stifle and suppress. Ag-gag laws criminalize whistle-blowers and undercover investigations of any animal enterprise by making it illegal to film or photograph abuse of animals, workers, and the environment, as well as making it illegal to possess or distribute such footage. These laws make it impossible to expose a systemic pattern of abuse without great personal risk.

As of March 2015, ag-gag bills have been passed in eight states and introduced in sixteen more states, with bills pending in several more.[42] Ag-gag bills are introduced with the heavy support of the corporation-dominated American Legislative Exchange Council (ALEC).[43]

"ALEC," says Bill Moyers in a *Moyers & Company* report, "is a nationwide consortium of elected state legislators working side by side with some of America's most powerful corporations. They have an agenda you should know about, a mission to remake America, changing the country by changing its laws, one state at a time. ALEC creates what it calls 'model legislation,' pro-corporate laws its members push in statehouses across the nation. ALEC says close to a thousand bills, based at least in part on its models, are introduced each year. And an average of two hundred pass. This has been going on for decades."

Congressman Mark Pocan of Wisconsin puts it this way: "The ALEC is a corporate dating service for lonely legislators and corporate special interests [and] eventually the relationship culminates with some special interest legislation and hopefully that lives happily ever after as the ALEC model. Unfortunately what's excluded from that equation is the public."[44]

One of ALEC's model bills, the Animal and Ecological Terrorism Act (not to be confused with AETA, the Animal Enterprise Terrorism Act,) is clearly a precursor of the ag-gag laws. House Bill 2095 of Missouri, coincidentally also called the Animal Ecological Terrorism Act, criminalizes anyone entering an animal enterprise "to take pictures with the intent to commit criminal activities or defame the facility or its owner." This phrase is taken verbatim from ALEC's model legislation.[45]

And as Ryan Shapiro, a leading Freedom of Information activist, points out, "There's a relationship also between these ag-gag laws and the Animal Enterprise Terrorism Act, because if you commit a crime, any crime, including violating an ag-gag bill, on a state level, then you can be prosecuted federally as a terrorist under the Animal Enterprise Terrorism [Act]."[46]

Undercover investigations are a fundamental tradition of American journalism, providing uncensored access to institutions and subjects that would otherwise remain concealed—often for good reason—from the public eye. The Pulitzer Prize, between 1960 and 1979, was awarded five times to projects that involved undercover reporting. Undercover investigations in the United States have exposed the truth about—among many other things—slavery, human trafficking, prisons and jails, mental asylums, hospitals, the Ku Klux Klan, homelessness, sweatshops, voter fraud, prostitution, and pedophiles.[47] Whistleblowers such as Chelsea Manning, Edward Snowden, and Thomas Drake have shone light on national security and citizen surveillance. And, of course, there is the food processing industry. In 1994, Tony Horwitz was awarded the Pulitzer

Prize for National Reporting for his undercover work as a poultry processor, writing for the *Wall Street Journal*. And a 2001 *New York Times* Pulitzer-winning series included Charlie LeDuff's work in a pork processing plant.[48]

Undercover investigations exposing the conditions and abuse of "animal enterprises," carried out by groups such as Mercy For Animals, the Humane Society of the United States, PETA, and Compassion Over Killing have lead to criminal convictions around the country. Their undercover videos show workers smashing in the heads of cows with hammers and pickaxes,[49] beating and sexually abusing pigs, electroshocking pregnant sows and slamming piglets on the ground, stomping on turkeys' heads and breaking their necks,[50] and illegally burning the ankles of horses with chemicals, along with egg-laying hens caged next to the rotting bodies of other chickens.[51]

"Although these investigations have certainly led to criminal charges across the country," Will Potter said on *Democracy Now!*, "much of what these investigators are documenting are actually standard industry practices. I think most people would be shocked to learn that there is not one federal law that protects farm animals during their lives. . . . So, to put this another way, there are about nine billion animals killed every year for food in this country by an industry with virtually no government oversight and no accountability. These undercover investigators are really the only meaningful way that American consumers have a right to know how their food is produced and to have a check and balance on a multibillion-dollar industry."[52]

"If you think this is an animal welfare issue, you have missed the mark," said Amanda Hitt, director of the Government Accountability Project's Food Integrity Campaign, in *Mother Jones*. "This is a bigger, broader issue. [Ag-gag laws] are also stopping environmental whistleblowing; you are also stopping workers' rights whistleblowing. . . . You have given power to the industry to completely self-regulate."[53]

"This is really about a corporate campaign," Potter said in another article on *Democracy Now!*, "to demonize their opposition and to use terrorism resources to shut down a movement."[54]

Will Potter's name kept coming up in my research on government and corporate crackdowns on environmental and animal rights activists. He has written for publications as diverse as the *Chicago Tribune*, *Foreign Policy*, *Herbivore*, the *Washington Post*, *WIRED*, *Legal Affairs*, and *Rolling Stone*. He is the author of *Green Is the New Red: An Insider's Account of a Social Movement Under Siege*, which explores and exposes how environmental and animal rights activists came to be targeted as ecoterrorists. Potter was invited to speak

before the U.S. Congress about the Animal Enterprise Terrorism Act. He also spoke before
the Australian Parliament about "ag-gag" bills. Definitely someone I wanted to talk to.

Potter is a thin, lanky guy with horn-rimmed glasses, a sharp chin, and a prominent
Adam's apple. I spoke with him at length in Washington, D.C., where he's based. Why,
I wanted to know, are environmental and animal rights activists considered the number
one domestic terror threat in the country?

"I think a big part of it is that [the environmental and animal rights movements],
more than any other social movements today, are directly threatening corporate
profits," Potter said. "They're threatening [profits] each time they release an undercover video that shows systemic animal welfare abuses. They are threatening it each
time they release animals from laboratories and fur farms. They threaten it each
time they convert someone to a vegan diet and a lifestyle change where they're
embracing compassion and refusing to purchase products from industries that are
destructive to the environment.

"The animal agriculture industry is one of the most powerful industries on the
planet," Potter continued. "I think most people in this country are aware of the influence of money and industry on politics. We see that clearly on display with this industry
in particular. . . . At every level, [the animal agriculture] industry has an overwhelming
influence on how business is handled and how they're policed.

"Around the country, as people are becoming more aware of how their food is
produced and where it comes from and the environmental impacts of those decisions,
people have been understandably outraged. There's been some really damning media
coverage in mainstream outlets [and the] industry has fought back in a variety of ways.
One of them has been food libel laws and food safety lawsuits. . . . This came to a head
with Oprah Winfrey, when she [talked] about mad cow disease.

"There are a couple of attempts in different states to roll back the Freedom of
Information Act protections, specifically as they apply to animal agriculture. A lot
of this is done in the name of national security because they're saying if terrorists
found out about locations of factory farms that have a massive amount of chemicals
on supply, this could be a public safety danger.

"Now of course, the real danger is to their profits. They don't want people to find
out all the chemicals that are entering the water supply, the heavy use of antibiotics, the
pollution, the water run-off into the broader ecosystem. It's all being masked in libel and
food safety and food security rhetoric.

"In the last couple of years, there has been a wave of legislation that people have
called ag-gag. We're seeing new legislation being introduced that not just criminalizes

taking photographs or video of factory farms and animal cruelty, they criminalize documenting environmental abuses in a wide range of industries, from fracking, mining, automobile production, in addition to industrial agriculture, any corporation you can think of. . . . Other corporations are seeing the value of cracking down on whistleblowers. When we open into our legislative process the possibility of corporations making themselves immune from public scrutiny and from bad press, that's something all corporations want to take part in.

"We see that on display with groups like the American Legislative Exchange Council (ALEC), a corporate front group that literally drafts legislation by corporations about environmental issues, energy, animal agriculture, food safety, food sustainability, that are [then] introduced around the country," Potter continued. "People have no idea that not only did corporations lobby for these bills, they actually wrote them. They're buying their way into our courthouses and into the law.

"As corporations were lobbying for the Animal Enterprise Terrorism Act, they had a secretive coalition, which wasn't available to the public, that someone happened to leak to me. When you log in [to the website], you see a list of corporations [involved in the coalition]. The animal agriculture industry was very heavily represented. So was the pharmaceutical industry.

"We're living in an age right now," Potter adds, "where, when it comes to our personal information as people, as citizens, it's all up for grabs. When we try to find out what corporations are doing, and what politicians and what law enforcement are doing, it's suddenly illegal.

"If you're facing one of these prosecutions for slander or food libel, you're going up against people who have massive legal resources. It's just overwhelming, the amount of money at their disposal, and you have nothing. I think that fear is a big part of the tactic as well with these lawsuits to try to deter people from speaking out.

"When we try to find out how factory farms and how animal agriculture is polluting the environment, they try to claim exemptions to that information either under national security terms or public safety, trademark issues, business—'it's a business secret.'"

I asked Potter about the impact of corporations on traditional journalism and how these crucial subjects have been covered.

"Look at the coverage that comes out consistently," Potter said. "It's ignoring some of the pressing issues of our time. It's ignoring the environmental impact of animal agriculture. It's ignoring the civil liberties implications of all the things we're discussing. This industry [journalism] is dominated by a handful of corporations. They're not always directly directing what media coverage is happening, but that institutional pressure is there. Everyone who works in newsrooms knows it and feels it. It limits the field of discussion.

"Part of being a journalist is having the courage to stand behind your research and your evidence and say, 'No, one [side] *is* wrong. Corporations that are trying to say that their actions are not affecting the planet, it's just flat-out wrong. There's no evidence supporting this. To shy away from that because of the financial influence of these industries is really I think a failure of journalism."

"Why is it, do you think," I asked Potter, "that for the longest time animal agriculture and its impact on the environment, it just wasn't on the radar, wasn't up for discussion? Even someone who's doing great environmental work and really committed to it, like Bill McKibben, one of the leading environmentalists of our time?"

"I think fear is a driving force in how we're thinking about these environmental issues," Potter replies. "I do not believe that most people don't think this is a problem. I think people really know this is a problem.

"Ten years ago, there might have been a question about what is the leading cause of climate change or whether even climate change is a problem, whether it even exists. Right now, you can go to the world's top media outlets. You can get on Google. You can type in 'leading causes of climate change' and you pop up *New York Times* stories, BBC, CNN, reports from the United Nations talking about the leading causes of climate change in report after report as being agriculture.

"This is not hidden information anymore. If we choose to ignore that, it's not because the information is not there. It's because we don't have the courage to acknowledge who's responsible for the problem. It's easier to not do that because it is an escape. It gets us out of having to confront the difficult questions."

"What do we do now?" I ask. "Are we at risk by doing this project?"

"We have to move forward with what we're doing," Potter said, "with the belief and the resolution that what we're doing is right. We're exposing what people need to know. [Your readers] right now are doing that work as they're engaging with these issues, like you should in a democracy. I don't think we should cede that ground one bit."

INTERVIEW WITH THE ANIMAL AGRICULTURE ALLIANCE

Was this why Al Gore, even during his vice-presidency, didn't address the issue of animal agriculture and failed to talk about it in his film, *An Inconvenient Truth*, or his organization, the Climate Reality Project? Was this truth just too inconvenient, even for him? I felt let down by the man who inspired me on this entire path.

I knew I needed to talk to an animal agriculture lobbying group to see what they had to say. If they could silence the government, are they influencing and making connections in these environmental groups as well?

Animal Agriculture Alliance, one of the biggest livestock lobby groups in America, agreed to an interview. Greenpeace wouldn't give us an interview, but Animal Agriculture Alliance would. Now that is saying something.

I met with Emily Meredith, who at the time of our interview was director of communications for Animal Agricultural Alliance and is currently the vice-president of animal care at the National Milk Producers Federation. PR News honored her in 2014 as a "Rising PR Star" in the "30 and Under" category for her work with Animal Agricultural Alliance, where she increased mention of the Alliance in the news media by 75 percent in one year and 365 percent in another.[55]

"Animal Agriculture Alliance is a membership-driven organization," Meredith told me, "so we represent all the protein groups that all have trade associations who help fund us. What we really seek to do here is correct a lot of the misinformation that is consistently spread by groups that really want to bring about the end of animal agriculture and the consumption of meat, milk, and eggs in this country."

"Why do they want to do that?" I asked.

"A lot of the activist groups, it's their goal to support a vegan world," she said. "They'll use whatever means possible to bring about the end of animal consumption in this country. Really, it's good for their bottom lines to drive this anti-agriculture agenda."

"Can you talk about why you think U.S. agriculture is more sustainable?"

"It's because we use advanced genetics, advanced healthcare, and we feed our animals optimal diets. Our industry as a whole is producing more product with fewer animals and fewer resources, meaning that we are more sustainable than the developing countries."

"Is that because of the different things they're feeding the cows in this country?" I asked.

"I wouldn't want to comment on the feed, I don't think," Meredith said. "That's just not an area that's in my wheelhouse."

"Is it possible to feed nine billion people by 2050 on the amount of animal consumption that Americans eat?" I asked her.

"If we can replicate the model we have here in the United States around the world, it's very doable to have continued meat consumption around the world."

"What do you say to the accusations of certain studies that say animal agriculture is responsible for about 90 percent of rain forest destruction?"

"We don't have rain forests in the United States."

"Well, we're dealing with global issues though."

"I can't speak to any livestock production issues outside the United States."

"Can you talk about the role of GMOs [genetically modified organisms] in sustainability?"

"People hear the word 'GMOs,' and that's a really scary term. Again, I think agriculture has kind of struggled to explain what that means, but in reality what we've done is to use technology to make advancements in how we raise crops and how we raise animals. On the animal side, what we do see is these advanced genetics to really breed an animal that's healthier and able to feed a large number of people and is more efficient in how it consumes feed and the end product.

"We're not going to feed the world going back to how it was one hundred years ago, where all the animals were pasture fed," Meredith went on. "We didn't just move animals inside and just implement these large, vertically-integrated systems because of sustainability. It certainly reduces the environmental impact while improving animal well-being and food safety."

"So you're saying that animals like it just as much, being inside?" I ask. "The chickens and the cows like being inside just as much as pasture, grass-fed?" I thought of the sows in their metal gestation crates, unable to turn around for their entire four-month pregnancies and the broiler chickens crammed into their windowless warehouses, sitting in their own excrement for their seven weeks of life.

"In a lot of cases, it's been a significant improvement in their well-being," Meredith repeated, "just in terms of the amount of care they can get, individualized care. When you look at pig production in this country, we've moved the pigs inside and they live a very nice life. They have climate control, it never gets too hot, it never gets too cold, they have individualized feeding systems, they get individual attention every day by the workers that are specifically trained to handle those animal in the best way possible. Really, there have been a lot of improvements. I think it's important to remember that 98.5 percent of farms are family owned. But whether you're indoors or outdoors, in a red barn or a metal barn, the values are inherently the same, those values are tried and true."

Meredith is right that the vast majority of farms in the country are owned by families or individuals—87 percent, according to the EPA's 2007 agricultural census[56]—although the EPA points out that "family farm" does not mean "small farm." But Meredith's statistic co-exists with the fact that factory farms—only 13 percent of the farms in the country—produce 99.9 percent of the country's chicken raised for meat,

97 percent of our laying hens, 99 percent of turkeys, 95 percent of pigs, and 78 percent of cattle.[57]

"Is there any way to visit a slaughterhouse?" I asked Meredith. "Maybe one that's more humane?"

"They're all humane. In fact, there are federal inspectors at every stage of that process when the animals reach the slaughterhouse facility."

"Is it possible to visit? I contacted a couple of slaughterhouses, and they were like, no way."

"Well, it would be like somebody saying, can I come to your home and just hang out and watch what you do everyday? With a camera rolling, peppering you with questions? Do the two of you just leave your studio unlocked every day? It's the same. These are private businesses, and many of them, their homes are right there, this is their home and these are their babies."

"Can you talk a bit about the so-called 'ag-gag' laws prohibiting the filming of animal operations?"

"The impetus for that has come from farmers and ranchers who are really looking for protection against these groups that use very deceptive and manipulative tactics to really bring about the end of their way of life. We call them farm protection. And again, as I mentioned, the danger is that these groups really have an agenda, looking to pad their pockets and I think it's very trendy lately to beat up on agriculture, as I mentioned."

"What's wrong with showing footage of something bad?"

"Well, we don't want groups that are very contrary to our purpose coming in and misrepresenting the truth about the industry."

"Does the meat and dairy industry ever support or donate to environmental non-profits?" I ask.

Meredith blinks. She looks over at Kay Smith, the president and CEO of Animal Agriculture Alliance, who is sitting outside the camera frame. "I don't know that I would want to comment on that," Meredith says, shaking her head. "I don't know."

Smith speaks off-camera. "I don't know that we would know what they donate to or don't donate to." Meredith continues to shake her head, blinking rapidly and pressing her lips together.

I try again. "Does the meat and dairy industry ever support or donate to Greenpeace?"

Meredith looks over at Smith again and lets out a kind of laugh. She adjusts her glasses. "Again, I don't know that I would feel comfortable . . . "

MAD COW DISEASE

Will Potter had mentioned the infamous cattle lawsuit against Oprah Winfrey. In April 1996, Winfrey had several guests on her talk show to discuss food safety in the United States, including Howard Lyman, a former cattle rancher and then-president of Earth Save International. Mad cow disease was causing a firestorm in the media. Lyman told a stunned audience, "A hundred thousand cows per year in the United States are fine one night, then [found] dead the following morning. The majority of those cows are rounded up, ground up, and fed back to other cows. If only one of them has mad cow disease, it has the potential to affect thousands. Remember today, in the United States, 14 percent of all cows by volume are ground up, turned into feed, and fed back to other animals. . . . These are USDA statistics, they're not something we're making up."

Winfrey and her audience were revolted at Lyman's revelation that the beef industry was turning cows into cannibals. Winfrey said, "Cows are herbivores. They shouldn't be eating other cows. . . . It has just stopped me cold from eating another burger."[58]

The U.S. beef industry instantly pulled $600,000 in advertising from Oprah's network.[59] Two months after the show with Lyman aired, Winfrey, her production company Harpo Productions, and Lyman were served with a lawsuit demanding $20 million dollars for damages and punitive fines,[60] filed by a group of Texas cattlemen led by billionaire Paul Engler, owner of Cactus Feeders, Inc. This made Winfrey and Lyman the first individuals sued under the Texas statute, the False Disparagement of Perishable Food Products Act of 1995. They were charged with making "slanderous" statements about beef, causing those in the cattle industry to suffer "shame, embarrassment, humiliation, and mental pain and anguish."[61] The lawsuit stated that the behavior of Winfrey and Lyman "goes beyond all possible bounds of decency and is utterly intolerable in a civilized community."[62]

Thirteen states currently have food disparagement laws. Conviction of food disparagement in Colorado can send you to prison.[63] They are also known as food libel laws and, with variations, permit a food supplier or manufacturer to sue any individual or organization that makes disparaging remarks about their product.[64]

The initial lawsuit against Winfrey and Lyman lasted two years, but in the end, after a jury deliberation of less than six hours in the cattle capital of Texas, Amarillo, they were found not guilty and not liable for damages.[65]

"Lyman's opinion," ruled the Court, "was based on truthful, established fact." The court noted that Lyman's and Winfrey's statements were the same conclusions reached by the FDA nine months later.[66]

The decision was appealed by the Texas cattlemen and moved to Federal Court, where, after almost six years and millions of dollars in legal fees, the federal judge finally dismissed the case with prejudice.

John Stauber, executive director of the Center for Media and Democracy, speaks in the documentary *Mad Cowboy*, based on the book of the same name by Lyman:

"The trial [of Lyman and Winfrey] was . . . the very first time that these food disparagements were used to try and shut up media coverage of a critical issue. And the trial succeeded in getting the media to stop looking critically at mad cow disease. What's frightening about the food disparagement laws is that they're patently unconstitutional. They're the single biggest threat to free speech and the first amendment that I've seen in my lifetime.[67]

I went to talk with Mr. Lyman. At seventy-five, he still looks like a linebacker, with a boxer's nose, broad shoulders, and a cowboy's drawl. I was particularly intrigued that he came from "the other side," as a fourth-generation dairy farmer and cattle rancher.

"I was born on the largest dairy farm in the state of Montana in 1938," Mr. Lyman told me. "Grew up my entire life on a livestock farm, went to Montana State University, got a degree in agriculture, came back and started a mega-agricultural endeavor where I had 10,000 acres of crop, 7,000 heads of cattle, and about 30 employees. I spent 45 years of my life in animal agriculture, and so I've been there, done that."

In his documentary, *Mad Cowboy*, Lyman describes how he got to where he is now:

> My grandfather bought this land. Ever since I was a little kid, this was home. . . . And we were organic farmers; everything we did, we did in conjunction with nature. I always wanted to be a farmer. I loved that more than anything, and I thought, to be a better farmer, to do more, the thing to do was to go to Montana State University and get a degree in agriculture. I was absolutely immersed in herbicides, pesticides, hormones, and medications. . . . And I will never forget, I came home with a degree in agriculture, and I said to my father, I said, "Move over, Pop—we're going to turn this one-horse farm into an agribusiness. . . . And the thing that resonates through my mind today . . . he said, "Our job is to work with nature." And I said, "That's old-fashioned." My great-grandfather, my grandfather, my father, they were organic farmers. I came home a chemical junkie.

Lyman, believing in this new world of chemical agriculture, inundated his farm with herbicides like 2,4,5-T, also known as Agent Orange, insecticides that fell into the feed and water of the cows and were absorbed through their backs, and chemical fertilizer. He pumped his cattle full of antibiotics and growth hormones.

In 1979 he became paralyzed from the waist down due to a tumor on his spinal cord. For the first time, he doubted what he was doing to his farm. His brother had died of cancer in 1969. Could his brother's death, and his own tumor, be connected to the chemical cocktails he had flooded his land and his animals with?

The night before the operation to remove the tumor, he wondered, *Can I save what I profess to love?* That night, certain that he would never walk again, he made a promise to himself to spend the rest of his life telling the truth to anyone who would listen about how we are killing the thing we love the most—the land, our earth.

I asked Lyman about the Oprah lawsuit in Amarillo, Texas.

"When I was on the *Oprah* show, we had the food disparagement law,"[68] Lyman said. "The food disparagement law in my opinion was unconstitutional, but what it basically said was that it was against the law to say something you knew to be false about a perishable commodity. I didn't say anything on the *Oprah* show I thought to be false. I went there and told the truth. Now, it took five years and hundreds of thousands of dollars to extricate myself from the lawsuits from the cattle industry, but if I was to go on the *Oprah* show today, say exactly the same thing today that I said back then, I would be guilty. For me, when they were talking about the food disparagement law, it was the fact of whether I told the truth or not. You can go today and tell the truth and you will be guilty because if you cause a disruption in the profits of the animal industry you're guilty under the Animal Enterprise Terrorism Act."

"Do you think there is any concern about us making this documentary and book?" I asked him.

"Of course! If you don't realize right now that you're putting your neck on the chopping block, you better take that camera and throw it away."

Whoa. Okay.

"Are you ever concerned," I ask him, "[about] being in this movie or book, or the other interviews that you do?"

"Oh, sure," Lyman says. "But you look at the facts. Here I am. I'm an old retired fart. I'm seventy-five. By the time they would drag me through court again, I'd probably be too feeble to eat my oatmeal, and so I wouldn't really care about it. I'm going to stand up and do everything I can do, every day that I have, the rest of my life, to inform the American people that if they don't take their own future in their own hands and are unwilling to go against the greed of corporations and reclaim our food supply, that we probably have no right to consider ourselves a free people anyway. So, I'm going to do what I can do. I'm going to do it every day, and if they want to sue me, so be it. I've been there before and I don't care."

"Awesome." I'm awed. I'm inspired. This guy is great.

"If we're going to see the changes that have to happen," Lyman continued, "so that we end up with a planet that our children and grandchildren can live long on, it's going to have to come from the grassroots. It's as simple as, *you have to live the kind of life you'd like to see the future be.* If you're going to be one of the customers of the people that are destroying the planet, you're voting with your dollars so there is no future for our children and our grandchildren."

"Do you really feel the situation is that dire?" I ask him.

"I would say today that the situation is probably, on a scale of 1 to 10, a 9.5. I think in my heart that the young people will rise up and cause the changes that need to happen, but I will tell you right now, we're going 100 miles an hour and we're approaching the cliff. There's never been a more dire time in the history of humanity than right now. I totally believe that the number one goal of every breathing human today should be to correct the problem so we're steering away from that cliff."

"So what are your thoughts," I ask him, "on grass-fed farms and this movement toward sustainable animal agriculture?"

"The question is *Should we eat animals?* whether they're pasture-raised, or feed-lot-raised, or whether you fed them on a milk bottle. There is no place, in my opinion, in the human body for animal products, period. If you're going to try and appease people with some sort of a throwaway line like, 'Well, we're opposed to the feedlots, but grass-fed ones, they're all right,' that's a bunch of crap."

"We've actually come across a number of studies that say greenhouse gas emissions are higher with grass-fed animals than feedlots," I said. "It requires just more resources in general. What are your thoughts on that? Could factory farming actually be more sustainable?"

"Absolutely not," Lyman replied. "Is it cheaper? Is monoculture agriculture cheaper to produce? Absolutely. But then factor in how we're destroying our infrastructure, the soil, the water, the groundwater. You tell me that this factory agriculture is good for us and our future? That's not true. It's absolutely not true. When you factor in all of the costs, it costs more for our future.

"The fact of it is," Lyman went on, "that the majority of people involved in animal agriculture are really good people, good hardworking people. They care. They are environmentalists in their own belief. I'm not going to eat their product. I'm not going to convince somebody else to eat their product, but they are doing what they think is right and they've been hoodwinked by the multinational corporations just as much as everybody else. But don't ever put them down as people who are trying to do things that are wrong or they're trying to destroy the environment. They just don't know."

I thought of Erik and Doniga Markegard, their kindness, and their sincere belief that livestock has no carbon footprint. "It always seems to come down to information and education," I say.

"Let me tell you something," says Lyman. "Somebody posted on the Internet one night about an easy way to get a green card. Next day, they had three million responses. You've got a machine that can share information with millions of people overnight. You have the capability to change the world far more than I ever had. I used to go out on the platform and I would see two to five hundred people every night. The Internet, you can go out and have two hundred million people view what you did overnight. It's a new ballgame. What's happening right now with the NSA, and reading the email and all that, it isn't accidental. They're trying to figure out how to control the Internet. You're still operating in the period of time [when] that water is still free-flowing. I don't know how much longer [it will last]."

"You guys are young," Lyman says. "You got a lot of years ahead of you. What you have to look at is, what do you think is the right thing to do. I totally believe, with every fiber of my being, that you cannot be an environmentalist and consume animal products. It's just totally opposed. *You can't be an environmentalist and eat animal products, period.* Kid yourself if you want. If you want to feed your addiction, so be it, but don't call yourself an environmentalist. We're approaching this point where we're going to have to make a decision. What is it that's going to make this planet more livable for Homo sapiens?"

I let out my breath. "You're awesome." That's all I can think of to say. I'd like to hug the guy.

I received a voice mail on my phone while we were conducting interviews. It was one of the potential financial backers for the project: "Hey, sorry we didn't get back to you earlier. I have some bad news. Unfortunately, we are no longer able to fund your project. We had a meeting and, due to the growing controversial subject matter, we have some concerns and have to pull out."

CHAPTER EIGHT

ETHICS, DAIRY, AND EGGS: CHOOSING LIFE OVER DEATH

I was scared. When I learned about the activists being killed in Brazil, I was disturbed, but I felt removed, safe. But to learn about American activists and journalists getting targeted by the animal agriculture industry, the FBI, the Department of Homeland Security, all kinds of anti-activist legislation—and then my funding getting dropped? I was genuinely worried and it hit close to home.

Was this why no one was willing to talk about the issue?

I was beyond frightened to imagine what could possibly happen if I pursued this subject any further. It seemed the only decision to make was to put my research down and walk away. Was I really willing to face lawsuits, harassment, repression, and possibly prison for exposing this subject?

But then I realized this issue was way bigger than any personal concern I could ever have for myself. This was about all life on Earth hanging in the balance of our actions. You either live for something or die for nothing, as cliché as it is. My conscience gave me no choice.

I decided then to surrender not to fear but to the truth. I couldn't be like these environmental organizations and sit silently by while the planet was being eaten alive right in front of our eyes. I had to stand up and continue on.

BACKYARD FARMS

I needed to know more about sustainability. Factory farming was out. Grass-fed, pasture-raised farms were out. But what about backyard farming, operations on a simple, miniature scale, with the animals practically a part of the family?

I arranged to meet Bill Phillips, a backyard farmer. He had sandy brown hair and wore camouflage pants and a red T-shirt with a large American flag printed on it. He had a sheepish, self-effacing air and a shy smile. His yard was filled with a jumble of things—a large motorboat covered by a tarp, a wheelbarrow, white plastic lawn furniture, and small stacks of cardboard boxes. He was going to show me a "culling" that day.

"I have forty-two ducks," Phillips told me. "I started off with three ducks three years ago, and then those burgeoned into a population. I buy a seventy-five-pound bag of seed for duck feed. That seed bag will last me right now . . . about two weeks. The ducks now that we're going to be culling are about two years old."

Phillips started walking toward the flock of ducks. "When you're living with them, they get used to you," he said. I don't know anything about ducks, but I thought these did seem alarmed as Phillips approached them. They scrambled out of the way, flapping their wings and kicking up dust, quacking rapidly and herding together against a wall, moving quickly away from Phillips. He finally cornered three of them behind a garbage can.

"Easy, easy, easy, easy," Phillips said to the ducks. He inspected the belly of the duck in his right hand. "Okay. We're going to keep you." He tossed that duck into the air. It fluttered away. "Run," he said to the other ducks on the ground. He held two ducks by the neck in his left hand. Their wings flapped. "These two go first."

He took the ducks to a makeshift chopping block, a large square piece of rough plywood on top of a lawn table. A big plastic green bowl stood on the table.

Phillips held up one duck for me to see, gripping it tightly so its wings couldn't move. The duck's head, which was free, looked down at the ground, motionless. I held the second duck. It, too, was not moving. Its feathers were very soft.

I asked Phillips how smart ducks are.

"Compared to a chicken, they're probably the same," he said.

The University of Bristol in England has shown that in multiple tests of cognitive and behavioral intelligence, chickens outperform dogs, cats, and four-year-old humans.[1]

Phillips carefully pressed the duck, belly down, against the plywood, and used one hand to secure its body, pinning the wings down. He stretched the duck's neck out with his other hand. "All righty. Okay. Right there." He picked up a small hatchet, and the duck raised its head. He pressed its head down again.

Phillips struck the hatchet down three times where the duck's neck met its body. The duck's foot, the one I could see, splayed out as the hatchet came down. Phillips dragged the blade hard the third time, pulling it over the duck's neck, trying to cut through the tissue, and then quickly ripped the head off, tearing the last piece of connective skin. The duck's foot flapped and paddled after the decapitation. I could also see the wings trying to expand underneath Phillips's hand.

Phillips quickly took the convulsing headless body and turned it upside down in the plastic green bowl to catch the blood. There wasn't as much as I expected. The severed head lay in the bottom of the bowl, the beak slowly opening and closing.

A little girl was watching. "How could that still be alive?" she asked, as the duck's legs jerked violently.

"Hmm?"

"How could that still be alive?"

"They're not. That's nerves. A nerve reaction."

Phillips held the carcass over the bowl a while longer. "Five years old or something like that, I think [I] was," he said, "the first time my dad came out and made us watch as we [butchered] rabbits. We had raised probably a couple dozen rabbits each year, then we would take those rabbits and skin them and clean them up, and keep them for food."

He took a pair of orange-handled shears and cut off the duck's wings and feet as he talked. He de-feathered and washed the small body with a trickle of water from a garden hose. It was hardly a handful of meat—it could have fit inside a football. It now looked like it was ready to be packed on a Styrofoam tray for the supermarket, with its purplish-red flesh and white, goose-bumpy skin.

Phillips seemed completely unmoved by the slaughter process, but I wondered if it had always been that easy.

"Was it hard the first time you butchered an animal?" I asked hesitantly.

"As a young kid, I was kind of . . . I don't want to say it was hard, but it was kind of . . ." He paused. "Some of the rabbits I had named"—he nervously laughed—"so I was kind of like, going . . ." Phillips made a sound and a troubled expression. He looked down.

"But . . ." He shrugged, with resignation, and something like sadness in his voice. "After doing it a couple times, you just learn it's something that has to be done."

Phillips took the second duck and arranged him belly down on the plywood, in the blood of the other duck. He took careful aim with the hatchet. "Not the fingers," he joked. The hatchet came down.

I sat in my apartment afterward. I looked at the Tibetan prayer flags I had strung up across the hall entrance a long time ago and the purple lotus sculpture on my coffee table. *Dar Cho* are the Tibetan words for prayer flag. "Dar" means to increase life and all good things. "Cho" means all living, sentient beings.[2]

I'd been so caught up in the environmental destruction caused by animal agriculture, I had never truly understood the obvious reality—that every single one of these animals was killed. That a life is taken every time. Nor did I truly comprehend that fact while I was overwhelmed and nauseated by the horrors of the factory farm—it took the "humane" death of two healthy, lively ducks on a sunny afternoon to make me understand. It was always a disconnected, abstract fact of eating meat, but when it became personal, face-to-face, the story changed.

I just can't do it, I kept thinking as I sat there. I couldn't have taken the hatchet and brought it down on the necks of those ducks. If I can't do it, I don't want someone else doing it for me.

And then when you bring sustainability into the equation—well, Phillips said he uses 75 pounds of feed every 2 weeks for 42 ducks. Although I suppose it's now 40 ducks. So it's about a pound of feed per week, per duck. There's 52 weeks in a year, he kills them when they're about 2 years old, so that's 104 weeks of feed, let's say 110 weeks. You get about a pound, a pound and a half of meat per duck. So it's 110 pounds of food to produce one to one-and-a-half pounds of meat. On a sustainability issue, it's 100 to 1; 100 pounds of edible plant food to create one pound of meat.

But when it gets to this point, it's not even about sustainability, it was just . . . I didn't feel good inside. It was the first time I'd ever seen that.

I thought of something I'd asked Howard Lyman during our interview. "Mr. Lyman, have you ever killed an animal yourself?"

"Yeah," he answered. "Have I ever killed an animal? I've killed all kinds of them. Thousands of animals. From small gophers, deer, elk, bear, raccoons, cows, horses, pigs, chickens, turkeys. Have I killed animals? Yeah. Am I proud of it? No. Would I ever do it again? No. For me, there's never been a time in my life that I've ever felt more comfortable about who I am than right now. I know today that no animal has to die for me to live. I feel good about that. Every morning I get up, I have a bowl of oatmeal. I don't have to kill my oatmeal. Will I ever eat so that somebody else will kill an animal for me? No."

"Can you recall the first time you killed an animal?" I asked.

"No. I mean, I was probably three years old and it was probably some mouse running across the floor. I don't remember."

There's something chilling in how, from a young age, the idea of death and killing is both abstract, removed, and acceptable.

Will Tuttle, in his book *The World Peace Diet*, writes, "Because cruelty is inescapable in confining, mutilating, and slaughtering animals for food, we have been forced from childhood to be distracted and inattentive perpetrators of cruelty. . . . As infants, we have no idea what 'veal,' 'turkey,' 'egg,' or 'beef' actually are, or where they come from. . . . We find out slowly, and by the time we do, the cruelty and perversity involved seem natural and normal to us."

"Because we are adept at disconnecting from the suffering we impose on animals," Tuttle continues, "we naturally and inevitably become adept at disconnecting from the suffering we impose on hungry people, living biosystems, war-ravaged communities, and future generations."[3]

I began reading the work of Gary L. Francione, a leading and controversial voice in the modern animal rights movement, and a Board of Governors Distinguished Professor of Law and Philosophy at Rutgers School of Law. He and his partner, Anna Charlton, founded the Abolitionist Approach to Animal Rights, arguing for the abolition—as in, the total eradication—rather than the regulation or reduction of animal exploitation. Many animal activists spend their energy working for more humane treatment for animals (often marginal, minuscule changes). This, ironically, allows corporations to put labels on their products like "free-range," "cage-free," and "ethically raised," which only make people feel better about buying animal products. Francione calls this kind of animal rights, "tidying up the concentration camps."[4] You see why he's controversial.

Other animal rights activists, including organizations like the Humane Society and writers such as Peter Singer and Jonathan Safran Foer, write about how to use animals more kindly. Francione and Charlton believe that human beings simply have no right to use animals as property or resources at all. Abolitionist Approach also rejects all forms of violence and injustice and considers all forms of oppression and abuse to be interconnected. In an interview with Chris Hedges on Truthdig, Francione explains his stance:

> Most animal rights activists argue that "using them is not the problem, the problem is how we treat them." My view is that using them *is* the problem. It does not matter how well we treat them. Obviously, it is worse to impose more suffering than less suffering, but that does not mean it is all right to *use* them in a "humane" way. If someone sneaks into your room while you are sleeping and blows your brains out and you do not feel a thing, you are still harmed. You may not have suffered. But you have been harmed.
>
> These are fundamental issues of justice. These are fundamental issues that require that we take nonviolence seriously. You cannot speak about nonviolence and stick violence into your mouth three times a day. . . . It is impossible to participate multiple times a day in victimizing the vulnerable and supporting the suffering and death of sentient others for trivial reasons and not have it make a profound impact. It means we accept the injustice of violence. It means injustice is not taken seriously. Injustice fails to motivate us. Violence works when we otherize groups of beings and put them on the "thing" side of the line between persons and "things." The paradigmatic example of this is what we do to nonhuman

animals. What we do with animals is a model for our exploitation of everyone else. What we do to animals allows us to treat other humans like animals. If we stop otherizing nonhumans, it becomes impossible to otherize humans.

The word "moral," which Francione uses a lot, makes me uncomfortable. I don't think I'm alone in this. It's old-fashioned. It sounds judgmental. It conjures up images of Sunday school, and church ladies with big hair and cat-eye glasses. So I looked it up.

The *Oxford English Dictionary* defines moral as "concerned with the principles of right and wrong behavior and the goodness or badness of human character." The principles of right and wrong behavior. Francione is correct. There's no way around it: it is a moral fact that inflicting unnecessary suffering is wrong.

And another mind-bogglingly simple fact: we all agree on it! This issue is not about changing people's core beliefs.

In *Mind If I Order the Cheeseburger?*, Sherry F. Colb writes, "[V]egans and non-vegans share the basic values that underlie veganism. . . . Vegans observe that institutions that surround the production and consumption of food and clothing actively disguise the truth about what happens to the animals we use, precisely because that truth would deeply offend so many consumers, vegan and non-vegan alike.

"Like others I know," Colb continues, "I became vegan as an adult, not because my values changed but because I came to understand much of what I did in my daily life was falling short of reflecting those values."[5]

It's obvious that suffering and death are involved when animals are raised for meat. After all, they have to be killed for their flesh to be eaten. But I always thought of dairy and eggs as a kinder way to get animal protein. Cows don't die when they're milked, and chickens aren't killed when they lay their eggs.

But then I came across a quote from Professor Francione: "There is more suffering in a glass of milk than in a pound of steak."[6] What?

Kids grow up with peaceful images of dairy farms, of a placid cow at dawn, munching grass, while the farmer sits on an upturned bucket, squirting the milk rhythmically into a metal pail, before the cow goes off to join the other cows grazing on the green hillside. I think I first saw this on *Sesame Street*.

I knew, after visiting the Clover dairy farm, that this was not the reality of milk production in the United States—but I still had no idea what really happens to dairy cows.

The American dairy industry is far, far worse than the beef industry when it comes to the abuse and suffering of the animals.[7]

We are not taught in school that cows, like all mammals, including female humans, need to be pregnant before they can "give" milk, despite, or maybe because of, the fact that the dairy industry has been providing free "educational materials" to schools since the 1920s.[8] We grow up assuming that having udders full of milk is the result of being a cow, not the result of being a pregnant female mammal. It seems remarkable to me that anyone can be a feminist, fighting for the rights of women, and also drink milk and eat eggs. The dairy and egg industries are massive global businesses built on the reproductive systems of enslaved female animals.

Because there's no money to be made from keeping a cow that doesn't give milk, farmers manipulate the reproductive systems of very young female cows with hormones—enormous amounts of estrogen and prostaglandin—so that they can be impregnated long before they are sexually mature. In a human context, these cows are still children.[9]

"Dairy farmers," writes Colb in *Mind If I Order the Cheeseburger?*, "regularly and forcibly place each dairy cow into what is sometimes called a 'rape rack,' a device on which animals are restrained while they are inseminated."[10] Farmers use a sperm gun, which is shoved elbow-deep into the cow's vagina before it is fired.[11]

One of the most devastating things about the dairy industry, says Colleen Patrick-Goudreau in her lecture, "Debunking the Myths of Veganism," given in Oakland in 2013, "is that [the cows'] offspring were incidental. That they were only there because the cows had to be impregnated, so that she would be stimulated to lactate. And that was devastating, because then the question is, what happens to the babies? After nine months, the baby's born, after nine months, all she wants is her baby, and if he's male . . . they're useless in an industry that exploits the female reproductive system. And so they're sent to slaughter right away."[12]

"The veal industry was literally born out of the dairy industry," says Gene Baur (formerly Bauston), of Farm Sanctuary. "It was developed to take advantage of the unwanted male calves born to dairy cows."

Approximately 4.5 million male calves are born annually in American dairies.[13] Female calves are usually raised to go into the same system of reproductive slavery as their mothers, or if there are too many, they will be sold for veal along with the males. Veal calves are chained at the neck and locked into crates so tiny they cannot move—to prevent muscle growth and make their flesh more "tender"—when they are only a few days or weeks old. They live in darkness, immobilized in these crates, for three or four months, before they are slaughtered.

Even dairy farmers admit that cows suffer horribly when their calves are taken away from them, bellowing, sometimes for days, pacing the area where they gave birth and not eating.[14]

Soon after giving birth and having her newborn taken away, a cow is impregnated again on the "rape rack," and the cycle of birth, loss, and lactation repeats itself for three to five years. When her milk production declines, usually after about five years, and the cow no longer makes enough milk to be profitable to the farmer, she is considered "spent," and is sent to slaughter, usually ending up as cheap hamburger meat, pet food, glue, leather, or gelatin.[15] The average natural life-span of a cow is twenty to twenty-five years.[16]

"A dairy farmer cannot make a living from this work unless he subjects a cow to pregnancy, removes her calf from her side, and then slaughters the mother cow once her milk production diminishes," Colb writes. "These are each unavoidable aspects of dairy farming."[17]

I had seen and heard this for myself from my short visit to Bivalve Dairy Farm. John Taylor had openly admitted that this is the fate of all dairy cows, regardless of whether they are grass-fed or factory farmed.

Weeks before filming the backyard duck slaughter, I had scheduled another interview with a woman who raised chickens in her backyard for eggs. Her hens had stopped producing eggs and she had already killed all but one, saving that slaughter for me to witness. I didn't know how I was going to possibly go through another killing. Watching animals lose their lives right in front of me was too much to bear. The night before that interview, I wrestled with what to do. When morning came, I had a solution.

I arrived at the interview early and explained to the woman, apologetically, that I couldn't stand to watch another animal be killed. I pleaded with her to give me the last hen. She looked at me strangely and then asked, with what seemed like genuine concern, what would happen to this chicken if I took her. I found it odd that she was worried about whether I would take proper care of an animal that she was ready to kill that afternoon. Luckily I had an answer. I had arranged to take the hen to Animal Place, a sanctuary for farm animals. She finally agreed, sparing the hen's life. The woman probably thought I was a granola-eating, tree-hugging San Fran–Berkeley hippie in Birkenstocks. I guess she wouldn't be too far off . . .

I didn't have a carrier or even a box for the chicken, but I was afraid that the woman would change her mind if I asked for one. I left quickly and placed the sweet, calm hen in the passenger seat of my van. And then I drove very, very carefully to Animal Place.

I couldn't believe how comfortable and curious my new friend was, riding shotgun after having just been spared another (metaphorical) shotgun. I really wanted to take her home, but I knew that probably wasn't the greatest idea, so I drove on to Animal Place. It was the best thing for my friend.

"Animal Place is a farm animal sanctuary in Northern California that focuses on rescuing animals from the animal agriculture industry," David Phinney, the then–animal care coordinator of Animal Place, told me. I handed the hen over to David, who cradled her in his heavily tattooed arms. "A lot of people don't realize that meat-breed chicken,"—Phinney pointed to a large white rooster standing close by—"like this guy behind us, they're generally slaughtered at about forty-two days old, whereas chickens that are bred for egg production are killed when their productivity starts to decrease, when they start laying fewer eggs, and that generally happens about eighteen months to twenty months, even though chickens will live many years longer than that." We stood in a large shaded yard, with many chickens of different colors as Bella, Phinney's rescued black-and-white, three-legged pitbull, ambled around with the chickens.

Phinney had been directly involved in the rescue of more than 12,000 chickens used by the egg industry and explained all about the horrors of industrial egg production, which mirrored the horrors of the dairy industry: another system of female reproductive slavery. Every year, 250 million male chicks are born in the United States[18] and are either thrown alive and conscious into meat grinders, which mince them, alive, into fertilizer or pet food, or gassed, or tossed into large plastic bags, where they suffocate under the weight of other discarded chicks.[19] "They are not broiler [meat] chickens, and so will not grow fast enough or big enough to be used for their meat, and are therefore completely worthless to the industry." Phinney noted. But like broilers, the female layer chicks, at about a day old, have roughly half their beaks chopped off with a hot blade without anesthetic. This causes so much pain that the heartbeat of a chick undergoing this operation will increase by more than one hundred beats a minute.[20] Layer hens are debeaked for the same reason that broiler chickens are: because when they are kept in continual, close confinement, they will tear one another apart out of severe stress and frustration.

After twenty weeks the female chicks mature and are transferred from the hatcheries to egg farms.[21] They are crammed into tiny "battery" cages so tight they cannot spread their wings, four to eight chickens per cage, and kept there for the rest of their short lives. The cages are arranged in long rows and stacked four or five tiers high, with the urine and feces of the chickens on the top tiers falling on those below.[22]

"If you haven't been in a hen plant, you don't know what hell is," an undercover activist said in *Rolling Stone*. "Chicken shit is piled six feet high, and your lungs burn like you took a torch to 'em."[23]

"To get a sense of a hen's life in a battery cage," Bruce Friedrich, director of advocacy and policy of Farm Sanctuary, writes in the *Huffington Post*, "imagine spending your entire life in a wire cage the size of your bathtub with four other people. You wouldn't be able to move, so your muscles and bones would deteriorate. Your feet would become lacerated. You would go insane. That's precisely what happens to laying hens."

And if one or more of your four fellow prisoners died, they would simply be left in the cage with you to rot. Again and again, investigations have discovered dead, decaying, sometimes mummified flattened birds in the battery cages, jammed in or trampled underfoot by the living chickens.[24]

A hen's body is destroyed by extreme osteoporosis from laying around three hundred eggs (wild chickens lay less than twenty eggs) a year.[25] Her uterus will often protrude out of her body from the daily exertion of egg laying, her feet and legs are deformed and painfully ingrown into the wire floor of the cage, constant filth and distress have caused swollen head syndrome and fatty liver syndrome, and ammonia rising up from the heaps of fecal material beneath the cages has caused disorders of her lungs and eyes.[26] It usually takes about two years for her to be "used up." And then she is, like the unproductive dairy cow, considered "spent," and it is time for her to be slaughtered for chicken soup or baby food, tossed into a plastic bag to suffocate,[27] or thrown alive into the same grinder that kills male chicks.[28]

I also interviewed Phinney's colleague, Marji Beach, Animal Place's education director. We sat in the Animal Place yard with the rescued chickens. She explained that it makes no difference where you buy your eggs. Caged, cage-free, free-range, it doesn't matter, she said. "We have rescued thousands of hens from 'free-range' farms that were destined for slaughter," she told me. There is no legal definition in the United States for what 'free-range' means, and there is no regulation regarding the size, quality, or time spent outdoors. "Free-range" egg producers still debeak their female chicks, kill the males, and slaughter the hens when they no longer lay enough eggs to make a profit for the company.[29]

"When it comes to the words 'natural,' 'organic,' and 'free range' . . . federal law is and always was toothless," Steve Bjerklie, who edited *Meat and Poultry* magazine for fifteen years, wrote in the *Sonoma County Independent*. "It doesn't guarantee a thing . . . Poultry companies use 'free range' strictly as a marketing gimmick. . . . 'Natural' is another meaningless term. . . . By USDA's standards a Burger King Whopper is natural."[30]

But what about backyard eggs? The same hatcheries that stock factory farms also supply backyard chicken coops.[31] Every time a hobbyist sends out a mail order for chicks to start a backyard flock, they support and demand the continuation of an industry built on the instant death of the males and the prolonged suffering and eventual death of the females. All laying hens, including those raised in backyard coops, have been selectively bred to lay eggs until exhaustion, extreme osteoporosis, and uterine prolapse.[32] Chickens, if allowed to, will frequently eat their unfertilized eggs to regain the nutrients and minerals that egg-laying depletes from their bodies. They often become very distressed when their eggs are taken, in any situation.[33]

Farmers and corporations will continue to selectively breed female chickens and selectively kill male chickens as long as there is demand for eggs, whether they are laid in a backyard coop or in a battery cage.

Sherry Colb brings up some challenging questions about the ethical consequences of consumer demand:

> [O]ur consumption of animal products asks producers to create, harm, and kill more animals. The animal we consume may already be dead, but other animals who will be created and used for food in the future are not. By consuming the dead animal (or products, such as dairy and eggs, that necessarily involve the killing and hurting of animals) right now, we demand that more animals be killed tomorrow. . . . We are inclined to rationalize what we do, and we experience what social psychologists call "cognitive dissonance" when we sense a conflict between our own regular, day-to-day behavior and our deeply held values.[34]

I used to be proud to say, "Yeah, I eat everything." It made me seem like someone who was open to all options, who wasn't picky, and, frankly, way more fun to be with than someone with "restrictions." But I'm starting to hear that statement, "I eat everything," in a different way now.

I don't want to eat genetically modified, highly processed and refined, artificially flavored and colored food that is saturated with chemicals, growth hormones, antibiotics, and contaminated with fecal matter. I don't want to eat cruelty. I don't want to eat suffering and violence. I do not want to support an industry and a way of life that "eats everything," including our besieged planet. I do not want to support an industry responsible for the decimation of our rain forests, the spreading dead zones in the ocean, the draining of our finite freshwater supply, and the depletion of our land. I do not want to support an industry that imprisons and kills living beings that want to live just as much as I do, or an industry that turns the very bond between an incarcerated mother and her child into a profitable commodity.

I finally had to face up to the fact that all my life, I had been living in a way that did not reflect my own deeply held values regarding compassion, violence, injustice, and life itself. The way I had been living my life was a betrayal of my own core beliefs.

It was time to change that.

CHAPTER NINE

HEALTH: SKIP THE MIDDLE ANIMAL

I knew I had to stop eating all animal products. But all I knew was the standard American diet I grew up on, the one promoted by every teacher and doctor I ever had. I felt a little scared turning away from it, jumping into the unknown. I wanted to help the planet be sustainable, but I also needed to sustain myself.

Is it even possible to be a healthy vegetarian or vegan?

I went to see Dr. Michael Klaper, a physician with the TrueNorth Health Center in Santa Rosa, California, who lectures frequently on diet and health. It's hard to tell how old he is, but he's been practicing medicine for more than forty years. He's a tall, thin man, with a trim white beard and bright brown eyes. He spent his childhood summers on a dairy farm in northern Wisconsin. I spoke with him in his office.

"Is it possible to be a healthy vegetarian or vegan?" Dr. Klaper asks, echoing my question to him. "I became vegan . . . let's see . . . thirty-two years ago, now. I run several miles every day, I go biking forty, fifty miles through the countryside, I work long hours. I feel great. It's nice waking up with a light, trim body every day. So many of my friends and patients are thriving ever since their transition to a vegan diet. So yes. I've seen vegan moms go through healthy vegan pregnancies and deliver healthy vegan children and raise them to tall, full-size, intelligent vegan adults. Yes. Certainly all the nutrients are there in the plant kingdom to do this. That is correct.

"Now, I've spent forty years in general practice," Klaper continued, "cleaning up the wreckage of a small group of grim diseases—obesity, diabetes, high blood pressure, clogged arteries, and a whole bunch of inflammatory '-itises': arthritis and colitis and other inflammatory conditions of the body. That's the vast majority of what most

Western physicians see. I watch billions of dollars get spent trying to find the cause of childhood obesity, the cause of type II diabetes, and the cause of clogged arteries. Makes me want to get the biggest soapbox I can, go down to Washington D.C., stand on it, and yell loudly, 'It's the food!' The American diet causes disease. If I have a patient who has headaches, I'd say, 'When do you get headaches?'

"'Every time I hit myself in the head with a hammer, Doctor.'

"'Maybe you don't want to keep doing that.'

"Same thing: 'Gee, Doc, when I keep eating the fatty, salty, sugary food, my blood pressure goes up, and I get more obese. Why do you think that's happening?'

"To use an automotive analogy, you're driving your car, and the diesel fuel is cheaper than the gas fuel. You fill your gas tank up with diesel fuel. Diesel fuel is oily. It doesn't burn cleanly. You turn on your engine. It coughs and sputters, and black smoke comes out the back. You put it in gear, and it lurches forward 10 yards and stops. The mechanic says, 'What are you using for fuel?' You say, 'Kerosene. It's cheaper.' He says, 'Try gasoline.' They drain the kerosene out of the tank, clean off the spark plugs, and fill it up with high-octane gasoline. You turn on the engine. Runs great. 'Wow, that mechanic cured my car's disease.' The car did not have a disease. The engine malfunctioned because you put too oily a fuel through a fuel system not designed to handle it. The filter's clogged up and the piping system's clogged up."

"If it's that simple," I say, "why don't we get taught this, why don't all the doctors say this?"

"That is such an important question," Klaper said. "For one thing, nutrition is the poor sister of medical education. The doctor thinks, 'If a patient has nutritional problems, I'll send them to a dietician. I'm a doctor. I deal with broken arms and deliver babies. Nutrition is sissy stuff.' There's an institutional disregard-slash-contempt for nutrition. Which is ironic, because these young physicians who go into these specialties, whether it's gastroenterology or cardiology, they're going to be treating nutritionally based diseases.

"Med students don't have much time for nutrition. I think I had four lectures on nutrition in med school. You don't make any money off it, that's for sure. It starts there. In fact, a lot of people make a lot of money to keep that high fat, high salt, high sugar food stream going through the country. And the meat and dairy industry is right there in medical education, in all levels of education, saying that it's good for you, and milk is nature's perfect food, et cetera, and we ate it as kids growing up. Many of us are treating our colleagues as a result. There's a huge inertia. It means that your mother was wrong.

"I tell people, look, most Americans eat a piece of animal flesh two or three times a day. Bacon and eggs for breakfast. Cheeseburgers for lunch. Chicken for dinner. Every four or six hours, a piece of animal flesh is going down American throats. Not even mountain lions eat flesh three times a day, and yet we *homo sapien* naked apes gorge on flesh nonstop, and it's killing us."

"Do you think anyone should be consuming dairy?" I ask. I still have trouble believing that cow's milk, which I've been told all my life is a cornerstone of a healthy diet, could be bad for me.

"I really don't. When you think about it"—Dr. Klaper sighs heavily—"the purpose of cows' milk—I did most of my growing up on a dairy farm in Wisconsin—is to turn a sixty-five-pound calf into a four-hundred-pound cow as rapidly as possible. Cows' milk is baby calf growth fluid, is what the stuff is. Everything in that white liquid . . . the hormones, the lipids"—he counts them off on his fingers—"the proteins, the sodium, the growth factor, the IGF [insulin-like growth factor-1] . . . Every one of those is meant to blow that calf up to a great big cow or it wouldn't be there. And whether you pour it on your cereal as a liquid, whether you clot it into yogurt, whether you ferment it into cheese, whether you freeze it into ice cream—it's *baby calf growth fluid*." He sighs again. "And women eat it and it stimulates their tissues and it gives women breast lumps,[1] it makes the uterus get big and they get fibroids and they bleed, and they get hysterectomies and they need mammograms, and it gives guys man boobs.[2] Cows' milk is the lactation secretions of a large bovine mammal who just had a baby. It's for baby calves," he says again with emphasis. He smiles and says, "I tell my patients to go look in the mirror. Do you have big ears? Do you have a tail? Are you a baby calf? If you're not, don't be eating baby calf growth fluid at any level. There's nothing in it people need!"

I left Dr. Klaper's clinic feeling like someone from hundreds of years ago who finally learns that the earth is round and not flat. I've been told all my life, from doctors, teachers, nurses, and my parents, not to mention all those celebrities in the *Got Milk?* ads, that I have to drink milk to get my calcium, so I can have strong bones. Where will I get my calcium?

"I have seen real fear in people who contemplate not consuming cows' milk, and contemplate not feeding their children cows' milk," Colleen Patrick-Goudreau says in her lecture, "Debunking the Myths of Veganism." "But I ask you, what is calcium? It's a mineral. And where are minerals found? In the ground, in the earth, in the soil. And why do cows have calcium in their milk? Because they eat the grass. . . . They're *supposed* to eat grass. Three out of four cows raised specifically for dairy are not consuming grass,[3] and so that the dairy industry can live up to the marketing claims that it's a

Calcium Found in Vegetables vs. Milk

(milligrams [mg] per 100 calories)

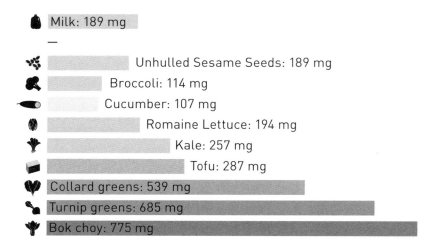

Milk: 189 mg

Unhulled Sesame Seeds: 189 mg
Broccoli: 114 mg
Cucumber: 107 mg
Romaine Lettuce: 194 mg
Kale: 257 mg
Tofu: 287 mg
Collard greens: 539 mg
Turnip greens: 685 mg
Bok choy: 775 mg

high-calcium food, what do they do to [the cows'] feed? They supplement their feed." Patrick-Goudreau pauses. "*You* could supplement *your* feed. We'd skip a lot of problems. You don't even have to supplement your feed; you could go right to the source and get your calcium from the green leafy vegetables, the highest source of calcium."[4]

Calcium from green leafy vegetables? We don't get taught this in school. Dr. Joel Fuhrman, an internationally recognized expert on nutrition and health, includes in his *New York Times* best-selling book, *Eat to Live*, a chart listing the amounts of calcium contained in one hundred calories of various foods.

Let's just say I was surprised.

Milk comes in at a respectable 189 milligrams (mg) of calcium per 100 calories, above unhulled sesame seeds (170), broccoli (114), and cucumber (107). But the calcium content of milk is whupped by romaine lettuce (194), kale (257), tofu (287), collard greens (539), turnip greens (685), and bok choy (775). Yes, bok choy has 775 mg of calcium per 100 calories, and cows' milk has 189.[5] That's a vegetable with more than four times as much calcium as milk.

Here in the United States, we drink more cow's milk and consume more dairy per person than in most countries in the world. And calcium, as we are all told from childhood, builds strong bones. But a 2000 study, *Worldwide Incidence of Hip Fracture in Elderly Women: Relation to Consumption of Animal and Vegetable Foods*, shows that one of the highest rates of hip fractures in the world belongs to American women, fifty and older.

Countries with higher rates of fractures are those that consume even more dairy, such as in northern Europe—particularly Sweden and Norway[6]— Australia, and New Zealand.[7]

Osteoporosis, a common bone disease that results in weak and brittle bones, often caused by low levels of calcium, is frequently seen in older women. A high rate of hip fractures is a dependable sign of osteoporosis. Doctors and dieticians will frequently recommend that women, after menopause, increase their dairy consumption—and therefore their calcium intake—in an effort to stave off osteoporosis.

But why do the countries with the highest levels of dairy consumption also have the highest rates of bone fractures in a demographic particularly vulnerable to osteoporosis?

"Epidemiologic studies," writes Dr. Fuhrman in *Eat to Live*, "have linked osteoporosis not to low calcium intake but to various nutritional factors that cause excessive calcium loss in the urine."[8]

Topping the list of dietary factors that induce calcium loss in urine?

Animal protein.[9]

A report done by the Yale School of Medicine in 1992, which used information on women over the age of 50, from 34 separate surveys, in 16 countries, that were published in 29 peer-reviewed research journals, found that 70 percent of the bone fracture rate was caused by eating animal protein.[10]

More recent research tells the same story. In their 2009 book, *Building Bone Vitality*, authors Dr. Amy Joy Lanou of the University of North Carolina and Michael Castleman conducted an extensive review of the scientific literature on bone health. They discovered that "two-thirds of clinical trials show that milk, dairy foods and calcium supplements do not prevent fractures." The high fracture rates in the countries that consume the most dairy products, Lanou and Castleman conclude, are because "these affluent Western countries also consume the most meat, poultry and fish."[11]

Eating animal protein, which contains sulfur-based amino acids, makes human blood and body tissues more acidic. In an effort to neutralize the acid, the body pulls calcium, an alkaline substance that neutralizes acid, out of the bones, and eventually the calcium leaves the body in the urine.[12] So essentially, with cow's milk, calcium does come into the body, but even more calcium comes out.

A study examining the capacity of fruits and vegetables to neutralize acids in the body, led by Dr. Bess Dawson-Hughes from the Jean Mayer USDA Human Nutrition Research Center on Aging at Tufts University, was published in January 2014 in the *Journal of Clinical Endocrinology and Metabolism*. The study concluded that eating more fruits and vegetables, and therefore increasing the alkaline content of the body, should be studied as a safe, low-cost way to prevent osteoporosis.[13]

Plant protein, which has less sulfur-based amino acids, can still cause calcium loss through the urine, but vegetarian and vegan diets in general are usually more alkaline, while animal-based diets are usually more acidic.[14] A study done in 2000 by the Department of Medicine at the University of California, San Francisco compared the rate of bone fractures to the ratio of vegetable to animal protein dietary intake. The study used eighty-seven surveys from thirty-three countries. It found that a high ratio of vegetable to animal protein intake was clearly associated with a correspondingly low or non-existent rate of bone fractures.[15] And the Study of Osteoporotic Fractures Research Group, also at the University of California, San Francisco, studied more than 1,000 women over the age of 65 for 7 years and found that the women who had the highest ratio of animal protein to plant protein in their diets had 3.7 times more bone fractures than the women with the lowest animal to plant protein ratio. The women with the high animal to vegetable ratio also lost bone mass nearly 4 times faster than the women with the lowest ratio.[16]

Even the National Dairy Council admits the connection, with a protective disclaimer: "Excess dietary protein, particularly purified proteins, may increase calcium excretion, although this effect is controversial."[17]

And it turns out meat, dairy, and eggs can cause ailments much worse than brittle bones.

"Today," writes Dr. Fuhrman, "the link between animal products and many different diseases is as strongly supported in the scientific literature as the link between cigarette smoking and lung cancer."[18] Those diseases include, as Dr. Klaper mentioned, heart disease, hypertension, high cholesterol, diabetes, obesity, and cancer.

Dr. T. Colin Campbell, like many advocates of a plant-based diet, grew up believing firmly in the benefits of eating animals and their secretions. Like Dr. Klaper, he was raised on a dairy farm. "I started at the opposite end of the spectrum [from a plant-based diet]," he writes in *The China Study*, "as a meat-loving dairy farmer in my personal life and an 'establishment' scientist in my professional life. I even used to lament the views of vegetarians as I taught nutritional biochemistry to pre-med students."[19]

He doesn't like the words "vegan," or "vegetarian," believing that people who use those labels have chosen to eat that way for ideological, political reasons. Dr. Campbell is all about nutrition and the science behind it.

"The idea is that we should be consuming whole foods," he told the *New York Times* in 2011. "We should not be relying on the idea that genes are determinants of our health. We should not be relying on the idea that nutrient supplementation is the way to get nutrition, because it's not. I'm talking about whole, plant-based foods. The effect it produces is broad for treatment and prevention of a wide variety of ailments, from cancer to heart disease, to diabetes."[20]

To many people, Whole Foods is the name of a super swanky, super fun supermarket. In terms of nutrition, whole foods are simply foods that are as close to their natural form as possible and minimally processed. Plant-based whole foods retain the fiber, phytochemicals, and nutrients that are often removed during processing. Not all plant-based foods are whole foods, though—potato chips, for instance, while usually vegan, are not whole foods! Fresh fruits and vegetables are a cornerstone of a whole-foods diet, but it also means, for instance, choosing whole grains (like brown rice) instead of refined grains (like white rice).

THE CHINA STUDY

Dr. Campbell was one of the lead researchers and scientists of the China-Cornell-Oxford Project, more commonly known as the China Study. The *New York Times*, in May 1990, called the project "the most comprehensive large study ever undertaken of the relationship between diet and the risk of developing disease," and stated that the study was "challenging much of American dietary dogma." Most famously, the *New York Times* called the China Study "the Grand Prix of epidemiology."[21]

The China Study was a collaboration between Cornell University, Oxford University, the Chinese Academy of Preventive Medicine, and the China Cancer Institute. The data used by the study spanned from the early 1970s through the early 1990s.[22] The researchers went into 65 rural and semi-rural counties in China; they chose rural areas because they wanted to study people who had, for the most part, lived in the same area and eaten the same food for most of their lives. An average of 90 to 94 percent of the adults in each county lived in the same county they were born in. The scientists collected data from 6,500 adults using questionnaires, blood tests, urine samples, food sample analysis, and food logs. There were 367 variables in the study, which were then all cross-referenced with one another.

"Nowhere else [than in China]," the *New York Times* reported on Campbell's study in 1990, "is there a genetically similar population with such great regional differences in disease rates, dietary habits and environmental exposures. For example, cancer rates can vary by a factor of several hundred from one region of China to another. These large regional variations in China highlight biologically important relationships between diet and disease."[23]

By the end of the study, the researchers had compiled "more than 8,000 statistically significant associations between lifestyle, diet and disease variables."[24] The data alone, published by Cornell University Press, filled 920 pages. "Among the first tantalizing findings are these," the *New York Times* reported. "Obesity is related more to what people eat than how much. Adjusted for height, the Chinese consume 20 percent more calories than Americans do, but Americans are 25 percent fatter. The main dietary differences are fat and starch. The Chinese eat only a third the amount of fat Americans do, while eating twice the starch.

"Eating a lot of protein, especially animal protein, is also linked to chronic disease," the *New York Times* continued. "Americans consume a third more protein than the Chinese do, and 70 percent of American protein comes from animals, while only 7 percent of Chinese protein does. Those Chinese who eat the most protein, and especially the most animal protein, also have the highest rates of the 'diseases of affluence' like heart disease, cancer and diabetes."[25]

Campbell and his research team discovered, among many other findings, that the counties that consumed the most meat, milk, eggs, fish, fat, and animal protein had the highest blood cholesterol, while those that consumed mostly plant-based food had the lowest blood cholesterol.

Dietary cholesterol is found only in food made from animal flesh and animal secretions.[26] And a high daily intake of animal protein in rural China during the study was still very low by American standards—about the same amount found in three McDonald's Chicken McNuggets.[27] Even with this relatively low intake of animal protein and dietary cholesterol, the China Study found that "one of the strongest predictors of Western diseases [diseases of affluence, i.e., coronary heart disease, cancer, diabetes] was blood cholesterol."[28]

HEART DISEASE

Heart disease is the number one cause of death in the United States. According to the American Heart Association, about one in every three deaths in America is caused by heart disease, stroke, and other cardiovascular diseases. In fact, cardiovascular disease kills more people than all forms of cancer combined.[29]

We now know that the single greatest risk factor for heart disease is a high level of blood cholesterol. The single biggest factor in raising blood cholesterol levels is eating saturated fat. "The correlations between cholesterol levels, saturated fat intake, and heart disease are among the strongest and most consistent in the history of world medical research," John Robbins writes in *The Food Revolution*. "This is why every authoritative health body in the world, from the American Heart Association to the World Health Organization to the National Heart, Lung, and Blood Institute, is calling for reductions in saturated fat consumption."[30] The American Heart Association tells us, "The majority [of saturated fat] comes mainly from animal sources, including meat and dairy products."[31]

The Framingham Heart Study, a project of the National Heart, Lung, and Blood Institute, is an ongoing, long-term study that surveys the residents of Framingham, Massachusetts, in an effort to identify the patterns and risk factors of cardiovascular disease. The study began in 1948 and is now on its third generation of subjects. The Framingham Study led to the identification of many of the now widely known risks of heart disease.[32]

Dr. William Castelli, the director of the study, says "We've never had a heart attack in Framingham in 35 years in anyone who had a cholesterol under 150."[33] It is a statement echoed by Dr. Bill Roberts and Dr. Caldwell Esselstyn Jr. both highly prominent heart-disease physicians and researchers.[34] To put that information in context, the average cholesterol level in the United States is 210. The average cholesterol level of vegetarians (who eat dairy and eggs) in the United States is 161. The average cholesterol level of vegans in the United States is 133.[35]

"Some criticize this exclusively plant-based diet as extreme or draconian," Dr. Esselstyn writes on his website. He is a doctor at the Cleveland Clinic, rated the best cardiac care center in the country by US News and World Report.[36] "Webster's dictionary defines draconian as 'inhumanly cruel.' A closer look reveals that 'extreme' or 'inhumanly cruel' describes not plant-based nutrition, but the consequences of our present Western diet. Having a sternum divided for bypass surgery or a stroke that renders one an aphasic invalid can be construed as extreme; and having a breast, prostate, colon, or rectum removed to treat cancer may seem inhumanly cruel. These diseases are rarely seen in populations consuming a plant-based diet."[37]

And what about when people say, "I can't do anything about it, heart disease runs in my family"?

"It's true that a small percentage of patients have a hereditary form of arteriosclerosis [hardening and thickening of artery walls] in the sense that in their immediate family and their parents' and grandparents' families, there is a high incidence of atherosclerosis [plaque build-up in arteries] and coronary heart disease. . . . But that only constitutes about five percent of the cases. Most people (who develop heart disease) don't really have a hereditary disease." That's Dr. Michael Debakey, director of the Cardiovascular Research Center and a pioneer in heart transplants, bypasses, and the artificial heart, in Robbins's book, *The Food Revolution*.[38]

In 1985, Dr. Esselstyn, a celebrated heart surgeon frustrated at the lack of emphasis placed by the medical community on disease prevention, launched a study that, as

Dr. Campbell writes in *The China Study*, "has gotten the most spectacular results ever recorded in the treatment of heart disease."[39]

Esselstyn wanted to see what would happen to people with serious, established heart disease if they went on a whole-food, very low-fat, plant-based diet. He also used a very small amount of cholesterol-lowering medication. His first goal was to reduce the blood cholesterol level of the participants to under 150 milligrams per deciliter (mg/dL). He started with twenty-three patients. They "were to avoid oils, meat, fish, fowl, and dairy products, except for skim milk and nonfat yogurt."[40] For the next five years, they all met every two weeks, during which Dr. Esselstyn would take blood tests, and check blood pressure and weight. After the first five years, Esselstyn recommended that the patients remove skim milk and yogurt from their diet.

Five of the patients left within two years. The eighteen who remained had all started the study with serious heart problems. In the eight years prior to beginning the study, these eighteen patients had experienced a collective forty-nine coronary events, such as heart attacks, strokes, bypass surgery, angioplasty, and angina. Their average blood cholesterol level was 246 mg/dL. That average blood cholesterol level dropped during the study to 132 mg/dL, well below 150 mg/dL, which Dr. Esselstyn, Dr. Bill Roberts, and Dr. William Castelli all said was the figure below which they had never seen a heart attack occur in anyone.

Even more striking was that in the eleven years after beginning the study, there was one single coronary event among the eighteen subjects. And that single coronary event occurred to a patient who drifted away from the low-fat, plant-based diet. This patient experienced angina (chest pain caused by reduced blood flow to the heart). He went back on the diet prescribed by the study. The angina stopped, and there were no further problems. Remember that in the eight years prior to the study, there were forty-nine collective coronary events. If you consider only the patients who followed Dr. Esselstyn's diet, then the takeaway is that among eighteen people with severe heart disease, there were forty-nine coronary events in eight years on a standard, animal-based diet, versus zero—ZERO—events in eleven years on a low-fat, plant-based diet.

Not only can a plant-based diet prevent and control heart disease, it can often reverse it. Eleven of Dr. Esselstyn's patients agreed to an angiography, a kind of X-ray of specific arteries. They discovered that they had gained a 7 percent opening in their clogged arteries. A 7 percent increase in the diameter of an artery leads to at least 30 percent greater blood flow.[41] And ultimately, unobstructed blood flow is the key to preventing heart attacks and strokes.

From the American Dietetic Association position paper on vegetarian diets: "Studies indicate that vegetarians [the ADA includes vegans as a subcategory of vegetarians] often have lower morbidity and mortality rates. . . . Not only is mortality from coronary artery disease lower in vegetarians than in nonvegetarians, but vegetarian diets have also been successful in arresting coronary artery disease. Scientific data suggest positive relationships between a vegetarian diet and reduced risk for . . . obesity, coronary artery disease, hypertension, diabetes mellitus, and some types of cancer."[42]

CANCER

Another startling finding from the China Study was the relationship between blood cholesterol and cancer. "As blood cholesterol levels decreased from 170 mg/dL to 90 mg/dL," Dr. Campbell writes, "cancers of the liver, rectum, colon, male lung, female lung, breast, childhood leukemia, adult leukemia, childhood brain, adult brain, stomach and esophagus (throat) decreased. Most Americans know that if you have high cholesterol, you should worry about your heart, but they don't know that you might want to worry about cancer as well."[43]

Dr. Campbell uses the analogy of seeding a lawn to explain the three stages of cancer: initiation, promotion, and progression. "Initiation," Dr. Campbell writes, "is when you put the seeds in the soil, promotion is when the grass starts to grow and progression is when the grass gets completely out of control, invading the driveway, the shrubbery and the sidewalk."[44]

Chemicals called carcinogens trigger initiation by mutating healthy, normal cells into cells with cancerous potential. Initiation, with very few exceptions, is permanent and irreversible.[45]

Dr. Campbell explains how the cancer cells develop:

> But just like seeds in the soil, the initial cancer cells will not grow and multiply unless the right conditions are met. The seeds in the soil, for example, need a healthy amount of water, sunlight and other nutrients before they make a full lawn. If any of these factors are denied or are missing, the seeds will not grow. . . . This is one of the most profound features of [cancer] promotion. *Promotion is reversible, depending on whether the early cancer growth is given the right conditions in which to grow.* This is where certain dietary factors become so important. These dietary factors, called promoters, feed cancer growth. Other dietary factors, called anti-promoters, slow cancer growth. . . . It is a push-pull process. The profound importance of this reversibility cannot be overemphasized.[46]

As with heart disease, genetics can rarely be blamed entirely for cancer. A prominent report by Sir Richard Doll and Sir Richard Peto of the University of Oxford on the links between diet and cancer was prepared in 1981 for the U.S. Congress. It concluded that only about 2 to 3 percent of total cancer risk is due to genetics.[47]

PROTEIN AND VITAMINS ON A VEGAN DIET

In our culture, protein is meat and meat is protein. "But where do you get your protein?!" is probably the question vegans hear most frequently. Stereotypes of the pale, weak, skinny vegan abound.

Patrick-Goudreau, who's an engaging, spontaneous, and often very funny speaker, says in her lecture "Debunking the Myths of Veganism," "Protein, everyone's obsessed with protein. Do me a favor, please raise your hand if you've ever heard of heart disease," she deadpans. "Anyone ever hear of diabetes? Or know anyone with high blood pressure? Know anyone with high cholesterol? Anybody know anybody with kwashiorkor?" she asks without missing a beat. "Raise your hand nice and high, you know someone with kwashiorkor?"

No one in her audience has heard of kwashiorkor. "Really??!" She opens her eyes wide in mock amazement.

"You'd think you would, we're so obsessed with protein deficiency, we're so concerned about the vegetarians not getting their protein. Protein deficiency is called kwashiorkor, that's the scientific term for protein deficiency. Kwashiorkor. We've seen people with kwashiorkor only when we've seen appeals from hunger organizations, and we see children with distended bellies. . . . They have kwashiorkor. They're not getting any protein. They're not getting any *nutrients*, because they're not getting any food. The only time we see true kwashiorkor in developed nations is when someone's anorexic and quite literally not eating any food. That's the only time we see kwashiorkor. We don't have diseases of deficiency in developed nations. That's not our problem. All of the diseases . . . that you knew about? Those are all diseases of excess . . . and that's all related to the animals we're consuming, and the animal secretions we're consuming."[48]

"The protein is in the grains and the beans and the nuts and the seeds and the greens and the fruit. Everything has protein in it," Dr. Klaper said to me, confirming Patrick-Goudreau's point. "If you're eating whole plant foods, not Cokes and Twinkies, but if you're eating whole plant foods, and you're eating 1,800 to 2,000 calories a day, you're going to be getting 60 or 70 grams of high-grade protein.

It's easy to get enough protein. It really isn't a concern. In forty years, I've never seen a protein-deficient patient on a 'healthy' North American diet. Not a concern.

The Food and Nutrition Board of the Institute of Medicine, after extensive research, determined that the U.S. Recommended Dietary Allowance (RDA) for daily protein intake is approximately 0.8 gram per kilogram of body weight (g/kg).[49] Athletes, children, adolescents, pregnant and lactating women, as well as individuals who are underweight or recovering from surgery or burns, need more.[50]

The 0.8g/kg of body weight figure includes an extra allowance to take into account the various digestibilities of food, as well as a 25 percent increase to fill the requirements of different individuals, and then a bit more on top of all that, just to cover all the bases. Tofu, refined grains, textured soy protein, and meat substitutes contain protein that is equally digestible as that found in animal protein. Vegans eating a lot of these foods can use the traditional number of 0.8g/kg for their protein needs. If you're eating mostly whole-plant foods, some dieticians suggest eating 10 to 15 percent more protein because of different protein digestibility. So if you're on a vegan diet made up mostly of whole, unprocessed foods, then the figure of 0.9 gram of protein per kilogram of body weight is recommended.[51]

What does this all mean mathematically? Brenda Davis and Vesanto Melina, both registered dieticians, in their excellent nutritional guide, *Becoming Vegan: The Complete Guide to Adopting a Healthy Plant-Based Diet*, provide these two easy-to-follow equations to figure out your own protein RDA:

Weight in pounds (___ lbs.) divided by 2.2 to give weight in kilograms = ___ kg.

Multiply ___ kg times 0.9 to give your recommended daily protein intake in
     grams = ___ grams.

(For ease in calculation, you may use 1 gram protein per kilogram body weight.)

Using this method, for someone weighing 135 lbs.:

135 lbs. ÷ 2.2 = 61 kg.

61 kg × 0.9 = 55 grams.

With that in mind, one cup (248 grams) of firm tofu contains 40 grams of protein. One cup of 2 percent cow's milk contains 8.1 grams of protein, and one medium egg contains 5.5 grams.[52] You'd probably also be surprised to find out that 100 calories of broccoli contain 11.1 grams of protein, while 100 calories of steak contain 6.4 grams.

Most of the calories in meat are from fat. Most of the calories from green vegetables come from protein. Dr. Joel Fuhrman makes this great point: gorillas, elephants, rhinos, hippos—these huge, solid animals, who are exponentially stronger than humans, are herbivores. There is clearly plenty of muscle-building protein in the vegetation they eat.[53]

Protein in Animal Products vs. Vegetables
(grams [g] per 1 cup)

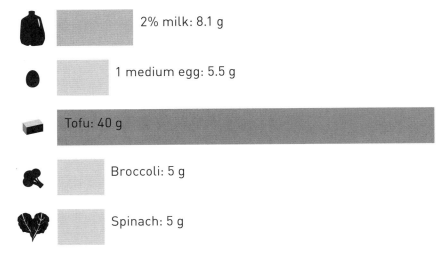

2% milk: 8.1 g

1 medium egg: 5.5 g

Tofu: 40 g

Broccoli: 5 g

Spinach: 5 g

Here are a few other plant-based ways to get 10 grams of protein:[54]

◆ 2 cups of cooked broccoli or spinach

◆ 3 to 4 cups of cooked kale, raw broccoli, or mung-bean sprouts

◆ 4.5 cups of cooked mushrooms

◆ 11 cups of romaine lettuce

You can also get plenty of protein from nuts and seeds (for example, almonds, cashews, pumpkin seeds, sunflower seeds), soy milk, almond milk, quinoa, brown rice, barley, millet, oats, oranges, bananas, tempeh, seitan, corn, cauliflower, potatoes, bean sprouts, and beans (like lentils, black beans, soybeans, and chickpeas).[55]

Another statement vegans often hear, usually after the protein question, is, "But you have to at least eat fish!"

Fish is brain food, we hear; fish is the perfect protein. Fish oil is the third most popular supplement in the United States, after vitamins and minerals, and is taken by at least 10 percent of Americans.[56] Most of the people who take fish-oil supplements believe that the oil will protect their arteries from plaque build-up.

"But there is one big problem," the *New York Times* reported in 2015. "The vast majority of clinical trials involving fish oil have found no evidence that it lowers the risk of heart attack and stroke."[57]

"I think that the era of fish oil as medication could be considered over now," said Dr. Gianni Tognoni of the Institute for Pharmacological Research in Milan, the lead author of one of the clinical studies cited by the *Times*.[58]

Dr. Klaper writes on the potential effects of fish oil and the simple alternative:

> The oil of a fish's liver is one of the strangest substances to consider eating. The liver of any animal is the chemical detoxifier for the body, and thus concentrates all the pollutants consumed by that animal. The oil squeezed from fish livers may contain high levels of hydrocarbon toxins such as PCBs and dioxins. People who use fish oil "to protect their arteries" may actually be poisoning themselves with hydrocarbons, and thus increasing their cancer risk from these dietary oils. The better solution is to keep one's arteries clear by not loading the blood with saturated animal fats in the first place. People who do not eat saturated animal fats generally have a much lower risk of clogging their arteries. Fish is not "brain food"—in fact, it now may well have become just the opposite, as mercury poisons the brain and nerve cells.[59]

It isn't just the livers of fish that absorb contaminants. A fish's entire body is an intensely concentrated package of toxins. Would you drink water laced with heavy metals like arsenic, cadmium, chromium, lead, and mercury? Add some radioactive substances like strontium 90, toxins like PCBs and cancer-causing dioxins, and then stir in some human and animal feces with the attendant E. coli bacteria for flavor.[60] Would you drink that? If not, you probably don't want to eat the flesh of fish that have absorbed and intensely concentrated all those "healthy" substances. The solution is simple—just eat less saturated fats. That will benefit you more than any amount of fish oil ever could.

A common, and old, misconception about vegetarian or vegan diets is that plant proteins must be carefully combined to create "complete" proteins with all the essential amino acids, in the right amounts, that would normally be found in animal products. This is a myth, long disproved, that is still widespread not only among the public but also in the medical community and sometimes even in the vegetarian community. It scares many people away from plant-based diets.

Jeff Novick, a registered dietician, wrote an article in 2003 for *Health Science*, the membership magazine of the National Health Association, explaining where the nutritional bogeyman of "protein complementing" came from, and how it refuses to go away. The myth was started by the 1971 book *Diet for a Small Planet*, by Frances Moore Lappé. Lappé was a sociologist trying to deal with world hunger; she was not a medical doctor, a nutritionist, or a physiologist.[61] In the 1981 edition of her book, Lappé retracted her original statement about protein complementarity:[62]

> In 1971 I stressed protein complementarity because I assumed that the only way to get enough protein . . . was to create a protein as usable by the body as animal protein. In combating the myth that meat is the only way to get high-quality protein, I reinforced another myth. I gave the impression that in order to get enough protein without meat, considerable care was needed in choosing foods. Actually, it is much easier than I thought.

The question of protein quality, which is related to the myth of protein combining, also comes up when plant-based diets are discussed. Animal proteins are considered a "higher" quality because they are similar to our own proteins, with the right amounts of amino acids, and can be synthesized very efficiently by our bodies. The plant proteins are considered "lower" quality.

High-quality protein, however, is not as great as it sounds.

"Can you guess what food we might eat to most efficiently provide the building blocks for our replacement proteins?" Dr. Campbell asks in *The China Study*. "The answer is human flesh. Its protein has just the right amount of the needed amino acids."

That would be a tough marketing campaign, even for the PR champions of the animal agriculture industry.

Quality, in this context, means how efficiently specific food proteins promote growth. But efficiency and growth are not the same as good health. Anyone with cancer will tell you that rapidly growing cells are not always welcome. There is a growing mountain of evidence that "low-quality" plant protein, which builds new proteins slowly but steadily, is the healthiest type of protein.[63]

One very important nutrient that people cannot get from plants is Vitamin B12. It is not plant-based. It is also not animal-based. It grows on bacteria and fungi.[64] If we didn't wash our vegetables so thoroughly, drink such purified water, and ferment our foods in such sanitary conditions, we would get B12 from soil, water, and fermented foods. People who eat animal products get B12 because the animals eat dirt and manure along with their feed, and B12 finds its way into their milk and flesh.[65] Vegans need to get their B12 from supplements and/or fortified foods. Only a little bit can be absorbed at one time, so large amounts are not necessary. B12 is particularly important during pregnancy, infancy, and early childhood.[66]

Deficiency can cause fatigue, depression, confusion, inability to concentrate, irritability, tingling and numbness in the fingers, arms, and legs, and in extreme cases, lack of sensation and paralysis. B12 deficiency can also lead to the clogging of arteries with plaque, leading to heart attacks and strokes.[67]

So vegans—especially pregnant and/or nursing vegans—take your B12 supplements and fortified foods! But B12 deficiency is not solely a vegan issue—according to the USDA, close to two-fifths of the US population may have marginal levels of B12, even those who consume high levels of animal products.[68]

Other nutrients besides protein and calcium that are often doubted to be sufficient in a plant-based diet are riboflavin, iron, zinc, and omega-3 fatty acids. Let's just check them off here:

✓ Riboflavin, also known as vitamin B2, can be found in plentiful supply in leafy green vegetables, asparagus, mushrooms, sweet potatoes, legumes, peas, almonds, peanuts, bananas, whole grains, breads, sea vegetables, nutritional yeast, fortified soy milks, cereals, and flour.[69]

✓ Iron from plants has a lower bioavailability than iron from animal products, so people on a plant-based diet may need to eat more, though iron deficiency is actually more common in meat eaters than vegans. Vegans can get their iron from black beans, chickpeas, lentils, soybeans, aduki beans, tofu, tempeh, barley, quinoa, veggie meat substitutes, almonds, cashews, flaxseed, hazelnuts, pine nuts, pumpkin seeds, sunflower seeds, apricots, and blackstrap molasses. Eating foods high in vitamin C at the same time helps your body increase its absorption of iron.[70] Remember that dairy, which has very little iron, can actually prevent iron absorption—research shows that eating cows' milk or cheese can decrease iron absorption from a meal by up to 50 percent.[71]

✓ Zinc-rich plant foods include whole grains, nuts and seeds, and legumes like beans, lentils, peas, soybeans, and peanuts.[72]

✓ Omega-3 fatty acids, which are usually marketed as coming from fish, can be obtained from flaxseed or flax oil, walnuts, cauliflower, hummus, brussels sprouts, hemp seeds, chia seeds, canola oil, perilla oil, and purslane, among many other plant sources.[73] Another great source, and my personal favorite, is veggie DHA algae oil pills. This gives you the exact same omega-3 fatty acids right from the purified source where fish get theirs: algae. For those of you with a sweet tooth, there are also delicious flavored flaxseed oils: chocolate mint, strawberry, caramel. . . . They taste pretty fabulous on almond ice cream.

✓ Vitamin D deficiency is a global problem, affecting both non-vegans and vegans. The major natural source of vitamin D for humans is sunshine absorbed through the skin.[74] Factors such as skin color, age and body fat, the application of sunscreen, the time of day, year, and geographical location, as well as the clothing worn, can all affect the actual production of vitamin D in the body.[75] Foods containing vitamin D are not that common; plant sources include mushrooms and tofu, and animal foods include egg yolk, fatty fish, dairy, and beef liver.[76] Cows' milk, soy and grain milks, and cereals are frequently fortified with vitamin D—it has a big effect on calcium absorption, regulation, and cell function.[77] Vitamin D2 is usually of plant origin and D3 is usually of animal origin,[78] though there are now some vegan sources of D3 from lichen commercially available. It makes no real difference to the human body whether the source of vitamin D is through sunlight on the skin or by dietary intake. D2 and D3 are both effective, though you may require slightly more D2 to reach the same level of concentration as D3.[79] It's a good idea, whether you are eating a plant-based or animal-based diet, to take a vitamin D supplement and eat foods fortified with it, especially if you don't get a lot of sunlight or wear sunscreen regularly.

A few other tips for the transition to a plant-based diet:

◆ Give it at least a month. Your taste buds have a memory of about three weeks. Dairy—cheese in particular—will probably prompt the most cravings. Casein, the primary protein in cows' milk (the same casein found in many studies to be a cancer promoter), breaks apart during digestion into opiates—yes, opiates—called casomorphin.[80] This is a naturally addictive, soothing substance, also found in human milk, which accounts for the blissed-out faces of breastfeeding human infants. That's why you're craving cheese. As with other opiates, just say no.

◆ You may experience an upset stomach for the first week or two. This is normal and will go away.

◆ Don't be afraid to call restaurants ahead of time to ask if they can make vegan accommodations or ask what the chef can do once you get there. You can also mix and match from the existing menu. Speak up for yourself!

◆ Bring your own food on airplanes, trains, etc. They might have a "strict vegetarian" option available, but there's no guarantee it will be anything other than iceberg lettuce.

◆ When cooking beans, boil them on medium-high heat for ten minutes, and scoop off the foamy stuff that rises to the top. That will cut down significantly on your, ahem, methane emissions after eating the beans. Add a bay leaf or two for digestion.

◆ Shop your veggies by color—could you use more green/orange/purple to round out your meal? This isn't just about aesthetics—the different colors of vegetables indicate the presence of different phytochemicals. The bigger the variety of phytochemicals and nutrients, the better.

- If you like to bake, there are many commercial egg replacers out there. For that matter, there are delicious vegan versions of pretty much any animal-based food available (eggs, butter, mayonnaise, grated parmesan, marshmallows— yes, you read that right—vegan s'mores are the bomb!).

- Take the first month to really educate yourself. There are tons of books, websites, online videos, lectures, and documentaries on every aspect of being vegan—health and nutrition, animal welfare, the environment, spirituality, lifestyle. Check out the recommended reading list at the end of this book for a place to start. There's a lot of information out there, so take it slow, and don't get overwhelmed.

- Keep in mind, as Colleen Patrick-Goudreau says, "To make a difference, you might have to be different."

So here's the bottom line, from the American Dietetic Association (now the Academy of Nutrition and Dietetics, and the world's largest organization of food and nutritional professionals):[81]

> Well-planned vegan and other types of vegetarian diets are appropriate for all stages of the life-cycle including during pregnancy, lactation, infancy, childhood, and adolescence. Vegetarian diets [the ADA classifies vegan diets under the label "vegetarian"] offer a number of nutritional benefits including lower levels of satu-rated fat, cholesterol, and animal protein as well as higher levels of carbohydrates, fiber, magnesium, potassium, folate, antioxidants such as vitamins C and E, and phytochemicals. Vegetarians have been reported to have lower body mass indices than non-vegetarians, as well as lower rates of death from ischemic heart disease, lower blood cholesterol levels, lower blood pressure, and lower rates of hyperten-sion, type 2 diabetes, and prostate and colon cancer.

"The question is not," Patrick-Goudreau says, "'Where do vegans get their pro-tein?'—the question is 'Why have we all been taught that we need to go through an animal to get the nutrients that the animals get, because the animals eat plants?' . . . We need to skip the middle animal and go directly to the source. And you can do this with every single nutrient that everyone questions."[82]

After I learned all this information, I felt as if a great weight had been lifted off my shoulders. I was seeing the world through a different lens. There are so many things in our society that we accept as true, simply because everyone around us believes them— our parents, our friends, our teachers, our medical professionals. We don't question those things until we are forced to. Well, I was forced to confront the "facts" because

I wanted to live in a sustainable way. But we are all, now, being forced to confront the facts, whether we know it yet or not. Time is running out for our planet. We have to break away from the animal agriculture industry and find another way to feed ourselves. Luckily, that way happens to be *much* healthier—for us as individuals, for our societies, and for our planet.

CHAPTER TEN

VEGANIC (STOCKFREE) AGRICULTURE: FEEDING A GROWING WORLD

It was a relief to hear I didn't have to eat any animal products to be healthy and even thrive, but I still thought you needed animal manure to grow organic plants. It turns out, there's an entire movement with people growing vegetables and food without any animal inputs.

I visited Earthworks Urban Farm in Detroit, where they're working with and growing food for the low-income community. It is also Detroit's only certified organic farm.[1]

"'Earthworks' has two meanings," their mission statement declares. "First, 'Earthwork' from a military perspective is an earthen barricade to protect from an advancing attack. The concept of our Earthworks is that it protects the environment and us by showing people how to live in harmony with nature by assisting in building relationships of mutual benefit. Second, 'Earthworks' reflects the work that the Earth does. In this sense, we value the Earth's work and recognize ourselves as shareholders in the natural economy of energy exchange (goods and services) in this living system."

"It is a working study in social justice, as well as in being more connected to the food we eat," the statement continues.[2]

I met with Shane Bernardo, their outreach coordinator, who grew up in Detroit just a few blocks from where Earthworks stands now. He had black hair, olive skin with stubble, and wore a dark pink hoodie and jeans. We sat in one of Earthworks' small fields under the sun, with rows of small green potato plants rising up out of the soil.

"We tend to see ourselves as individuals in a bubble," Bernardo reflected, "and forget that we inhabit this land and this Earth with other creatures, so we have to learn how to share more, I guess."

Bernardo brought me over to meet Jah Muhammad, one of the urban gardeners. "Jah is here, he's working on his garden," Bernardo said. Muhammad wore glasses and a navy cap and a T-shirt. His garden had an improvised sign made from a galvanized metal plate, with "The JAH Patch" hand-painted in black.

"You'll be surprised what you can do with [what] seems to be not a lot of space," Muhammad said to me. "[This is] about a four-by-eight-foot plot."

It did seem to be a very small space. Smaller than a modest front lawn, for sure. But there were several rows of vegetables growing, some with tall grasses and leaves, others closer to the ground.

"What's your goal this year?" I asked him. "How much do you think you can grow?"

"I would push for a hundred, at least," Muhammad said.

"A hundred pounds?"

"At least. At least."

"That's amazing." It really was. Could one hundred pounds of vegetables really come out of that tiny plot of land?

Bernardo then showed me the greenhouse, built with semi-opaque plastic sheeting instead of glass. A hand-painted wooden sign with stenciled letters read, "GROWING HOPE GREENHOUSE." They had a lot of dark-green, curly kale growing in there, and some other big-leafed plants I couldn't identify. I love kale.

"The one full year after this was constructed," Bernardo told me, "we doubled our yield to more than 14,000 pounds of food."

"14,000 pounds?" That seemed incredible. "On about how many acres?"

"About two and a half."

"So as much food as we produce and we grow, or the Earth helps us grow," Bernardo went on, "we also have to return those nutrients back to the soil. We like to think of our work as being regenerative, that we're putting as much life-giving substance in the ground as we're taking out."

I asked if they used animal manure for fertilizer. Bernardo explained that properly composting animal manure under the USDA organic certification is a complicated and time-consuming process, because poorly composted manure has real health risks to human beings. Instead, Earthworks uses vegetable compost.

"So it's just, kind of healthier and safer to use vegetarian or vegetable composting and stuff for fertilizer?" I asked.

"Yeah. That's what we found, but also because it takes less time, and it's a lot easier to manage."

"A lot easier. And the soil is just as rich?"

"Yeah. Absolutely."

This kind of farming is called veganic, stockfree, vegan organic, or plant-based farming. No synthetic chemicals are used, like pesticides, herbicides, synthetic fertilizer, GMOs, or growth regulators. This is familiar territory to anyone who knows about organic farming. But veganic farming also does not use animal manure or any slaughterhouse by-products, including blood meal, bone meal, feather meal, or fish emulsion.[3]

These slaughterhouse by-products are cheap, easily available, and overwhelmingly abundant, due to the continual killing and rendering of billions of animals in the country's CAFOs. But, apart from the horrible suffering of these animals, their rendered parts and fecal matter contain the residue of steroids, antibiotics, growth hormones, as well as disease-causing intestinal and parasitic bacteria like salmonella and E. coli. E. coli, for example, can be transferred to crops through the use of manure as fertilizer, which has lead to E. coli outbreaks in humans who eat the contaminated vegetables.[4]

This leads to some disturbing realizations about organic produce. Ron Khosla, who, along with his wife, Kate, founded Huguenot Street Farms, a seventy-seven-acre veganic farm in New Paltz, New York, told *USA Today* that the number one source of nutrients on many of the country's organic farms is CAFO-produced manure.

"You think you are getting these clean happy vegetables, but more often than not they're grown in waste from factory farms," Khosla said. "The animals . . . were fed non-organic feed laced with hormones and antibiotics. Those products bio-accumulate in the animals and it's present in their waste as well."[5]

On their website, Huguenot Street Farms states their outlook clearly:

> Really, we are just "cutting out the middle man." The middle man in this case is the cow, chicken, horse, pig, or wh[o]ever. What is their manure made from anyway but plant materials? There is no "magic" that goes on inside the animal that makes their manure better for the soil or plants than if we used the base material. In fact, it is quite the opposite if you are using factory-farmed wastes! Organic crops grown using factory-farmed manures and offal are now PROVEN to take up the toxic products used in those factory farms! People buying USDA-Certified Organic products and thinking they are avoiding the chemicals that poured onto factory farms (and into confinement factory-raised animals) are being horribly fooled. It has become too common for some organic vegetable farms (especially the big ones that now grow most all the organic produce you buy in grocery stores) to rely almost exclusively on slaughterhouse by-products (chicken manure, blood, bone, and fish meal) to get nutrients to their plants. The idea of supporting these industries in any way, and putting what we consider to be toxic waste products onto our otherwise clean fields, seems completely counter to our goal of organic clean living.[6]

Instead of slaughterhouse by-products, veganic farmers use "green manure," or plant compost, as fertilizer, as well as mulch, chipped branch wood, ground-up rock powders, and other techniques like crop rotation.[7] Biological pest control, such as beetle banks, is used instead of chemical pesticides. Beetle banks are strips of land planted with grasses to provide shelter and habitat for helpful birds, animals, and insects.[8] Parasitic wasps, for instance, control the caterpillar population that would otherwise eat the crops.

Veganic farming also helps sequester carbon in the soil, helping to fight global warming. Iain Tolhurst, who owns Tolhurst Organic, a stockfree (veganic) organic farm in the UK, explains:

> And because we're building carbon in the soil, very small increases in organic content in the soil [have] a huge effect in terms of carbon entrapment, in fact [soil] is one of the biggest carbon sinks possible. So it's not only good for animals, it's also very good for carbon capture, which is awfully good for climate change. So we're building organic material, and the only way to build organic material long-term is through plants. You cannot do it through manure, because manure dissipates into the environment very quickly, it gets broken down. Whereas plants, and the fruits in the ground, will gradually decay and become carbon.[9]

Veganic agriculture, on top of all these benefits, is also cheaper than conventional or organic farming.[10]

I went to visit Dr. Greg Litus, a veganic farmer with a PhD in horticulture, who tended a three-acre veganic garden there.[11] I'm fascinated and, frankly, pretty dismayed at what I'm learning about organic produce. I had always thought "organic" meant safe, healthy, and sustainable. Maybe Dr. Litus would be able to enlighten me.

"Most people who buy organic produce approach it from this concern for the environment," he told me. "A lot of them don't understand the agricultural systems that support that organic produce that they get on the shelf. They don't understand that almost all organic systems [use] the waste products or the body parts of animals to make those systems work. They don't need to use them and some organic systems will choose not to use them but almost all of them do—because those by-products are cheap and easy to get.

"If you ask somebody if they knew that their [organic] tomato was the result of a factory chicken farm, they would just be confused," Litus continued. "It takes an understanding of agriculture and horticulture to recognize all of the components that go into those tomatoes. They are building a 'sustainable' system off of something that's not sustainable. If you say we can use fish emulsion in our organic system, let's think about where that fish emulsion comes from. You don't see a sustainable system on that end. If we can use blood meal in our system, let's look where the blood meal comes from—it's not coming from a sustainable system. It's coming from a completely twisted system that is depleting the planet.

"There is absolutely no doubt," Litus went on, "that using animal body parts or wastes, dairy compost, or blood meal, or bone meal, or concentrated fish grows a lot of food. It has the nitrogen, the phosphates, it has the calcium, magnesium, all these things that we put into the soil that we harvest out with our tomatoes and squashes and melons and peas, which have to be replaced. You can replace it with by-products of the animal industry—but you don't have to. The veganic method works just as well. It's just about building good, strong soil and microbial communities that can biodegrade these grasses and other plant matter.

"The veganic method is much more efficient than bringing animals out here first to eat this, and then for us to try to contain their wastes or process their bodies, and then to take that back to our vegetable production. If you are going to run all of this plant biomass through an animal first, you are going to lose some of the fertility along the way."

I asked Litus about the big environmental groups—I've never seen any of them raise the issue of veganic farming.

"There are all of these environmental groups," Litus said, "many, many of them who work on specific issues associated with the outcome of agricultural production, whether it's dead zones in the ocean or whether it's toxic runoff into groundwater systems or land degradation and loss of habitat, species loss and everything else.

"They all focus on one aspect of it, but if you have dead zones in the Gulf of Mexico and you don't change the way you conduct agriculture up in the Mississippi valley, then you don't control the problem. They are just trying to tweak the system [while] keeping it pretty much the same."

I had learned that veganic agriculture, using green manure, has a long history that stretches back to the Greek, Roman, and Chinese civilizations, when there weren't domesticated animals producing large amounts of manure to use as fertilizer.[12] But today, apart from a handful of veganic farms, is veganic agriculture catching on?

"In the Midwest," Litus said, "in the grain-producing states all the way into Canada, where they grow a lot of wheat, they are actually moving toward veganic practices. This is an amazing thing to see, because these people are not doing it from a cultural perspective of compassion. They are doing it because they are trying to grow a lot of wheat with the minimum amount of inputs in a location that works really well if you cover crop [use green manure or plant compost]. What they'll do before they grow their wheat is, they'll come in and they'll cover crop [use vegetable compost] with a variety of different grasses and pea species.

"Then they'll turn that into the soil and grow their wheat there without having to bring in animal inputs for fertility. Occasionally they have to add some mineral phosphates. The system can be adapted to all parts of the country; it's clear that that can be done. There are a lot of veganic growers in the UK, a very different climate than here. In fact there is an organization in the UK that actually certifies farms that are stockfree.

"They are very productive; they've been doing it for decades. It can be done there, it can be done up in the Midwest, it can be done on the West Coast.

"All the benefits that come from the vegetarian lifestyle, from the environmental to the health benefits, [will] build on each other to the point where this animal agriculture industry becomes part of history.

"Not only is organic more compassionate—it's also more efficient," Litus continued. "In a society with this many billions of people, we need to be as efficient as possible. Some people might say, if we embrace this primitive approach of only wild animals everywhere and we go back to a hunter-gatherer system, that sounds great, but that was ten million people on the entire continent. Maybe a little bit more, a little bit less. No one really knows.

"Today, now, we have what? We have 320 million in the United States, 25 million in Canada, another hundred and so many million in Mexico? So North America is up to almost 450 million people. Trying to figure out a way to bring animal agriculture into balance with 450 million hungry people is impossible."

How about bringing animal agriculture into balance with 7.3 billion hungry people worldwide? Some people would say the problem isn't really animal agriculture, but actually human overpopulation.

"This is amazing," John Jeavons, director of the Grow Biointensive Mini-Farming program for Ecology Action, told me. "I didn't believe it when I first learned it, but 216,000 more people are born to the planet every day.[13] *Every day*. It's extraordinary. But what's really extraordinary is, you need, per day, 34,000 new acres of farmable land. It's not happening." And Jeavons's statistic is assuming people only eat plants and farm biointensively. Fifteen times more land—minimally—is needed otherwise.[14]

In 1812, there were 1 billion people on the planet. In 1912, there were 1.5 billion. Then, just 100 years later, our population exploded to 7 billion humans.[15] This number is rightly given a great deal of attention, but an even more important figure when determining world population is the world's *70 billion* farm animals raised by humans.

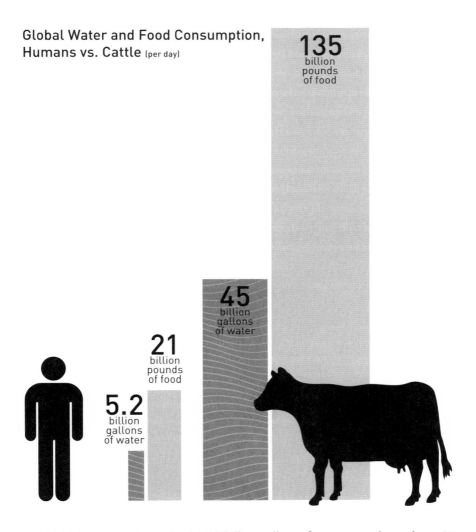

Global Water and Food Consumption, Humans vs. Cattle (per day)

135 billion pounds of food

45 billion gallons of water

21 billion pounds of food

5.2 billion gallons of water

The human population drinks 5.2 billion gallons of water every day and eats 21 billion pounds of food.[16] But just the world's 1.5 billion cows alone drink 45 billion gallons of water every day and eat 135 billion pounds of food.[17] This isn't so much a human population issue, it's a humans-eating-animals-population issue.

Environmental organizations not addressing this is like health organizations trying to stop lung cancer without addressing cigarette smoking. But instead of secondhand smoking, it's secondhand eating, which affects the entire planet. In all of my interviews, nearly every doctor, author, researcher, or experienced industry veteran told me the same thing.

"We're growing enough food right now in the world to feed about twelve billion people,"[18] Dr. Will Tuttle told me. "We only have seven billion people. We have roughly a billion people starving every single day. Worldwide, 50 percent of the grain and legumes that we're growing, we're feeding to animals. So they're eating huge amounts of grain and legumes. In the United States, it's closer to 70, 80,[19] depending on which grain it is, 90 . . . About 90 percent of the soybeans."[20]

"Eighty-two percent of the world's starving children live in countries where food is fed to animals in the livestock systems that are then killed and eaten by more well-off individuals in developed countries such as the United States, UK, and in Europe,"[21] Dr. Richard Oppenlander said, echoing Dr. Tuttle's statements. "You can produce, on average, fifteen times more protein from plant-based sources than from meat[22] on any given area of land using the same type of land, whether it's a very fertile area in one area of the world or it's an area that's depleted."

"The fact of it is," Howard Lyman told me, "we could feed every human being on the planet today an adequate diet if we did no more than take the feed that we are feeding to animals and actually turn it into food for humans.[23] So somebody trying to justify GMOs? That's like trying to give a drowning man a drink of water. Anytime somebody tells you that we can't grow food for humans on the land that we're growing feed for animals—that is somebody who is smoking the number one crop out of California. The fact of it is, if you can grow corn to stuff down the throat of an animal, you can actually grow corn and feed it to a human."

"As the world population continues to grow to almost nine billion people," I asked during my interview with Michael Pollan, "do you foresee someday that we might just completely have to stop eating meat altogether?"

"I don't know that we'll completely stop," Pollan said. "I think that the amount of meat eaten will decline. There's no way to support nine ounces per person per day, which is what Americans are eating now. If the Chinese alone decide they want to eat that much—and they *have* decided they want to eat that much—there isn't . . . We just can't. We don't have enough world to produce the grain to generate that much meat. I think a plant-based diet is the most sustainable."

"Could you throw out a number for animal-based protein, like an ounce, a number that nine billion people can eat, for the planet to not only sustain itself, but to thrive?" I asked.

"I don't think I know enough," he said. "But yeah, it would be on the order of a couple ounces a week, you know? It's not going to be the way we're eating it now. We're gorging on meat. We're eating huge amounts."

Pollan is right that more and more nations, including China, the world's most heavily populated country, are emulating the affluent United States and demanding greater and greater amounts of animal products. China was a net exporter of grain in the 1990s, but is now one of the biggest grain importers in the world.[24] The *International Business Times* reported that China's wheat imports, from December 2012 to December 2013, increased by 5,319 percent,[25] while their overall grain imports, according to the USDA, almost doubled between 2012 and 2013.[26] According to Lester Brown, the founder and president of the Earth Institute, and whose personal papers were requested by the Library of Congress in 1986 because his writings "have already strongly affected thinking about problems of world population and resources,"[27] this amazing increase, although influenced by a poor growing season and bad weather, is primarily driven by the rising demand for meat among the growing wealthy population of China, and the desire to raise that meat at home.[28]

That is bad news for the rest of the world, especially for the world's poor.

"As Chinese eat more grain-fed meat, the country's need for grain will continue to grow," stated the Worldwatch Institute. "This . . . could quickly make China the world's leading grain importer. . . . China cannot import the grain it needs without driving world grain prices up, leaving the 1.3 billion people in the world who subsist on $1 a day at risk."[29]

Of course, it isn't only China. The same story is played out in countries like Russia, Thailand, Egypt, Jordan, Israel, Libya, Saudi Arabia, Guatemala, Costa Rica, and many others.[30] The true struggle is between the world's wealthy and their desire to eat animal protein, often as a status symbol, and the 805 million people who struggle with hunger every day, the 868 million who are undernourished, and the 1.2 billion living in severe poverty.[31]

"In a world where an estimated one in every six people goes hungry every day," says the Worldwatch Institute, "the politics of meat consumption are increasingly heated, since meat production is an inefficient use of grain—the grain is used more efficiently when consumed directly by humans. Continued growth in meat output is dependent on feeding grains to animals, creating competition for grain between affluent meat eaters and the world's poor."[32]

"[The world's poor] cannot compete for grain with the cattle and chickens of the world's wealthy people," said Joel Cohen, head of the Laboratory of Populations at Rockefeller University. "The extremely poor are irrelevant to international markets; they are economically invisible. But they are people nonetheless."[33]

The United Nations estimates, in a low population projection, that there will be almost eight billion people on the planet by 2050. Their high population estimate is 10.5 billion by 2050.[34]

Back in 1996, when the world's population was a mere 5.8 billion,[35] Paul Ehrlich, the Stanford professor who wrote *The Population Bomb*, said, "By almost any standard, we are beyond carrying capacity [the number of people the planet can theoretically support] now; but that doesn't mean we can't still go beyond that capacity for some time."[36]

How can we be beyond carrying capacity? And how could that continue "for some time"?

"We're accomplishing this by depleting oil reserves by using lots of petroleum-based fertilizers," explained David Pimental, who is on the Emeritus Faculty of Cornell University's College of Agriculture and Life Sciences. "We're switching to high-yield farming practices that often cause massive soil erosion. And we're drying up irreplaceable aquifers by irrigating vast amounts of cropland. By doing this, we're managing to feed growing numbers of people over the short term. But every year we do this, we are reducing the earth's capacity to support its population over the long term."[37]

That's basically the definition of unsustainability.

Pimental and Henry Kendall, a Nobel Prize–winning physicist and co-founder of the Union of Concerned Scientists, collaborated on a study in 1992 to examine whether the global food supply could feed the world with the projected growth in population. Pimental and Kendall found that "If humans, especially in developed countries, moved toward more vegetable protein diets rather than their present diets, which are high in animal protein foods, a substantial amount of grain would become available for direct human consumption."[38]

"If present food distribution patterns persist," Kendall and Pimental concluded, "the chance of bettering the lot of the majority of the world's peoples vanishes. The likelihood of a graceful and humane stabilization of world population vanishes as well. Fertility and population growth in numerous developing countries will then be forced downward by severe shortages of food, disease, and by other processes set in motion by shortages of vital resources and irreversible environmental damage."[39]

ANIMAL AGRICULTURE AND TAXES

In the United States, whether you are rich or poor, a meat-eater or a vegan, if you are a taxpayer, you are paying for the enormous hidden costs—billions of dollars—of animal food production. I spoke with David Simon, an attorney and the author of *Meatonomics*, about the concealed economics of animal agriculture, outside of a conference where he was presenting.

"I've added up the costs of animal food production that the producers don't actually bear themselves," Simon said. "These are the hidden costs—or the externalized costs—that they impose on society. Those are in categories like health care, environmental damage, subsidies, damage to fisheries, and even cruelty.

"If you take those externalized costs, which are about $415 billion,[40] if the meat and dairy industries were required to internalize those costs, if they had to bear those costs themselves, the costs of the retail prices of meat and dairy would skyrocket. A $5 carton of eggs would go to $13. A $4 Big Mac would go to $11.

"The problem with these externalized costs being imposed on society is that, whether you eat meat or not, whether you're an omnivore or an herbivore, you are paying part of the costs of somebody else's consumption. So that when somebody goes into a McDonald's and buys a Big Mac for $4, there is another $7 of costs that is imposed on society. I'm paying that. You're paying that, whether you eat meat or not."

"In the United States," Will Anderson writes in *This Is Hope*, "dairy is subsidized with our federal taxes. Price support for milk means the dairy animal agriculturalists will be paid a guaranteed minimum price per hundred pounds of milk the cows produce. There are a number of similar programs that buy up excess dairy products and make exporting them easier."[41]

That's not where I want my tax dollars going.

While everyone has to pay taxes that support the animal agriculture industry, not everyone has open access to healthy food. Many wealthy people have infinitely more access to healthy, fresh food than those in low-income communities, where there seem to be fast-food chains on every corner. The Earthworks farm in Detroit is an amazing example of what can be accomplished with a small bit of land and a great deal of cooperative spirit in a low-income community, but you don't see an Earthworks in too many inner cities.

I met with Lauren Ornelas, the founder and executive director of the Food Empowerment Project. She's been an activist for animal rights and food justice for two decades.

"Food justice is incredibly important," Ornelas told me, "because food touches all of our lives daily. We have to look at how [food] impacts everyone, from the waiters and waitresses and cooks at restaurants, to the produce workers who pick our food, to the animals who are suffering and dying so we can eat them. We have the responsibility to speak out against these injustices and make sure we hold those who are doing the exploiting accountable.

"We constantly put profit over people, and of course we put [profit] over non-human animals as well. It's all part of the same system. There can't be any justice when you have workers who aren't paid a living wage. There can be no justice when you have certain portions of a population that do not have the same access to healthy foods so they have higher rates of disease. There's no justice when certain portions of the population, predominantly people of color, are more impacted by contaminants because their communities tend to be in areas where you have more dumps, more toxic waste sites, [and] more oil refineries.

"You have, especially in communities of color and low-income communities, some of the worst food you could imagine in the school-lunch cafeterias. I compared the school-lunch program in East San Jose with the school-lunch program in Palo Alto. It was just amazing to see the difference. Salad bar and brown rice compared to fried chicken on a stick and syrup, or something like that."

And in some communities, economics and traditional culture have combined to steer people toward a meat-and-dairy-laden, sugary, high-fat diet. Dick Gregory, the comedian, civil rights activist, and vegan, has famously stated, "I personally would say that the quickest way to wipe out a group of people is to put them on a 'soul-food' diet. One of the tragedies is that the very folks in the Black community, who are most sophisticated in terms of the political realities in this country, are nonetheless advocates of soul food. They will lay down a heavy rap on genocide in America with regard to Black folks, then walk into a soul-food restaurant and help the genocide along."[42]

This just goes to show what lack of access—both to healthy food and to education about good diet—can do to a community. Nobody wants to be unhealthy, but in a lot of communities, it seems like there isn't much choice. Dr. Milton Mills, a leader in promoting healthy eating in African American communities, says, "What we call 'soul food'— it is actually plantation food. West Africans who were brought to America as slaves were forced to eat the literal garbage of the plantations on which they were enslaved . . . [it] is a dietary vestige of slavery . . . and *not* our cultural heritage."

Many white Americans still live by the idealized stick-to-your-ribs meat-and-potatoes diet. Neither is good for you—but culture rarely takes that into account. Education is needed to shake people from what they've grown up *in* and get them to actually *grow*.

It turns out there's a successful movement of sustainable, animal-alternative food producers based right here in California, funded by big names like Bill Gates and Biz Stone (co-founder of Twitter).

John Schindler founded and is CEO of Omega Creamery, a plant-based dairy, which creates milks and creams with proprietary blends of organic flax, rice, and hemp milk.

"We're making the Omega products and proving that we can make better-tasting food that is great for you, and it takes one twentieth of the land and resources that dairies do," Schindler told me.

Another plant-based alternative company is Beyond Meat. Their mission is to "create mass-market solutions that perfectly replace animal protein with plant protein."[43] The products of Beyond Meat are incredibly convincing vegan meat substitutes. I met with Ethan Brown, the founder and CEO of Beyond Meat. He's a tall, well-built man in a blue polo shirt, jeans, and a baseball cap. While he was growing up, he spent the weekends on his family's dairy farm, which made him ask, "Why do we eat protein the way we do?"[44]

"If I could tell you that you could have the fiber structure of meat," Brown said, holding out a small vegan piece of what looked, smelled, and tasted exactly like rotisserie chicken breast, while his kids chowed down at the kitchen table next to us, "the satiating bite of meat, the protein, and all the nutritional benefits of meat, without actually having animal protein itself, and by doing that, you can address climate change, you could address the human health epidemics that we're seeing, you could address animal welfare, and you could address natural resource conservation—would you make the change?"

Well, yeah.

"I try to encourage people to shift to plant protein," Brown said in an interview with *Fortune* magazine. "I think that's the [number] one thing that people can do in their lifetime to positively impact climate change."[45]

Next I went to see Josh Tetrick. He's a former football linebacker from Alabama and looks like he could also have been a GI Joe action figure model with his square jaw, chiseled features, and short brown hair. Tetrick was featured on *Fortune*'s 2014 "40 Under 40" list as the CEO and founder of Hampton Creek. Hampton Creek's mission is to replace eggs in our diet with plants. Their two main products right now are an egg-free mayo called "Just Mayo," and "Just Cookies," egg-free cookies.

When we spoke, Tetrick had just started Hampton Creek a year and a half before. I asked him why he did it.

"We are trying to upend the global egg industry," he said, "by finding plants out there in the world to replace battery cage eggs. I mean, who would have known that the end result of a hen's ovulation cycle can do all this insane stuff in food? It binds a cookie, it brings oil and water together in mayonnaise, and also coagulates like a scrambled egg. We scan the world's plants, and [have] found ones that could do all of those functionalities. 'Beyond Eggs' [Hampton Creek's vegan egg replacer] is a whole bunch of different plants and replaces the sweatshop eggs we're not too happy with."

"How's the nutritional value compared to an egg?" I asked.

"Pretty similar, except ours doesn't have cholesterol."

Tetrick told me more about his background, before he founded Hampton Creek.

"I've spent about seven years of my life in sub-Saharan Africa," he said, "working on environmental sustainability and with kids who live on the street, finding ways to get them in school. My best friend spends a lot of time working with some of the largest food companies in the world, and he tries to convince them to move toward more sustainable ways of doing things.

"He was frustrated because the people inside these companies got it. Like, they get that chickens are tortured. But if it's too expensive to do the good thing, then they don't do the good thing. And that's awful. Can we find a way so that the good thing is actually the extremely affordable thing? Hampton Creek kind of grew out of that conversation."

"So is Hampton Creek's main motivation from the animal ethics aspect?" I asked.

"My personal motivation is 'How do we alleviate massive amounts of animal suffering as quick as we possibly can?'" Tetrick said. "Other people in the company are more motivated by environmental sustainability—our head of biochemistry is really driven by a desire to reduce greenhouse gas emissions for the food system. Other people are more concerned about health. So there are different motivations for different people in the company, but personally, the reason why I'm doing it is because I think it's a really powerful way to relieve an unbelievable amount of suffering."

"Could you talk a little bit more about your time in Africa, the poverty you saw there, and food security issues?"

"Yeah, you bet. There are a lot of bizarre things about animal farming. Probably the most bizarre is that we actually give the animals we eat more food than we do the 1.3 billion people who go to bed hungry every single night. That's crazy. I spent seven years working in Liberia and Nigeria and Kenya and Ethiopia, working with kids who live out on the street. These kids are going to bed hungry every single night and that's not okay. If we can find ways to feed them in a much more affordable way, in a way that is also pretty nutritious, I think that's a big win in making our system a lot more sustainable.

"Also, around the world, as people rise up the income ladder, they begin to eat in a more unsustainable way. How do we reverse that? How do we find a way that, when they rise up the income ladder, they're actually eating in a sustainable way, too?"

"Yeah, yeah. They want to move the world toward a more sustainable place, but I think a big reason you're seeing Bill Gates and the Founders Fund and Khosla Ventures backing us is they see this current food system as being massively inefficient.

"Think about it. You have all these animals and all these cages that require all this feed and all this water and all this land, and they look at that like horse-and-buggy days, like what is this? They look at this like land lines in sub-Saharan Africa. Do we really need land lines anymore? Let's get on the cell phone bandwagon.

"So, we look at the food system like we look at health care or education. These are all broken systems. And the food system is even more broken, I think, than education and health care. It's broken because it's bad for the environment, awfully brutal to animals, and bad for our health. We got frustrated at the slow pace of change.

"Our philosophy is, 'Can we create an entirely new model that makes the existing model, which is to say factory farming, obsolete?' So it really emerges with this kind of ethos, let's end it through something that's ten times more affordable and ten times more sustainable.

"Our investors are interested in this because of the current food system's massive inefficiency and the potential for innovation to leapfrog all of that nonsense and make the world a little bit better and also create what I think will amount to a pretty successful business.

"This, what we are doing, is not about serving the vegans in San Francisco," Tetrick went on. "That is not what Bill Gates is invested in. This is about massively transforming how our society eats, because it is a necessity. It is because [we] cannot go on feeding the world in the way we are right now in a sustainable way, so our focus is: How do you feed people in Birmingham, Alabama, at the Piggly Wiggly? How do you feed people in Beijing, and how do you feed people in the subways in London? Some of these folks care about sustainability and they care about animal welfare, [but] some folks, like my dad, don't really care about either, but they care about insanely cheap, good food. That's fine. We've got something for them, too. But, you know, our focus isn't to have incremental change and make a little bit of money. Our focus is massive, transformative change."

"How does the energy efficiency compare, eating plants versus eggs or beef?"

"When you imagine all those egg-laying hens eating all that soy and all that corn," Tetrick said, "you have an energy conversion ratio of about 38 to 1, whereas, alternatively, you can find plants and you can grow those plants and you can convert those plants into food. The energy conversion ratio for the plants that we're using to replace eggs is about 2 to 1 compared to 38 to 1 for eggs.

"So we think the ultimate insight is taking the animal out of the system of food production. When you take the animal out, you also take the greenhouse gases out. You take the food safety issues out. You take the food scarcity out. But one thing that's amazing—you put our values back in. You put in values like compassion and integrity and kindness, values that are natural to human beings. You build that back into the story of our food."

There's a flourishing movement of veganic agriculture and plant-based alternatives to animal products that is churning just beneath the surface of what mainstream America sees. We're not hearing a lot about it yet, but it's there. And just like any social revolution, a seismic shift in how we feed ourselves seems impossible—until it becomes inevitable. Even now those alternatives are breaking through the crust of habit and tradition, and they're just gathering more strength, more momentum.

I often imagine how, in the not-so-distant future, eating animal products will be viewed as smoking is now viewed in our society. A few decades ago, everyone smoked. They smoked endlessly—at home, at work, in the car, around their kids, until science and lung cancer rates stepped in to wake people up.

The animal agriculture wake-up call is ringing now.

You awake yet?

CHAPTER ELEVEN

TRANSFORMING THE WORLD, ONE MEAL AT A TIME

To feed a person on an all-plant-based vegan diet for one year requires just one-sixth of an acre of land. To feed that same person on a vegetarian diet that includes eggs and dairy requires three times as much land. To feed a person on the average diet eaten by an American citizen, with high consumption of meat, dairy, and eggs, requires eighteen times as much land.[1]

This is because you can produce 37,000 pounds of vegetables on one and a half acres, but only 375 pounds of meat on that same plot of land.[2]

1.5 ACRES LAND = 37,000 POUNDS OF PLANT-BASED FOOD OR 375 POUNDS OF MEAT

The comparison doesn't end with land use. A vegan diet produces half as much carbon dioxide as an American omnivore,[3] uses 1/11 the amount of fossil fuels,[4] 1/13 the amount of water,[5] and 1/18 the amount of land.[6]

After adding all this up, I realized I had the choice—every single day—to save:[7]

✓ More than 1,100 gallons of water

✓ 45 pounds of grain

✓ 30 square feet of forested land

✓   The equivalent of 20 pounds of carbon dioxide

✓   And one animal's life.

Every. Single. Day.

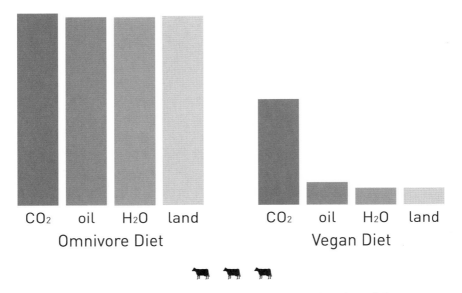

During this journey, I discovered a kaleidoscope of voices, but they all focus on one vision for our planet.

"If we all as a society did go vegan," Dr. Will Tuttle said to me, his eyes lighting up, "and we moved away from eating animal foods and toward a plant-based diet, what would happen? If we didn't kill all these cows, [chickens, pigs, and fish] and eat them, then we wouldn't have to [relentlessly] breed [them]. If we didn't breed them, then we wouldn't have to feed them. If we didn't have to feed them, then we wouldn't have to devote all this land to growing grains and legumes and so forth to feed to them. Then the forests could come back. Wildlife could come back. The oceans would come back. The rivers would run clean again. The air would come back. Our health would return."

What about stopping global warming with green technology?

"Renewable energy infrastructure, such as building solar and wind generators all over our country to reduce climate change, I mean, that's a pretty good idea," Dr. Richard Oppenlander said, "but it's projected to take at least twenty years and at least minimally $18 trillion to develop.[8] It's important to realize that we don't have that long of a time frame. We don't really have twenty years and we really don't have $18 trillion to develop these, so another solution to climate change . . . We could stop eating animals and it could be done today. It doesn't have to take twenty years and it certainly doesn't have to take $18 trillion—because it costs nothing."

With the elimination of animal agriculture, methane emissions would drop drastically. Thirty-five percent of methane produced by human beings and their activities comes from livestock.[9] And as Professor Kirk Smith told me earlier, if emissions are greatly reduced, methane levels in the atmosphere will drop within decades. With carbon dioxide, on the other hand, you don't see a difference in the atmosphere for about a century. And methane, as we know, has a global warming power eighty-six times greater than carbon dioxide.[10]

"Some people say, 'Well, let's fix carbon dioxide and then we can worry about the methane,'" Smith said. "Well, that's wrong . . . It's the other way around that actually makes sense. Do something about methane, because you get a response right away."

I looked back on all of the illuminating, inspiring, startling, and wonderful interviews of this project. I felt incredibly lucky that I was given a chance to go on this journey of investigation and discovery. It was as if I was hearing a symphony of voices all saying the same thing, weaving together into an urgent song that demands to be heard—before it's too late.

"We will not succeed until we stop animal agriculture," Will Anderson said simply. "And by succeed, I mean we will not save ecosystems to the extent necessary. We will not have enough food for people around the planet. We will not stop global warming. We will not stop pollution and the dead zones that run off all the fields of corn and soy that are grown to feed livestock. We will not stop the hunting of wolves and other predators."

"As a journalist," said Will Potter, "I really put an unwavering faith in the power of information and education. We need to know what's going on. We need to know the scope of the environmental impact, how both industrial operations and small-scale operations are contributing to that. Then we can use that to make our own choices.

"But we have to go further than we thought possible," Potter went on. "It's not enough to just sign a signature or click something online. It's not enough to just cast a vote every four years or to sign a petition every once in a while, or even mail a really big check. You also have to walk the walk. I don't mean this in a condescending way, because there's a lot of ways I need to change in getting my own values in line with my lifestyle. It takes a lot of courage and humility and selflessness to think about how we're acting ourselves and be the ones who take that first step. If we're not able to recognize our own impact and the choices that we're making in contributing to that [impact], we're not going to move that dialogue forward.

"We're talking about the future of the planet. Nothing could be bigger than that in terms of the weight that it has on all of us to take action. What do we do? To me, it's really inspiring to remember that the modern environmental movement itself is not very old. The amount of change in public consciousness, in policy, that's happened in that amount of time, it's incredible. I think we have to remind ourselves how much is getting done right now, how much potential is there."

"The single most effective thing anyone can do to help their own health and help the planet is to change to a plant-based diet, where your meal is not based on a piece of animal flesh. There's a whole world of delicious food," Dr. Michael Klaper said to me.

"Have fruit and oatmeal for breakfast and for lunch, a big salad and a hearty vegetable soup and a plate of greens or a bean burrito or a piece of veggie pizza with non-dairy cheese. Then for dinner: Italian or Chinese or east Indian or Thai. There's lots of cuisines, lots of ways to have fun with spices, but send that river, and lots of salads and fruits, through your system, and stop the dairy and the meat and the processed white flour products. Take a walk every day and laugh a lot and watch your body get healthier. It's a wonderful thing to see, and you can do it. You don't need a doctor to do that.

"We've seen a lot of things happen," Dr. Klaper reflected. "I grew up with the Berlin Wall in place, and I never thought I'd see that come down, and it came down within weeks. People just said, 'We can't stand for that anymore.' If enough people understand the cost of a meat-based diet, it would change everything."

"Now," John Jeavons said, "organic farming is one major positive step in the right direction, but we need to keep walking. We need to get beyond organics. We need to get to sustainability. We can do it, but we have to choose to do it."

"We become part of a gathering momentum of other people," Dr. Tuttle said. "That's what's happening. This is really what's happening. This is the news."

"Selflessness is a nice way to be," said Dr. Greg Litus. "It has all these benefits for yourself as well as the planet and other people. It's a beautiful way to live. Ecologically, it just feels better."

"Quietly and unmistakably," said Demosthenes Maratos, "the most powerful thing that someone can do for the environment [is to choose] to stop consuming animals and live a vegan lifestyle. No other lifestyle choice has a further reaching and more profoundly positive impact on the planet and all life on Earth."

I had come to a conclusion. The only way to sustainably and ethically live on this planet with seven billion other people is to live an entirely plant-based vegan diet. I decided that, instead of eating others, I'd eat for others. At first, like these environmental groups, I was afraid of what it would mean to change. But now I embrace it.

A distinction is often made in the vegan world between "ethical" veganism—that is, being vegan for the sake of the animals—and "environmental" veganism.

I don't believe that distinction exists.

Environmental veganism—being vegan for the sake of the planet, all life, and future generations—*is* ethical veganism. It isn't just about saving trees or pretty places—it's about preserving life, *all* life. It is about a commitment to non-violence not only toward animals and toward ourselves but toward our planet. If that isn't ethical, I don't know what is. And ultimately, all the arguments for ethical veganism have an environmental impact. Boycotting circuses that use exotic and endangered species will discourage taking those species out of their native ecosystems. Not using products tested on animals will allow us to reallocate the resources wasted feeding and housing the animals in laboratories. Not buying leather will decrease demand, which in turn saves thousands of gallons in water. The use of animals in any human industry is having a detrimental effect on our planet and truly must come to an end.

"For me," Howard Lyman told me, "it's treating the environment in such a way that it's better tomorrow than it is today. That's as straight as it comes. When I leave this planet, I'm going to leave my kids and grandchildren a place to live. Did I do what I could for them?"

That is ethical veganism, no doubt. Everything is connected. It is choosing life over death, for the animals, for ourselves, for all future generations. For the Earth.

All this talk about sustainability made it sound like our planet was on some sort of life support. I don't want her to simply survive or be sustained, but to *thrive*. Life today is not about sustainability. It's about thrive-ability. Planet Earth has given so much to us for so long. It was time to give back 108 percent of everything we have.

It felt good.

It was in alignment.

"Do you realize," Howard Lyman asked me, pinning me with his eyes, "seventy-five percent of Americans consider themselves to be environmentalists? You don't think we could solve this problem in a heartbeat? . . . All we would need is for the environmentalists to live what they profess and we'd be on a new course in the world.

"Do what you can do, as well as you can do it, every day of your life," he said emphatically, "and you will end up dying one of the happiest individuals that ever died. You're fortunate. I wish I knew what you know when I was your age, but I didn't. You can change the world.

"You *must* change the world."

RECOMMENDED READING AND VIEWING LIST

For the nutritional nuts and bolts of a plant-based diet, check out Brenda Davis and Vesanto Melina's *Becoming Vegan: The Complete Guide to Adopting a Healthy Plant-Based Diet*. There are several editions, ranging from the Express (distilled for busy vegans) to the Comprehensive (phonebook-sized for vegans who want to know everything).

I highly recommend *Vegan Freak: Being Vegan in a Non-Vegan World*, by Bob and Jenna Torres. Careful, though—it may make you laugh so hard your chocolate almond milk will come out your nose. It dispenses excellent advice on vegan lifestyles.

For help in dealing with all those curious questions from omnivores ("But, don't carrots have feelings? Wasn't Hitler a vegetarian? And what if I were starving to death on a desert island?"), *Eat Like You Care*, by Gary Francione and Anna Charlton, and Sherry Colb's *Mind If I Order the Cheeseburger?* are both brilliant.

On the health benefits of living vegan: *The China Study* by Dr. T. Colin Campbell and Thomas Campbell II, *Eat to Live* and *Disease-Proof Your Child: Feeding Kids Right*, both by Dr. Joel Fuhrman, and *The Food Revolution* by John Robbins. Also check out the documentary *Forks Over Knives*.

The World Peace Diet by Dr. Will Tuttle is a meditation on the philosophy and spirituality of being vegan. *Peaceable Kingdom* is a beautiful documentary about the emotional lives of animals and their connections to one another and to human beings. For animal rights, you can't go wrong with anything by Gary Francione.

For everything you never wanted to know about slaughterhouses, read *Slaughterhouse* by Gail Eisnitz and *Every Twelve Seconds* by Timothy Pachirat. They will give you nightmares and make you sick to your stomach.

And if you just can't get enough on animal agriculture and the environment, read *Comfortably Unaware* and *Food Choice and Sustainability*, both by Dr. Richard A. Oppenlander.

There's also a pretty good documentary out there called *Cowspiracy*.

NOTES

PROLOGUE

1. "Livestock Impacts on the Environment." Food and Agriculture Organization of the United Nations website. Spotlight November 2006. http://www.fao.org/ag/magazine/0612sp1.htm.

2. Kasper, Matt. "Next Steps to Reduce Methane Emissions from Landfills." Center for American Progress website. April 16, 2014. Accessed March 2015. https://www.americanprogress.org/issues/green/news/2014/04/16/88084/next-steps-to-reduce-methane-emissions-from-landfills/.

3. Goodland, Robert, and Jeff Anhang. "Livestock and Climate Change." WorldWatch.org website. November/December 2009. Accessed March 2015. https://www.worldwatch.org/files/pdf/Livestock%20and%20Climate%20Change.pdf.

4. Oppenlander, Richard A. " Freshwater Abuse and Loss: Where Is It All Going?" Forks Over Knives website. May 20, 2013. Accessed March 2015. http://www.forksoverknives.com/freshwater-abuse-and-loss-where-is-it-all-go.

5. Thornton, Philip, Mario Herrero, and Polly Ericksen. "Livestock and Climate Change." *Livestock Xchange*, International Livestock Research Institute (ILRI) website, 2011. Accessed March 2015. https://cgspace.cgiar.org/bitstream/handle/10568/10601/IssueBrief3.pdf.

6. Margulis, Sergio. "Causes of Deforestation of the Brazilian Amazon." Washington, DC: World Bank. © World Bank. 2004. Accessed March 2015. https://openknowledge.worldbank.org/handle/10986/15060.

7. "Animal Waste: What's the Problem?" U.S. Environmental Protection Agency website. http://www.epa.gov/region9/animalwaste/problem.html; Steinfeld, Henning, et al. "Livestock's Long Shadow: Environmental Issues and Options." Rome: Food and Agriculture Organization of the United Nations. 2006. Accessed April 2015. http://www.fao.org/docrep/010/a0701e/a0701e00.htm; http://comfortablyunaware.com/blog/biodiversity-and-food-choice-a-clarification/; "Risk Assessment Evaluation for Concentrated Animal Feeding Operations." U.S. Environmental Protection Agency website. http://nepis.epa.gov/Exe/ZyPURL.cgi?Dockey=901V0100.txt.

CHAPTER ONE

1. "Campaign Timeline: Historic Greenpeace Victories." Greenpeace website. http://www.greenpeacefund.org/timeline-victories/.

2. "Greenpeace Accomplishments in the U.S., 2000–2008." Greenpeace website. http://www.greenpeace.org/usa/wp-content/uploads/legacy/Global/usa/planet3/PDFs/passacantando-timeline.pdf.

3. "Global Greenhouse Gas Emissions Data." U.S. Environmental Protection Agency website. http://www.epa.gov/climatechange/ghgemissions/global.html.

4. Shindell, D. T., et al. "Improved Attribution of Climate Forcing to Emissions." *Science* 326 no. 5953. (2009): 716–18.

5. Johnson, K. A., and D. E. Johnson. "Methane Emissions from Cattle." *Journal of Animal Science* 73, no. 8 (1995). doi:/1995.7382483x. Calculation is based on 250–500 liters per cow per day, times 1.5 billion cows globally, yielding 99 to 198.1 billion gallons, or a rough average of 150 billion gallons of methane globally, per day.

6. "Industry Leaders, Including Energy Companies, Forge Partnerships to Advance Climate Solutions and Reduce Short-Lived Climate Pollutants." United Nations website. September 23, 2014. http://www.un.org/climatechange/summit/wp-content/uploads/sites/2/2014/05/INDUSTRY-PR.pdf.

7. "The Role of Livestock in Climate Change." Food and Agriculture Organization of the United Nations website. http://www.fao.org/agriculture/lead/themes0/climate/en/.

8. Steinfeld, Henning, et al. "Livestock's Long Shadow: Environmental Issues and Options." Rome: Food and Agriculture Organization of the United Nations, 2006.

9. "Role of Livestock in Climate Change." United Nations website. Accessed April 2015.

10. "Rearing Cattle Produces More Greenhouse Gases than Driving Cars, UN Report Warns." UN News Centre website. November 29, 2006. http://www.un.org/apps/news/story.asp?newsID=20772#.VZ6tX8ZVhBd.

11. Walsh, Bryan. "The Triple Whopper Environmental Impact of Global Meat Production." TIME.com. December 16, 2013. http://science.time.com/2013/12/16/the-triple-whopper-environmental-impact-of-global -meat-production/.

12. "Food, Farm Animals and Drugs." Natural Resources Defense Council website. http://www.nrdc.org/food /saving-antibiotics.asp.

13. Calculation is based on Worldwatch Institute analyses that 51 percent of greenhouse gases are attributed to animal agriculture (http://www.worldwatch.org/node/6294).

14. Oppenlander, Richard A. *Food Choice and Sustainability.* Minneapolis, MN: Langdon Street, 2013; "What's the Problem?" United States Environmental Protection Agency website. http://www.epa.gov/region9 /animalwaste/problem.html; "Livestock's Long Shadow: Environmental Issues and Options." Food and Agriculture Organization of the United Nations. 2006. http://www.fao.org/docrep/010/a0701e/a0701e00. htm; "Fire Up the Grill for a Mouthwatering Red, White, and Green July 4." Worldwatch Institute website. Accessed April 2015. http://www.worldwatch.org/fire-grill-mouthwatering-red-white-and-green-july -4th; "Risk Assessment Evaluation for Concentrated Animal Feeding Operations." U.S. Environmental Protection Agency—Office of Research and Development. 2004. http://nepis.epa.gov/Exe/ZyPURL. cgi?Dockey=901V0100.txt; "Biodiversity and Food Choice: A Clarification." *Comfortably Unaware* blog. June 9, 2012. Accessed April 2015. http://comfortablyunaware.com/blog/biodiversity-and-food-choice-a -clarification/; Ede, Sharon. "The Bomb Is Still Ticking. . . ." Post Growth Institute. November 8, 2010. Accessed April 2015. http://postgrowth.org/the-bomb-is-still-ticking/; Vaclav Smil. "Harvesting the Biosphere: The Human Impact." *Population and Development Review* 37, no. 4 (December 2011): 613–36. The proportions are of mass measures in dry weight.

CHAPTER TWO

1. Alexander, Kurtis. "California Drought: Gov. Jerry Brown Urges 20% Cuts." SFGate website. January 17, 2014.

2. Fountain, Henry. "California Drought Is Worsened by Global Warming, Scientists Say." *New York Times.* April 1, 2015.

3. Henson, Bob. "California Dryin.'" Atmos News. January 13, 2014. Accessed April 2015. http://www2.ucar .edu/atmosnews/perspective/10879/california-dryin.

4. "Water Conditions." California Department of Water Resources website. http://www.water.ca.gov /waterconditions/waterconditions.cfm.

5. "California's Water: Climate Change." Association of California Water Agencies website. http://www.acwa .com/content/climate-change/californias-water-climate-change.

6. "Governor Brown Declares Drought State of Emergency." Office of Governor Edmund G Brown Jr. website. January 17, 2014. http://gov.ca.gov/news.php?id=18379.

7. Nagourney, Adam. "California Imposes First Mandatory Water Restrictions to Deal With Drought." *New York Times.* April 1, 2015.

8. "April 2016 Drought News Release Archive." CA.gov website. http://ca.gov/drought/.

9. Nagourney. "California Imposes First Mandatory Water Restrictions."

10. Siders, David, and Jeremy B. White. "California Agriculture, Largely Spared in New Water Restrictions, Wields Huge Clout." *Sacramento Bee.* April 2, 2015.

11. Guo, Jeff. "Agriculture Is 80 Percent of Water Use in California. Why Aren't Farmers Being Forced to Cut Back?" *Washington Post.* April 3, 2015.

12. Catanese, Christina. "Virtual Water, Real Impacts: World Water Day 2012." EPA blog. March 22, 2012. http://blog.epa.gov/healthywaters/2012/03/virtual-water-real-impacts-world-water-day-2012/.

13. Baker, V. L. "Almost Half of the Average Californian's Water Footprint Is Due to the Consumption of Meat and Dairy." *Daily Kos.* March 23, 2015. http://www.dailykos.com/story/2015/03/23/1372642/--Almost-half -of-the-average-Californian-s-water-footprint-is-due-to-consumption-of-meat-and-dairy.

14. "More and Cleaner Water." Center for Science in the Public Interest. Accessed March 2015. http://www.cspinet.org/EatingGreen/pdf/arguments4.pdf.

15. Robbins, John. "2,500 Gallons All Wet?" EarthSave website. Accessed April 2015. http://www.earthsave.org /environment/water.htm.

16. "Draft Plan to Study the Potential Impacts of Hydraulic Fracturing on Drinking Water Resources." U.S. Environmental Protection Agency. February 2011. EPA/600/D-11/001/February 2011. http://yosemite.epa .gov/sab%5CSABPRODUCT.NSF/0/D3483AB445AE61418525775900603E79/$File/Draft+Plan+to+Study+t he+Potential+Impacts+of+Hydraulic+Fracturing+on+Drinking+Water+Resources-February+2011.pdf.

17. Pimentel, David, Bonnie Berger, David Filiberto, Michelle Newton, Benjamin Wolfe, Elizabeth Karabinakis, Steven Clark, Elaine Poon, Elizabeth Abbett, and Sudha Nandagopal. "Water Resources: Agricultural and Environmental Issues." *Bioscience* 54, no. 10 (2004): 909–18. Accessed March 28, 2015. doi:10.1641/0006 -3568(2004)054[0909:WRAAEI]2.0.CO;2; Barber, N.L., 2009, Summary of estimated water use in the United States in 2005: U.S. Geological Survey Fact Sheet 2009–3098, 2 p.

18. "Overview of Greenhouse Gases." U.S. Environmental Protection Agency website. http://epa.gov /climatechange/ghgemissions/gases/ch4.html.

19. "Water." Environmental Working Group website. http://www.ewg.org/meateatersguide/interactive-graphic /water/.

20. "Water Footprint of Crop and Animal Products: A Comparison." Water Footprint Network website. Accessed April 2015. http://waterfootprint.org/en/water-footprint/product-water-footprint/water-footprint-crop-and -animal-products/.

21. Strom, Stephanie. "California's Thirsting Farmland." *New York Times*. April 20, 2014.

22. "California's Extreme Drought, Explained." YouTube video, posted by *New York Times*. July 7, 2014. https://www.youtube.com/watch?v=rHWHuP91c7Y.

23. Nagourney, Adam. "As California Drought Enters 4th Year, Conservation Efforts and Worries Increase." *New York Times*. March 17, 2015.

24. Nagourney, Adam, and Jack Healy. "California Drought Tests History of Endless Growth." *New York Times*. April 4, 2015.

25. "Watering California's Farms." *New York Times*. April 4, 2015.

26. Gillis, Justin, and Matt Richtel. "Beneath California Crops, Groundwater Crisis Grows." *New York Times*. April 5, 2015.

27. Ibid.

28. Porter, Eduardo. "In Parched California, Innovation, Like Water, Has Limits." *New York Times*. April 7, 2015.

29. Holthaus, Eric. "10 Percent of California's Water Goes to Almond Farming. That's Nuts." Accessed April 2015. Slate.com. May 14, 2014.

30. "Are We Eating Too Much Protein?" Infographic in the *Huffington Post*. August 13, 2012.

31. Holthaus. "10 Percent of California's Water Goes to Almond Farming."

32. McWilliams, James. "Meat Makes the Planet Thirsty." *New York Times*. March 7, 2014.

33. Hanson, Blaine, "Irrigation of Agricultural Crops in California." PowerPoint presentation at UC Davis. http://www.arb.ca.gov/fuels/lcfs/workgroups/lcfssustain/hanson.pdf.

34. Holthaus. "10 Percent of California's Water Goes to Almond Farming."

35. Leithead, Alastair. "California Drought: Why Farmers Are 'Exporting Water' to China." BBC News, Los Angeles. February 19, 2014.

36. Oppenlander, Richard A. *Food Choice and Sustainability*. Minneapolis, MN: Langdon Street Press, 2013. Pg. 96.

37. Leithead. "California Drought."

38. Hanson. "Irrigation of Agricultural Crops in California."

39. Mekonnen, M. M., and A. Y. Hoekstra. "A Global Assessment of the Water Footprint of Farm Animal Products," *Ecosystems* 15 (2012): 401–15; Clark, William C. "Biomass Use, Production, Feed Efficiencies, and Greenhouse Gas Emissions from Global Livestock Systems." PNAS.org. October 13, 2013.

40. Oppenlander. *Food Choice and Sustainability*. Pg. 102.

41. "Report: Number of Animals Killed in US Increases in 2010." Farm USA. Accessed April 2015. http://farmusa.org/statistics11.html.

42. Oppenlander. *Food Choice and Sustainability*. Pg. 91.

43. Ibid. Pg. 92.

44. McDermott, Mat. "From Lettuce to Beef, What's the Water Footprint of Your Food?" Accessed April 2015. TreeHugger.com. June 11, 2009.

45. Oppenlander. *Food Choice and Sustainability*. Pg. 92.

46. Hoekstra, Arjen Y. "Water for Animal Products: A Blind Spot in Water Policy." *Environmental Research Letters* 9, no. 9 (2014). doi:10.1088/1748-9326/9/9/091003.

47. Oppenlander. *Food Choice and Sustainability*. Pg. 102.

48. Siders and White. "California Agriculture, Largely Spared."

49. Krulwich, Robert. "Born Wet, Human Babies Are 75 Percent Water. Then Comes The Drying." NPR. org. November 26, 2013.

50. Binns, Corey. "How Long Can a Person Survive Without Water?" LiveScience.com. November 30, 2012. Accessed April 2015.

51. Smolan, Rick, and Jennifer Erwitt. *Blue Planet Run*. San Rafael: Earth Aware, 2007. Pg. 32.

52. "Water Crisis." Water One World Solutions website. Accessed April 2015. http://www.wateroneworldsolutions .org/index.php?option=com_content&view=category&layout=blog&id=38&Itemid=59.

53. Oppenlander, Richard A. "Freshwater Abuse and Loss: Where Is It All Going?" Forks Over Knives website. May 20, 2013. Accessed April 2015. http://www.forksoverknives.com/freshwater-abuse-and-loss-where-is-it -all-going/.

54. "U.N. Raises 'Low' Population Projection for 2050." WorldWatch Institute website. http://www.worldwatch.org/node/6038.

55. "Mission 2012 Clean Water." Massachusetts Institute of Technology website. Accessed April 2015. http://web.mit.edu/12.000/www/m2012/finalwebsite/problem/groundwater.shtml.

56. Dimick, Dennis. "If You Think the Water Crisis Can't Get Worse, Wait Until the Aquifers Are Drained." National Geographic website. August 21, 2014. http://news.nationalgeographic.com/news/2014/08 /140819-groundwater-california-drought-aquifers-hidden-crisis/.

57. Steward, David. R. "Tapping Unsustainable Groundwater Stores for Agricultural Production in the High Plains Aquifer of Kansas, Projections to 2110." PNAS Plus—Physical Sciences—Sustainability Science. July 16, 2013. doi: 0.1073/pnas.1220351110.

58. Little, Jane Braxton. "The Ogallala Aquifer: Saving a Vital U.S. Water Source." Scientific American website. March 1, 2009. http://www.scientificamerican.com/article/the-ogallala-aquifer/.

59. Mufson, Steven. "Keystone XL Pipeline May Threaten Aquifer That Irrigates Much of the Central U.S." *Washington Post*. August 6, 2012.

60. Schneider, Jeffery A., "The Great Underground Sponge: Ogallala." Environmental Investigations. Accessed April 2015. http://www.oswego.edu/~schneidr/CHE300/envinv/EnvInv12.html.

61. "Mission 2012 Clean Water." MIT website.

62. Little. "The Ogallala Aquifer."

63. Oppenlander. *Food Choice and Sustainability*. Pg. 97.

64. Little. "The Ogallala Aquifer."

65. Oppenlander. *Food Choice and Sustainability*. Pg. 97.

66. Ibid. Pg. 98.

67. Ibid. Pg. 89.

68. Ayres, Ed. "Will We Still Eat Meat?" *Time*. November 8, 1999. *Washington Post*. September 12, 2013.

69. Steward. "Tapping Unsustainable Groundwater Stores."

70. Plumer, Brad. "How Long before the Great Plains Runs out of Water?"*Washington Post*. September 12, 2013.

71. Oppenlander. *Food Choice and Sustainability*. Pg. 111.

72. "Water Trivia Facts." U.S. Environmental Protection Agency website.

73. "Choosing Wildlife Forever." Michigan Land Use Institute. Accessed April 2015. www.mlui.org.

74. "Great Lakes: Basic Information." U.S. Environmental Protection Agency website. http://water.epa.gov/learn /kids/drinkingwater/water_trivia_facts.cfm; Oppenlander. *Food Choice and Sustainability*. Pg. 98.

75. Oppenlander. *Food Choice and Sustainability*. Pg. 111.

76. Erdman, Jon. "California's Snowpack at Record Early-April Low; Sierra Snow Survey Finds Bare Ground." The Weather Channel website. April 10, 2015. http://www.weather.com/climate-weather/drought/news /california-sierra-snowpack-record-low-april-2015.

CHAPTER THREE

1. "Erik Ethan Markegard Bio." Accessed March 2015. http://www.markegardfamily.com/erik/.

2. "Doniga Feliz Markegard Bio." Accessed March 2015. http://www.markegardfamily.com/doniga/.

3. "Shop." Markegard Family Grass-Fed website. Accessed March 2015. http://www.markegardfamily.com/ shop/.

4. Oppenlander, Richard A. *Food Choice and Sustainability*. Minneapolis, MN: Langdon Street, 2013. Pg. 80.

5. "U.S. Meat and Poultry Production & Consumption: An Overview." American Meat Institute website. www.meatinstitute.org/index.php?ht=a/GetDocumentAction/i/48781; Barnard, Neal. "Do We Eat Too Much Meat?" *Huffington Post*. May 25, 2011. http://www.huffingtonpost.com/neal-barnard-md/american-diet‹do -we-eat-too-much_b_805980.html; DeBruicker, Julia. "How Much Meat Do We Eat, Anyway?" Center for a Livable Future. March 21, 2011. Accessed April 2015. http://www.livablefutureblog.com/2011/03/how-much -meat-do-we-eat-anyway.

6. Vesterby, Marlow, and Kenneth S. Krupa. "Major Uses of Land in the United States, 1997." Resource Economics Division, Economic Research Service, U.S. Department of Agriculture. Statistical Bulletin No. 973. August 2001; Ibid.; "Rearing Cattle Produces More Greenhouse Gases than Driving Cars, UN Report Warns." UN News Centre. November 29, 2006. www.un.org/apps/news/story.asp?newsID=20772# .VcKzJvlViko.

7. "Economics of Beef." Beef.org. Accessed March 2015. http://www.beef.org/udocs/Beef%20Bytes%20 Economics.pdf.

8. Capper, Judith L. "The Environmental Impact of Grain-fed vs. Grass-fed Beef." April 27, 2012. www.academia.edu. /1720592/The_Environmental_Impact_of_Grain-fed_vs._Grass-fed_Beef.

9. Saperstein, Guy. "Cows, Rice Fields and Big Agriculture Consumes Well Over 90% of California's Water." Alternet.com. May 17, 2014. Accessed May 2015. http://www.alternet.org/cows-rice-fields-and-big -agriculture-consumes-well-over-90-californias-water.

10. Capper. "Impact of Grain-fed vs. Grass-fed Beef."

11. Chang, Samantha. "Experts Tout Grass-fed Beef as Healthier but Bad for Environment." Examiner.com. October 8, 2013.

12. "About Us." American Farmers for the Advancement and Conservation of Technology (AFACT). 2008. Accessed March 2015. http://itisafact.org/about-us/.

13. "American Farmers for the Advancement and Conservation of Technology." Source Watch. 2012. Accessed May 2015. http://www.sourcewatch.org/index.php?title=American_Farmers_for_the_Advancement_and _Conservation_of_Technology.

14. Saperstein. "Cows, Rice Fields and Big Agriculture."

15. "Global Greenhouse Gas Emissions Data." U.S. Environmental Protection Agency. http://www.epa.gov /climatechange/ghgemissions/global.html.

16. http://www.brilliantplanet.org/environmental-articles/. Accessed March 2015.

17. "About WWP." Western Watersheds Project. Accessed April 2015. http://www.westernwatersheds.org/about/.

18. Curit, Rachel. "Is Grass-Fed Beef Better? A Look Into How Much of America's Land Is Used for Cattle -Grazing." One Green Planet. July 22, 2014. Accessed March 2015. http://www.onegreenplanet.org /animalsandnature/america-land-cattle-grazing/.

19. "Cattle Grazing and the Loss of Biodiversity in the East Bay." Center for Biological Diversity. Berkeley, CA. http://www.biologicaldiversity.org/publications/papers/GRAZING-JM.PDF.

20. Ibid.

21. Ibid.

22. "Welcome to Clover County!" Clover Petaluma. 2015. http://www.cloverpetaluma.com/home/our-story/.

23. Adams, Mike. "Why It Takes 2,000 Gallons of Fresh Water to Produce One Gallon of Milk (transcript)." NaturalNews. June 2, 2008. Accessed May 2015. http://www.naturalnews.com/023341_water_milk_organic .html.

24. Hoekstra, Arjen Y. "The Hidden Water Resource Use Behind Meat and Dairy." doi:10.1016/j. wri.2013.03.001. http://waterfootprint.org/media/downloads/Hoekstra-2012-Water-Meat-Dairy.pdf.

25. "Farm Milk Production." USDA Economic Research Service website. 2012. http://www.ers.usda.gov/topics /animal-products/dairy/background.aspx#.VEmTg4vF-wk.

26. "Dairy Facts—Dairy Cows." Midwest Dairy Association website. http://www.midwestdairy.com/0t164p176 /dairy-cows/.

27. Lurie, Julia, and Alex Park. "It Takes HOW Much Water to Make Greek Yogurt?!" *Mother Jones*. March 10, 2014. Accessed March 2015. http://www.motherjones.com/environment/2014/03/california-water-suck.

28. Hanson, Blaine. "Irrigation of Agricultural Crops in California." PowerPoint presentation at UC Davis. http://www.arb.ca.gov/fuels/lcfs/workgroups/lcfssustain/hanson.pdf.

29. McWilliams, James. "Meat Makes the Planet Thirsty." *New York Times*. March 7, 2014.

30. "State Agricultural Profiles." U.S. Environmental Protection Agency website. http://www.epa.gov/region9/ag /ag-state.html.

31. U.S. Department of Agriculture. Agricultural Waste Management Field Handbook. Natural Resources Conservation Service (1992). Retrieved August 27, 2012.

32. Chastain, J. P. "Pollution Potential of Livestock Manure." Minnesota/Wisconsin Engineering Notes (1995).

33. "Background of Dairy Production in the U.S." U.S. Environmental Protection Agency website. http://www.epa.gov/oecaagct/ag101/dairybackground.html.

34. "Greenhouse Gas Emissions from the Dairy Sector: A Life Cycle Assessment." Food and Agriculture Organization of the United Nations. 2010. http://www.fao.org/docrep/012/k7930e/k7930e00.pdf.

35. Ibid.

36. "The Role of Livestock in Climate Change." Food and Agriculture Organization of the United Nations website. www.fao.org.

37. "Climate and Environmental Impacts." Environmental Working Group website. Accessed April 2015. http://www.ewg.org/meateatersguide/a-meat-eaters-guide-to-climate-change-health-what-you-eat-matters /climate-and-environmental-impacts/.

CHAPTER FOUR

1. Foer, Jonathan Safran. *Eating Animals*. New York: Back Bay Books, 2009. Pg. 107.

2. "Regulatory Definitions of Large CAFOs, Medium CAFOs, and Small CAFOs." U.S. Environmental Protection Agency website. http://www.epa.gov/npdes/pubs/sector_table.pdf.

3. "Industrial Livestock Production." Grace/Sustainable Table website. Accessed April 2015. http://www.sustainabletable.org/859/industrial-livestock-production.

4. "What Is a Factory Farm?" ASPCA website. Accessed March 2015. http://www.aspca.org/fight-cruelty/farm -animal-cruelty/what-factory-farm.

5. "Factory Farms: Overview." A Well-Fed World website. Accessed March 2015. http://awfw.org/factory-farms/.

6. "What Is a CAFO?" U.S. Environmental Protection Agency website. http://www.epa.gov/region7/water/cafo/.

7. "Animal Feeding Operations." U.S. Environmental Protection Agency website. http://www.epa.gov /agriculture/anafoidx.html.

8. "What Is a CAFO?" U.S. EPA website.

9. "Factory Farm Map." Food & Water Watch website. Accessed March 2015. http://www.factoryfarmmap.org/.

10. "Factory Farming: In the Beginning . . . Unintended Consequences." Factory-Farming.com. Accessed March 2015. http://www.factory-farming.com/factory_farming.html.

11. "Regulatory Definitions of CAFOs." U.S. EPA website.

12. Aillery, M., et al. "Managing Manure to Improve Air and Water Quality." USDA Economic Research Report 9. 2005; "Industrial Livestock Production," Grace/Sustainable Table. Accessed March 2015. www.sustainabletable.org.

13. "Factory Farming and the Environment." Farm Sanctuary. Accessed April 2015. http://www.farmsanctuary.org/learn/factory-farming/factory-farming-and-the-environment/.

14. Imhoff, Daniel, ed. *CAFO*. San Rafael: Earth Aware, 2010. Pg. 47.

15. U.S. Department of Agriculture, Natural Resources Conservation Service, and U.S. Environmental Protection Agency. "Unified National Strategy for Animal Feeding Operations." Draft. September 11, 1998; Imhoff. *CAFO*. Pg. 43.

16. Huffman, R. L., and P. W. Westerman. "Estimated Seepage Losses from Established Swine Waste Lagoons in the Lower Coastal Plain in North Carolina." *Transactions of the American Society of Agricultural Engineers* 38, no. 2 (1995): 449–53.

17. Rice, Pamela. *101 Reasons Why I'm a Vegetarian*. New York: Lantern Books, 2005. Pg. 5.

18. "Facts about Pollution from Livestock Farms." Natural Resources Defense Council website. http://www.nrdc.org/water/pollution/ffarms.asp.

19. "In the Aftermath of Floyd." North Carolina Riverkeepers & Waterkeeper Alliance website. Accessed March 2015. http://www.riverlaw.us/hurricanefloyd.html.

20. "Restoration and Spending Plan Marks Farm Natural Resource Damages Settlement." DEC Case# R6-20051021-44. November 7, 2014. http://www.dec.ny.gov/docs/fish_marine_pdf/mfarmresplfin.pdf.

21. "Facts about Pollution from Livestock Farms." Natural Resources Defense Council website. http://www.nrdc.org/water/pollution/ffarms.asp.

22. Imhoff. *CAFO*. Pg. 47; Hribar, Carrie. "Understanding Concentrated Animal Feeding Operations and Their Impact on Communities." CDC website. http://www.cdc.gov/nceh/ehs/docs/understanding_cafos_nalboh.pdf.

23. Imhoff. *CAFO*. Pg. 47.

24. Hribar. "Understanding Concentrated Animal Feeding Operations." CDC website.

25. "Waste Management." Grace/Sustainable Table website. Accessed March 2015. www.sustainabletable.org/906/waste-management.

26. Clancy, K. "Greener Pastures: How Grass-fed Beef and Milk Contribute to Healthy Eating." Union of Concerned Scientists. 2006.

27. Hribar. "Understanding Concentrated Animal Feeding Operations." CDC website.

28. Ibid.

29. "The Dangers of Factory Farming." Consumer Alert. Humane Farming Association. 2000.

30. Imhoff. *CAFO*. Pg. 162.

31. Ibid. Pg. 160.

32. Richards, Jennie. "The Life of a Factory Farm Chicken." Humane Decisions website. October 31, 2014. Accessed April 2015. www.humanedecisions.com/issues/animals-used-for-food/factory-farming/chickens/chicken-industry.

33. Imhoff. *CAFO*. Pg. 160.

34. Marcus, Erik. *Vegan: The New Ethics of Eating*. Ithaca: McBooks Press, 2001. Pg. 112.

35. "The Chicken Industry." PETA. www.peta.org.

36. Foer. *Eating Animals*. Pg. 131.

37. Marcus. *Vegan: The New Ethics of Eating*. Pg. 109.

38. Garces, Leah. "Why We Haven't Seen Inside a Broiler Chicken Factory Farm in a Decade." Food Safety News. January 24, 2013.

39. Marcus. *Vegan: The New Ethics of Eating*. Pg. 109.

40. Mallove, Zach. "Court Rules Against Meat Industry." Food Safety News. April 1, 2010.

41. Marcus. *Vegan: The New Ethics of Eating*. Pg. 109.

42. Ibid. Pg. 112.

43. Eisnitz, Gail A. *Slaughterhouse*. Amherst, NY: Prometheus Books. 2007, Pg. 163–4.

44. Foer. *Eating Animals*. Pg. 113.

45. Hofstad, M. S. *Diseases of Poultry*. 6th ed. Ames, IA: Iowa State University Press, 1972.

46. "Broiler Chickens." Canadians for Ethical Treatment of Farmed Animals. Accessed March 2015. http://cetfa.org/farm-animals/broiler-chickens/.

47. Ibid.

48. Richards. "The Life of a Factory Farm Chicken." Humane Decisions website.

49. "Pig Mutilation." Natural Pig Farming. 2013. Accessed April 2015. http://www.naturalpigfarming.com/pigmutilation.htm.

50. "Proper Way to Ear Notch Pigs." The Pig Site. May 13, 2004. Accessed April 2015. http://www.thepigsite.com/articles/1100/proper-way-to-ear-notch-pigs/.

51. "Pigs on Factory Farms." The American Society for the Prevention of Cruelty to Animals. Accessed April 2015. https://www.aspca.org/fight-cruelty/farm-animal-cruelty/pigs-factory-farms.

52. Video. "Helpless and Abused." *Rolling Stone* website. http://www.rollingstone.com/feature/belly-beast-meat-factory-farms-animal-activists.

53. Kennedy, Tom. "Undercover Investigation Reveals Disturbing and Inhumane Treatment of Factory Farm Animals." W5. December 7, 2012.

54. Eisnitz. *Slaughterhouse*. Pg. 220.

55. "Farm Animal Cruelty Glossary: Gestation." The American Society for the Prevention of Cruelty to Animals website. Accessed March 2015. https://www.aspca.org/fight-cruelty/farm-animal-cruelty/farm-animal-cruelty-glossary#gestation.

56. "Crammed into Gestation Crates." The Humane Society of the United States. http://www.humanesociety.org/issues/confinement_farm/facts/gestation_crates.html.

57. Philpott, Tom. "You Won't Believe What Pork Producers Do to Pregnant Pigs." *Mother Jones* website. July/August, 2013. Accessed March 2015. http://www.motherjones.com/environment/2013/06/pregnant-sows-gestation-crates-abuse.

58. Marcus. *Vegan: The New Ethics of Eating*. Pg. 116.

59. Philpott. "What Pork Producers Do to Pregnant Pigs." *Mother Jones* website.

60. Marcus. *Vegan: The New Ethics of Eating*. Pg. 117.

61. Ibid. Pg. 116.

62. "Farm Animal Cruelty Glossary: Gestation." ASPCA website.

63. Terris, Ben. "Why an Egg Amendment in Farm Bill Has Pig Lobbyists Flapping." *National Journal*. July 25, 2012. http://www.nationaljournal.com/blogs/influencealley/2012/07/why-an-egg-amendment-in-farm-bill-has-pig-lobbyists-flapping-25.

64. Ridgen, Bob. *The Economics of Pig Production*. Ipswich, UK: Farming Press Books, 1993. Pg. 515.

65. Ibid.

66. "Cows on Factory Farms." The American Society for the Prevention of Cruelty to Animals website. https://www.aspca.org/fight-cruelty/farm-animal-cruelty/cows-factory-farms.

67. Marcus. *Vegan: The New Ethics of Eating*. Pg. 134.

68. Ibid. Pg. 132.

69. "Cows on Factory Farms." ASPCA website.

70. Marcus. *Vegan: The New Ethics of Eating*. Pg. 135.

71. Ibid. Pg. 136.

72. Ibid. Pg. 135.

73. Lyman, Howard. *Mad Cowboy*. New York: Touchstone, 1998. Pg. 12–13.

74. "Cow Transport and Slaughter." PETA. http://www.peta.org/issues/animals-used-for-food/factory-farming/cows/cow-transport-slaughter/.

75. Eisnitz. *Slaughterhouse*. Pg. 102–4.

76. Foer. *Eating Animals*. Pg. 109.

77. Ibid. Pg. 132.

78. Marcus. *Vegan: The New Ethics of Eating*. Pg. 139.

79. Foer. *Eating Animals*. Pg. 133.

80. Marcus. *Vegan: The New Ethics of Eating*. Pg. 140–1.

81. Foer. *Eating Animals*. Pg. 133.

82. Eisnitz. *Slaughterhouse*. Pg. 166–8.

83. "Water in Meat and Poultry." United States Department of Agriculture website. http://www.fsis.usda.gov/wps /portal/fsis/topics/food-safety-education/get-answers/food-safety-fact-sheets/meat-preparation/water-in-meat- and-poultry/ct_index.

84. Eisnitz. *Slaughterhouse*. Pg. 20.

85. Solomon, Avi. "Working Undercover in a Slaughterhouse: An Interview with Timothy Pachirat." BoingBoing.net. March 8, 2012. Accessed April 2015. http://boingboing.net/2012/03/08/working-undercover -in-a-slaugh.html.

86. Schlosser, Eric. *Fast Food Nation*. New York: Perennial Books, 2002. Pg. 172.

87. Eisnitz. *Slaughterhouse*. Pg. 197–8, 203–4.

88. Ibid. Pg. 29.

89. Ibid. Pg. 132–3.

90. Ibid. Pg. 130.

91. Ibid. Pg. 90–1.

92. Foer. *Eating Animals*. Pg. 155–6.

93. Eisnitz. *Slaughterhouse*. Pg. 195–6.

94. 92 STAT. 1069—HUMANE METHODS OF SLAUGHTER ACT. October 10, 1978. www.animallaw.info /article/detailed-discussion-humane-methods-slaughter-act.

95. Ibid.

96. Eisnitz. *Slaughterhouse*. Pg. 101.

97. Marcus. *Vegan: The New Ethics of Eating*. Pg. 147.

98. 92 STAT. 1069—HUMANE METHODS OF SLAUGHTER ACT. October 10, 1978.

99. Eisnitz. *Slaughterhouse*. 243.

100. Ibid. Pg. 172.

101. Schlosser. *Fast Food Nation*. Pg. 173.

102. Schlosser, Eric. "The Chain Never Stops." *Mother Jones* website. July/August 2001. Accessed April 2015. http://www.motherjones.com/politics/2001/07/dangerous-meatpacking-jobs-eric-schlosser.

103. Eisnitz. *Slaughterhouse*. 304.

104. "Regulatory Definitions of CAFOs." U.S. EPA website.

105. Singer, Isaac Bashevis. *Enemies: A Love Story*. New York: Farrar, Straus and Giroux, 1972.

CHAPTER FIVE

1. "Environment." Pew Commission on Industrial Farm Animal Production. http://ncifap.org/issues /environment/; GAO/RCED-99-205 Waste Management Practices. July 26, 1999. http://gao.gov /archive/1999/rc99205.pdf.

2. GAO/RCED-99-205 Waste Management Practices. July 26, 1999.

3. Based on calculations of 1 pound of waste per 1 square foot at 1.4 billion tons.

4. "Louisiana Universities Marine Consortium." Press release. August 4, 2014. http://www.gulfhypoxia.net/. Actual number is more than 550 dead zones.

5. Smith, Melodi, and Jason Hanna. "Gulf of Mexico 'Dead Zone' Is the Size of Connecticut." CNN. August 5, 2014. http://www.cnn.com/2014/08/05/tech/gulf-of-mexico-dead-zone/.

6. Tuttle, Will. *The World Peace Diet*. New York: Lantern Books, 2005. Pg. 96.

7. "*Pfiesteria piscicida*: Facts about a Fish Killer." Sea Grant University of Delaware. October 1, 1997. http://www.udel.edu/db/pfiesteria%20flyer%20pdf/pfiesteria%20index/pfflyer.pdf.

8. "Factory Farm Map, 2007." FactoryFarmMap.org. Accessed April 2015.
   http://www.factoryfarmmap.org/#animal:all;location:CA;year:2007.

9. Worm, B., et al. "Impacts of Biodiversity Loss on Ocean Ecosystem Services." *Science* 314, no. 5800
   (November 2006): 787–790. doi:10.1126/science.1132294; DeNoon, Daniel. "Salt-Water Fish Extinction Seen
   By 2048." CBS News. November 2, 2006.

10. The number may be as high as 2.7 trillion animals: http://fishcount.org.uk/fish-welfare-in-commercial
    -fishing/estimate-of-fish-numbers; Montaigne, Fen. "Still Waters: The Global Fish Crisis." *National
    Geographic.* http://ocean.nationalgeographic.com/ocean/global-fish-crisis-article/.

11. "A Study of the Options for Utilization of Bycatch and Discards from Marine Capture Fisheries: Discards and
    Bycatch in Shrimp Trawl Fisheries." FAO Fisheries and Aquaculture Department. October 1997.
    www.fao.org/docrep/W6602E/w6602E09.htm.

12. Oppenlander, Richard A. *Comfortably Unaware.* New York: Beaufort Books, 2012. Pg. 51; "Utilization of
    Bycatch and Discards from Marine Capture Fisheries." FAO Fisheries and Aquaculture Department.

13. Goldenberg, Suzanne. "America's Nine Most Wasteful Fisheries Named." *The Guardian.* www.theguardian.com
    /environment/2014/mar/20/americas-nine-most-wasteful-fisheries-named; Smith, Zak, Margaretmary
    Gilroy, Matthew Eisenson, Erin Schnettler, Stephanie Stefanski. "Net Loss: The Killing of Marine
    Mammals and Foreign Fisheries." NRDC.org website. January 2014. R:13-11-B. www.nrdc.org/wildlife
    /marine/files/mammals-foreign-fisheries-report.pdf.

14. Watson, Paul. "Consider the Fishes." Veg News. March–April 2003. Pg. 27.

15. Oppenlander. *Food Choice and Sustainability.* Pg. 122–3.

16. Hance, Jeremy. "Using Fish as Livestock Feed Threatens Global Fisheries." Mongabay. November 17, 2009.
    http://news.mongabay.com/2009/1118-hance_fishmeal.html.

17. Ibid.

18. John Bostock, et al. "Aquaculture: Global Status and Trends." The Royal Society Publishing website. August
    16, 2010. doi: 10.1098/rstb.2010.0170.

19. "Fish to Pellets to Fish Again." Food & Water Watch. Accessed April 2015. http://www.foodandwaterwatch
    .org/common-resources/fish/fish-farming/fish-to-pellets-to-fish-again/.

20. Tuttle. *The World Peace Diet.* Pg. 100.

21. Poulter, Sean. "Salmon Health Alert." *DailyMail Online.* http://www.dailymail.co.uk/health/article-205547
    /Salmon-health-alert.html.

22. "Farmed Salmon and Human Health." Pure Salmon Campaign. Accessed April 2015. http://www.puresalmon
    .org/human_health.html.

23. Tuttle. *The World Peace Diet.* Pg. 101.

24. "Milestone: 50 Percent of Fish Are Now Farmed." LiveScience.com September 8, 2009. Accessed March 2015.
    http://www.livescience.com/5682-milestone-50-percent-fish-farmed.html.

25. "Overfishing: A Threat to Marine Biodiversity." UN News Center. Accessed March 2015. http://www.un.org
    /events/tenstories/06/story.asp?storyid=800; "General Situation of World Fish Stocks." Food and Agriculture
    Organization of the United Nations. http://www.fao.org/newsroom/common/ecg/1000505/en/stocks.pdf.

26. Oppenlander. *Food Choice and Sustainability.* Pg. 133.

27. Ibid. Pg. 134.

28. Ibid. Pg. 122.

29. "Krill Harvest Certification Upsets Conservationists." Globefish. Accessed March 2015.
    http://www.globefish.org/krill-harvest-certification-upsets-conservationists.html.

30. "Partnering for Success: McDonald's Announces Global Commitment on Deforestation." McDonald's. Press
    release. April 21, 2015. http://www.mcdonalds.ca/content/dam/Canada/en/in_the_community
    /McDonald-s%20-%20Partnering%20for%20Success.pdf.

31. Burton, Bob. "Something Fishy." PR Watch website. October 2, 2007. Accessed April 2015.
    http://www.prwatch.org/news/2007/10/6401/something-fishy.

32. Climate One Radio. Episode 2. Transcript: http://www.prx.org/pieces/80283/transcripts/183795.

33. Oppenlander. *Food Choice and Sustainability.* Pg. 130.

34. "Big-Fish Stocks Fall 90 Percent Since 1950, Study Says." National Geographic website. May 15, 2003. http://news.nationalgeographic.com/news/2003/05/0515_030515_fishdecline.html.

35. "Shark Fin Trade Myths and Truths: BYCATCH." Shark Savers website. Accessed April 2015. http://www.sharksavers.org/files/8613/3185/9956/Shark_Bycatch_FACT_SHEET_Shark_Savers.pdf.

36. Eriksson, Britas Klemens. "Does Overfishing Promote Algal Blooms?" Department of Marine Benthis Ecology and Evolution, Centre for Ecological and Evolutionary Studies, University of Groningen. doi:10.2861/57083; Kaplan, Matt. "Overfishing Linked to Algal Blooms." Nature.com. December 1, 2009. Accessed March 2015. http://www.nature.com/news/2009/091201/full/news.2009.1116.html.

37. Eriksson. "Does Overfishing Promote Algal Blooms?"

38. "What Are Phytoplankton?" National Ocean Service. Accessed March 2015. http://oceanservice.noaa.gov/facts/phyto.html.

39. Caciagli, Laura. "The 'Phytoplankton Effect.' New Insights from a Coupled Climate Model." CMCC.it. October 10, 2012.

40. Kaplan. "Overfishing Linked to Algal Blooms." Nature.com.

41. "Ocean Warming." Ocean Scientists for Informed Policy. Accessed March 2015. http://www.oceanscientists.org/index.php/topics/ocean-warming; Oppenlander. *Food Choice and Sustainability*. Pg. 117.

42. Oppenlander. *Food Choice and Sustainability*. Pg. 118.

43. Tuttle. *The World Peace Diet*. Pg. 101.

CHAPTER SIX

1. Elridge, Niles. "The Sixth Extinction." Action Bioscience website. Accessed April 2015. http://www.actionbioscience.org/evolution/eldredge2.html; "Mass Extinction of Species Has Begun." Macquarie University, Phys.org. February 23, 2006. Accessed April 2015. http://phys.org/news11151.html.

2. "Mass Extinctions: What Causes Animal Die-Offs?" National Geographic website. http://science.nationalgeographic.com/science/prehistoric-world/mass-extinction/.

3. Kolbert, Elizabeth. *The Sixth Extinction: An Unnatural History*. New York: Henry Holt and Company, 2014. Pg. 267.

4. Ibid. Pg. 267, 268.

5. Butler, Rhett. "Rainforest Diversity—Origins and Implications." Mongabay.com. July 27, 2006. Accessed April 2015. http://rainforests.mongabay.com/0301.htm.

6. "Tropical Rainforest." Blue Planet Biomes website. Accessed April 2015. http://www.blueplanetbiomes.org/rainforest.htm.

7. Oppenlander, Richard A. *Comfortably Unaware: What We Choose to Eat is Killing Us and Our Planet*. New York: Beaufort Books, 2012. Pg. 23.

8. Butler. "Rainforest Diversity."

9. Oppenlander. *Comfortably Unaware*. Pg. 24.

10. Kolbert. *The Sixth Extinction*. Pg. 151.

11. Steinfeld, Henning. "Livestock's Long Shadow: Environmental Issues and Options." Rome: Food and Agriculture Organization of the United Nations, 2006. www.fao.org; "How Eating Meat Hurts Wildlife and the Planet." Take Extinction off Your Plate website. Accessed April 2015. www.takeextinctionoffyourplate.com/meat_and_wildlife.html.

12. Margulis, Sérgio. "Causes of Deforestation of the Brazilian Amazon." World Bank, Washington, D.C. 2003. Accessed April 2015. https://openknowledge.worldbank.org/bitstream/handle/10986/15060/277150PAPER0wbwp0no1022.pdf?sequence=1.

13. Reid, Walter V. and Kenton R. Miller. "Keeping Options Alive: The Scientific Basis for Conserving Biodiversity." World Resources Institute, Washington, D.C. 1993. Accessed April 2015. http://pdf.wri.org/keepingoptionsalive_bw.pdf; "Avoiding Unsustainable Rainforest Wood." Rainforest Relief website. Accessed March 2015. http://rainforestrelief.org/What_to_Avoid_and_Alternatives/Rainforest_Wood.html.

14. "Facts about the Rainforest." Save the Rainforest website. Accessed April 2015. http://www.savetherainforest.org/savetherainforest_007.htm.

15. "What Is Deforestation?" Mongabay website. Accessed April 2015. http://kids.mongabay.com/lesson_plans /lisa_algee/deforestation.html.

16. "Rainforest Stats." Save the Amazon Coalition website. Accessed April 2015. http://www.savetheamazon.org /rainforeststats.htm.

17. Ibid.

18. Taylor, L. *The Healing Power of Rainforest Herbs.* Garden City Park, NY: Square One Publishers, 2004.

19. "Rainforests: Facts about Rainforests." The Nature Conservancy website. Accessed April 2015. http://www.nature.org/ourinitiatives/urgentissues/rainforests/rainforests-facts.xml.

20. "Crops of the Amazon and Orinoco Regions: Their Origin, Decline, and Future." Food and Agriculture Organization of the United Nations website. http://www.fao.org/docrep/t0646e/T0646E0j.htm.

21. "The Uncontacted Indians of Brazil." Survival International website. Accessed April 2015. http://www.survivalinternational.org/tribes/uncontacted-brazil.

22. "First Film Footage of Amazon Tribe." BBC News website. February 3, 2011. http://www.bbc.com/news/world -latin-america-12360013.

23. "Rainforest Stats." Save the Amazon Coalition website.

24. "Tropical Rainforest." Blue Planet Biomes website.

25. Oppenlander. *Comfortably Unaware.* Pg. 23.

26. Ibid. Pg. 25.

27. Ibid. Pg. 22.

28. "KFC Exposed for Trashing the Amazon Rainforest for Buckets of Chicken." Greenpeace website. May 17, 2006. Accessed April 2015. http://www.greenpeace.org/international/en/press/releases/kfc-exposed-for -trashing-the-a/.

29. Oppenlander. *Comfortably Unaware.* Pg. 26.

30. "UN Launches International Year of Deserts and Desertification." UN News Centre website. 2006. http://www.un.org/apps/news/story.asp?NewsID=17076#.VUFCS2a27oB.

31. "World Day to Combat Desertification." United Nations website. http://www.un.org/en/events /desertificationday/background.shtml.

32. Savory, Allan. "How to Fight Desertification and Reverse Climate Change." TED Talk video. Filmed Feb 2013. http://www.ted.com/talks/allan_savory_how_to_green_the_world_s_deserts_and_reverse_climate _change?language=en#t-1171109.

33. Monbiot, George. "Eat More Meat and Save the World: The Latest Implausible Farming Miracle." *The Guardian.* August 4, 2014.

34. Ibid.

35. Carter, John, et al. "Holistic Management: Misinformation on the Science of Grazed Ecosystems." *International Journal of Biodiversity,* 2014, Article ID 163431. http://www.hindawi.com/journals /ijbd/2014/163431/.

36. Savory. "How to Fight Desertification." TED Talk video.

37. McWilliams, James. "All Sizzle and No Steak." Slate.com. April 22, 2013.

38. Ibid.

39. Carter, et al. "Holistic Management: Misinformation."

40. Oppenlander, Richard A. *Food Choice and Sustainability.* Minneapolis, MN: Langdon Street Press, 2013. Pg. 63.

41. "Wild Horse Preservation: About." Wild Horse Preservation website. Accessed April 2015. http://wildhorsepreservation.org/about.

42. "Wild Horse Preservation: About." Wild Horse Preservation website.

43. "The USDA's War on Wildlife." Predator Defense website. Accessed April 2015. http://predatordefense.org/USDA.htm.

44. Maughan, Ralph. "Wedge Wolf Pack Will Be Killed Because of Its Increasing Beef Consumption." The Wildlife News. September 22, 2012. Accessed May 2015. http://www.thewildlifenews.com/2012/09/22 /wedge-wolf-pack-will-be-killed-because-of-increasing-beef-consumption/.

45. "Frequently Asked Questions about the Gray Wolf in the United States." The Humane Society website. http://www.humanesociety.org/animals/wolves/facts/faq_gray_wolf.html.

46. "10 Reasons We Need Wolves." *Mother Jones* website. Accessed April 2015. http://www.motherjones.com/slideshows/2011/04/wolves-protect-climate-change/staring-wolf.

47. "Lindsey Allen—Bio." Rainforest Action Network website. Accessed April 2015. http://www.ran.org/lindsey-allen.

48. "Indonesia: Palm Oil Expansion Unaffected by Forest Moratorium." USDA Foreign Agricultural Service website. 2013. http://www.pecad.fas.usda.gov/highlights/2013/06/indonesia/.

49. Butler, Rhett. "Amazon Destruction." Mongabay website. Accessed April 2015. http://rainforests.mongabay.com/amazon/amazon_destruction.html.

50. Yildiz, Ashley Schaeffer, "Eat Plan(e)t-Based on March 20, Join Meatout 2015!" Rainforest Action Network website. March 19, 2015. http://www.ran.org/meatout.

51. Ibid.

52. Butler, Rhett. "Rising Meat Consumption Pushes Farming Past Deforestation as Global Warming Driver." Mongabay website. January 18, 2015. Accessed April 2015. http://news.mongabay.com/2015/0118-afolu_emissions.html.

53. "Amazon Watch—Staff." Amazon Watch website. Accessed April 2015. http://amazonwatch.org/about/staff-and-board.

CHAPTER SEVEN

1. "Expanded Story of Sister Dorothy Stang." Sisters of Notre Dame de Namur website. 2010. Accessed April 2015. http://www.sndohio.org/sister-dorothy/Expanded-Story.cfm.

2. Dear, John. "Sr. Dorothy Stang, Martyr of the Amazon." National Catholic Reporter: The Independent News Source website. October 2007. Accessed April 2015. http://ncronline.org/blogs/road-peace/sr-dorothy-stang-martyr-amazon.

3. "Expanded Story of Sister Dorothy Stang." Sisters of Notre Dame de Namur website.

4. "Care for Creation: Commemorating the Life of Sr. Dorothy Stang, SNDdeN." The World Community for Christian Meditation website. Accessed April 2015. http://www.wccm.org/content/care-creation-commemorating-life-sr-dorothy-stang-sndden.

5. "Brazilian Rancher Jailed for Murder of American Nun Dorothy Stang." *The Guardian*. September 20, 2013.

6. "Expanded Story of Sister Dorothy Stang." Sisters of Notre Dame de Namur website.

7. Murphy, Roseanne. *Martyr of the Amazon: The Life of Sister Dorothy Stang.* Maryknoll, New York: Orbis Books, 2007.

8. Dear. "Sr. Dorothy Stang, Martyr of the Amazon."

9. Ibid.

10. Ibid.

11. "Brazilian Rancher Jailed." *The Guardian*.

12. Ibid.

13. Ibid.

14. "Deadly Environment." Global Witness website. April 15, 2014. Accessed April 2015. http://www.globalwitness.org/deadlyenvironment/.

15. Rudolf, John Collins. "Murder of Activists Raises Questions of Justice in Amazon." *New York Times*. May 28, 2011.

16. "Deadly Environment." Global Witness website.

17. Phillips, Tom. "Amazon Rainforest Activist Shot Dead." *The Guardian*. May 24, 2011.

18. Wallace, Scott. "Why Do Environmentalists Keep Getting Killed Around the World?" *Smithsonian*. February 2014.

19. Schuster, Henry. "Domestic Terror: Who's Most Dangerous?" CNN.com. http://www.cnn.com/2005/US/08/24/schuster.column/index.html.

20. Ibid. Pg. 46.

21. Plumer, Brad. "Eight Facts about Terrorism in the United States." The Washington Post website. April 16, 2013. http://www.washingtonpost.com/blogs/wonkblog/wp/2013/04/16/eight-facts-about-terrorism-in-the-united-states/.

22. Perliger, Arie. "Challengers from the Sidelines: Understanding America's Violent Far-Right." The Combating Terrorism Center at West Point website. November 2012. Accessed April 2015. https://www.ctc.usma.edu/wp-content/uploads/2013/01/ChallengersFromtheSidelines.pdf. Pg. 87.

23. Ibid. Pg. 86.

24. Ibid. Pg. 105–06.

25. Potter, Will. "If Right-Wing Violence is up 400%, Why is the FBI Targeting Environmentalists?" Green Is the New Red website. January 18, 2013. Accessed April 2015. http://www.greenisthenewred.com/blog/right-wing-violence-increase-west-point-study/6704/.

26. Potter, Will. Green Is the New Red: An Insider's Account of a Social Movement Under Siege. San Francisco: City Lights Books, 2011. Pg. 47.

27. Schuster. "Domestic Terror: Who's Most Dangerous?" CNN.com.

28. "'If a Tree Falls': New Documentary on Daniel McGowan, Earth Liberation Front, and Green Scare." Democracy Now! website. Accessed April 2015. http://www.democracynow.org/2011/6/21/if_a_tree_falls_new_documentary.

29. If a Tree Falls: A Story of the Earth Liberation Front. A film by Marshall Curry. 2011.

30. Ibid.

31. Merlan, Anna. "Daniel McGowan: The FBI's Least Wanted." The Village Voice website. September 25, 2013. Accessed April 2015. http://www.villagevoice.com/2013-09-25/news/fbi-least-wanted-daniel-mcgowan-environmental-liberation-front-operation-backfire-domestic-terrorism/.

32. "EXCLUSIVE: Animal Rights Activist Jailed at Secretive Prison Gives First Account of Life Inside a 'CMU.'" Democracy Now! website. June 25, 2009. Accessed April 2015. http://www.democracynow.org/2009/6/25/exclusive_animal_rights_activist_jailed_at.

33. Potter, Will. "'Animal Enterprise Terrorism 101' in Herbivore Magazine." Green Is the New Red website. November 17, 2007. Accessed April 2015. http://www.greenisthenewred.com/blog/aeta-101/313/.

34. "The Animal Enterprise Terrorism Act (AETA)." Center for Constitutional Rights website. November 19, 2007. Accessed April 2015. http://ccrjustice.org/learn-more/faqs/factsheet%3A-animal-enterprise-terrorism-act-%28aeta%29.

35. Pilkington, Ed. "Animal Rights 'Terrorists'? Legality of Industry-Friendly Law to Be Challenged." The Guardian website. February 19, 2015. Accessed March 2015. http://www.theguardian.com/us-news/2015/feb/19/animal-rights-activists-challenge-federal-terrorism-charges.

36. Potter. "'Animal Enterprise Terrorism 101.'" Green Is the New Red website.

37. "The Animal Enterprise Terrorism Act (AETA)." Center for Constitutional Rights website.

38. Kuipers, Dean. "Lawsuit Challenges Animal Enterprise Terror Law as Unconstitutional." Los Angeles Times. December 15, 2011.

39. "U.S. v. SHAC 7." Center for Constitutional Rights website. October 2011. Accessed April 2015. http://ccrjustice.org/us-v-SHAC7.

40. Pilkington. "Animal Rights 'Terrorists'?" The Guardian.

41. Ibid.

42. "Ag-Gag Bills at the State Level." The American Society for the Prevention of Cruelty to Animals (US) website. Accessed April 2015. https://www.aspca.org/fight-cruelty/advocacy-center/ag-gag-whistleblower-suppression-legislation/ag-gag-bills-state-level.

43. "Debate: After Activists Covertly Expose Animal Cruelty, Should They be Targeted with 'Ag-Gag' Laws?" Democracy Now! website. April 9, 2013. Accessed April 2015. http://www.democracynow.org/2013/4/9/debate_after_activists_covertly_expose_animal.

44. "United States of ALEC." Moyers & Company website. September 28, 2012. Accessed April 2015. http://billmoyers.com/segment/united-states-of-alec/.

45. Robberson, Tod. "'Animal Ecological Terrorism Act' Seeks to Protect Agricultural Abusers." The Dallas Morning News website. April 10, 2013. http://dallasmorningviewsblog.dallasnews.com/2013/04/animal -ecological-terrorism-act-seeks-to-protect-agricultural-abuses.html/.

46. "Why Did the FBI Label Ryan Shapiro's Dissertation on Animal Rights a Threat to National Security?" Democracy Now! website. March 25, 2014. Accessed April 2015. http://www.democracynow.org/2014/3/25 /why_did_the_fbi_label_ryan.

47. "Deception for Journalism's Sake: A Database. Undercover Reporting." New York University Digital Library website. Accessed April 2015. http://dlib.nyu.edu/undercover/archive/clusters.

48. Kroeger, Brooke. "IRE Journal—'Undercover Reporting: An American Tradition.'" Brooke Kroeger website. Spring 2014. Accessed April 2015. http://brookekroeger.com/ire-journal-undercover-reporting-an-american -tradition/.

49. Bittman, Mark. "Who Protects the Animals?" The New York Times website. April 26, 2011. http://opinionator.blogs.nytimes.com/2011/04/26/who-protects-the-animals/?_r=2.

50. Paden, Dan. "Giving Farmed-Animal Abusers Their Due." Common Dreams website. July 16, 2009. Accessed April 2015. http://www.commondreams.org/views/2009/07/16/giving-farmed-animal-abusers-their-due.

51. Oppel, Richard. "Taping of Farm Cruelty Is Becoming the Crime." The New York Times website. April 6, 2013. http://www.nytimes.com/2013/04/07/us/taping-of-farm-cruelty-is-becoming-the-crime .html?pagewanted=all&_r=2&.

52. "Debate: After Activists Covertly Expose Animal Cruelty?" Democracy Now! website.

53. Genoways, Ted. "Gagged by Big Ag." Mother Jones website. July/August 2013. Accessed April 2015. http://www.motherjones.com/environment/2013/06/ag-gag-laws-mowmar-farms.

54. "Green Scare: Animal Rights Activists Face Terrorism Charges for Freeing Minks from Fur Farm." Democracy Now! website. July 15, 2014. Accessed April 2015. http://www.democracynow.org/2014/7/15/green_scare _animal_rights_activists_face.

55. "AG Communicator Emily Meredith Honored as 30 & Under 'Rising PR Star.'" National Milk Producers Federation website. December 9, 2014. Accessed April 2015. http://www.nmpf.org/latest-news/press-releases /dec-2014/ag-communicator-emily-meredith-honored-30-under-%E2%80%98rising-pr-star%E2%80%99.

56. "Ag 101: Demographics." U.S. Environmental Protection Agency website. Accessed April 2015. http://www.epa.gov/agriculture/ag101/demographics.html.

57. Zacharias, Nil. "It's Time to End Factory Farming," The Huffington Post website. October 19, 2011. http://www.huffingtonpost.com/nil-zacharias/its-time-to-end-factory-f_b_1018840.html.

58. "Howard on 'The Oprah Winfrey Show' April 15th, 1996 (show segment transcript)." Mad Cowboy website. Accessed April 2015. http://www.madcowboy.com/02_OP_Transcript.000.html.

59. Robbins, John. The Food Revolution. San Francisco: Conari Press, 2010. Pg. 147.

60. Ibid.

61. Lyman, Howard F. Mad Cowboy: Plain Truth from the Cattle Rancher Who Won't Eat Meat. New York: Touchstone Books, 1998. Pg. 15.

62. Robbins. The Food Revolution. Pg. 147.

63. "Food-Disparagement Laws: State Civil & Criminal Statutes." Food Speak: Coalition for Free Speech website. March 19, 1998. Accessed March 2015. https://www.cspinet.org/foodspeak/laws/existlaw.htm.

64. "Change Food Libel Laws to Allow Us to Know the Truth About Our Food." Change.org website. Accessed March 2015. https://www.change.org/p/change-food-libel-laws-to-allow-us-to-know-the-truth-about-our- food.

65. Lyman. Mad Cowboy. Pg. 19.

66. Robbins. The Food Revolution. Pg. 148.

67. Mad Cowboy: The Documentary. A film by Michael Tobias. 2005.

68. "Food-Disparagement Laws." Food Speak: Coalition for Free Speech website.

CHAPTER EIGHT

1. Sanghani, Radhika. "Chickens 'Cleverer than Toddlers,'" The Telegraph website. June 19, 2013. http://www.telegraph.co.uk/news/science/science-news/10129124/Chickens-cleverer-than-toddlers.html.

2. "The Prayer Flag Tradition." PrayerFlags.com website. Accessed April 2015. http://www.prayerflags.com /download/article.pdf.

3. Tuttle, Will. *The World Peace Diet: Eating for Spiritual Health and Social Harmony*. New York: Lantern Books, 2005. Pg. 10–11.

4. Hedges, Chris. "All Forms of Life Are Sacred." Truthdig website. January 4, 2015. http://www.truthdig.com/report/item/all_forms_of_life_are_sacred_20150104.

5. Colb, Sherry F. *Mind If I Order the Cheeseburger? And Other Questions People Ask Vegans*. New York: Lantern Books, 2013. Pg. 53.

6. "Gary Francione: Animal Advocate.'" The Believer website. February 2011. Accessed April 2015. http://www.believermag.com/issues/201102/?read=interview_francione.

7. Lohan, Tara. "Got Milk? A Disturbing Look at the Dairy Industry." Alternet.com website. January 25, 2010. Accessed April 2015. http://www.alternet.org/story/145378/got_milk_a_disturbing_look_at_the_dairy _industry.

8. "Why Would Anyone Choose a Dairy Free Diet?" Healthy Vegan Weight Loss website. Accessed April 2015. http://www.vegan-weight-loss.com/dairy-free-diet.html.

9. Tuttle. *The World Peace Diet*. Pg. 117.

10. Colb. *Mind If I Order the Cheeseburger?* Pg. 42.

11. Tuttle. *The World Peace Diet*. Pg. 117.

12. "Colleen Patrick-Goudreau: Debunking the Myths of Veganism." YouTube video, posted by PacificVegan. April 24, 2013. https://www.youtube.com/watch?v=od_cqvr-ueY.

13. Lohan. "Got Milk?" Alternet.com website.

14. Colb. *Mind If I Order the Cheeseburger?* Pg. 42.

15. Tuttle. *The World Peace Diet*. Pg. 118.

16. "Factory Farming: Cows." Farm Sanctuary website. Accessed April 2015. http://www.farmsanctuary.org /learn/factory-farming/dairy/.

17. Colb. *Mind If I Order the Cheeseburger?* Pg. 43.

18. Ibid. Pg. 42.

19. Marcus, Erik. *Vegan: The New Ethics of Eating*. Ithaca, NY: McBooks Press, 2001. Pg. 102.

20. Tuttle. *The World Peace Diet*. Pg.126.

21. Marcus. *Vegan: The New Ethics of Eating*. Pg. 104.

22. Tuttle. *The World Peace Diet*. Pg. 125.

23. "In the Belly of the Beast." Rolling Stone website. 2013. http://www.rollingstone.com/feature/belly-beast -meat-factory-farms-animal-activists.

24. Friedrich, Bruce. "The Cruelest of All Factory Farm Products: Eggs from Caged Hens." Huffington Post website. January 14, 2013. http://www.huffingtonpost.com/bruce-friedrich/eggs-from-caged -hens_b_2458525.html; "In the Belly of the Beast." Rolling Stone website.

25. Colb. *Mind If I Order the Cheeseburger?* Pg. 45.

26. Tuttle. *The World Peace Diet*. Pg. 126.

27. Colb. *Mind If I Order the Cheeseburger?* Pg. 45.

28. Tuttle. *The World Peace Diet*. Pg. 126.

29. Ibid. Pg. 128.

30. Bjerklie, Steve. "Fowl Play." *Sonoma County Independent*. Metro Active. May 15, 1997.

31. "What's Wrong with Backyard Eggs?" PeacefulPrairie.org website. Accessed April 2015. http://www.peacefulprairie.org/backyard-eggs.html.

32. Colb. *Mind If I Order the Cheeseburger?* Pg. 46.

33. Francione, Gary L., and Anna Charlton. *Eat Like You Care: An Examination of the Morality of Eating Animals.* Charleston, SC: Exempla Press, 2013. Pg. 80.

34. Colb. *Mind If I Order the Cheeseburger?* Pg. 75.

CHAPTER NINE

1. "Health Concerns About Dairy Products." Physicians Committee for Responsible Medicine website. Accessed April 2015. http://pcrm.org/health/diets/vegdiets/health-concerns-about-dairy-products; Hicks, Cherrill. "Give up Dairy Products to Beat Cancer." The Telegraph website. June 2, 2014. http://www.telegraph.co.uk /foodanddrink/healthyeating/10868428/Give-up-dairy-products-to-beat-cancer.html.

2. Davidson, Garry. "Milk & Dairy for Guys with Man Boobs." Chest Sculpting website. Accessed April 2015. http://chestsculpting.com/milk-and-dairy-for-guys-with-man-boobs/; Renehan, Andrew G. "Insulin-like Growth Factor (IGF)-I, IGF Binding Protein-3, and Cancer Risk: Systematic Review and Meta-Regression Analysis." US National Library of Medicine National Institutes of Health website. April 24, 2004. http://www.ncbi.nlm.nih.gov/pubmed/15110491?dobt=Abstract.

3. Lohan, Tara. "Got Milk?: A Disturbing Look at the Dairy Industry." Alternet website. January 25, 2010. Accessed April 2015. http://www.alternet.org/story/145378/got_milk_a_disturbing_look_at_the_dairy _industry.

4. "Colleen Patrick-Goudreau: Debunking the Myths of Veganism." YouTube video, posted by PacificVegan. April 24, 2013. Accessed April 2015. https://www.youtube.com/watch?v=od_cqvr-ueY.

5. Fuhrman, Joel. *Eat to Live: The Amazing Nutrient-Rich Program for Fast and Sustained Weight Loss.* New York: Little, Brown, 2011. Pg. 145.

6. Dhanwal, Dinesh, et al. "Epidemiology of Hip Fracture: Worldwide Geographic Variation." US National Library of Medicine National Institute of Health website. Jan.–Mar. 2011. http://www.ncbi.nlm.nih.gov/pmc/articles/PMC3004072/.

7. Campbell, Colin T., and Thomas M. Campbell II. *The China Study: The Most Comprehensive Study of Nutrition Ever Conducted.* Dallas, TX: Benbella Books, 2006. Pg. 204.

8. Fuhrman. *Eat to Live.* Pg. 136.

9. Ibid. Pg. 137.

10. Campbell and Campbell. *The China Study.* Pg. 205.

11. Brody, Jane. "Exploring a Low-Acid Diet for Bone Health." The New York Times website. November 23, 2009. http://www.nytimes.com/2009/11/24/health/24brod.html?_r=1&.

12. Davis, Brenda, and Vesanto Melina. *Becoming Vegan: The Complete Guide to Adopting a Healthy Plant-based Diet.* Summertown, TN: Book Publishing Company. 2000. Pg. 93.

13. Brody. "Exploring a Low-Acid Diet for Bone Health." The New York Times website.

14. Davis and Melina. *Becoming Vegan.* Pg. 94.

15. Campbell and Campbell. *The China Study.* Pg. 206.

16. Ibid. Pg. 207.

17. "Absorption/Utilization Issues." National Dairy Council website. Accessed Aprl 2015. http://www.nationaldairycouncil.org/SiteCollectionDocuments/health_wellness/dairy_nutrients /CalciumAbsorptionpdf.pdf.

18. Fuhrman. *Eat to Live.* Pg. 133.

19. Campbell and Campbell. *The China Study.* Pg. 21.

20. Parker-Pope, Tara. "Nutrition Advice from the China Study." The New York Times website. January 7, 2011. http://well.blogs.nytimes.com/2011/01/07/nutrition-advice-from-the-china-study/?_r=0.

21. Brody, Jane. "Huge Study of Diet Indicts Fat and Meat." The New York Times website. May 8, 1990. http://www.nytimes.com/1990/05/08/science/huge-study-of-diet-indicts-fat-and-meat. html?scp=8&sq=%22T.%20Colin%20Campbell%22&st=cse.

22. Cornell University. "China-Cornell-Oxford Project." Wayback Machine Internet Archive website. Accessed April 2015. http://web.archive.org/web/20090223222003/http://www.nutrition.cornell.edu/ChinaProject/.

23. Brody. "Huge Study of Diet Indicts Fat and Meat." The New York Times website.

24. Campbell and Campbell. *The China Study.* Pg. 73.

25. Brody. "Huge Study of Diet Indicts Fat and Meat." The New York Times website.

26. Campbell and Campbell. *The China Study.* Pg. 77.

27. Ibid. Pg. 80.

28. Ibid. Pg. 77.

29. "Heart Disease and Stroke Statistics—At-a-Glance." American Heart Association (Heart.org) website. December 17, 2014. Accessed April 2015. http://www.heart.org/idc/groups/ahamah-public/@wcm/@sop/@ smd/documents/downloadable/ucm_470704.pdf.

30. Robbins, John. *The Food Revolution.* San Francisco: Conari Press, 2010. Pg. 16–7.

31. "Saturated Fats." American Heart Association (Heart.org) website. January 12, 2015. Accessed April 2015. http://www.heart.org/HEARTORG/GettingHealthy/NutritionCenter/HealthyEating/Saturated-Fats _UCM_301110_Article.jsp.

32. "History of the Framingham Heart Study." Framingham Heart Study website. Accessed April 2015. https:// www.framinghamheartstudy.org/about-fhs/history.php.

33. Robbins. *The Food Revolution.* Pg. 21.

34. Campbell and Campbell. *The China Study.* Pg. 79.

35. Robbins. *The Food Revolution.* Pg. 21.

36. "Hospital Rankings." US News (Health) website. Accessed April 2015. http://health.usnews.com/best-hospitals/rankings/cardiology-and-heart-surgery.

37. Esselstyn, Caldwell. "More than Coronary Artery Disease (continued)—Making the Change." Dr. Esselstyn website. Accessed April 2015. http://www.dresselstyn.com/morethan04_change.htm.

38. Robbins. *The Food Revolution.* Pg. 21.

39. Campbell and Campbell. *The China Study.* Pg. 126.

40. Esselstyn, Caldwell B., S. G. Ellis, S. V. Medendorp, et al. "A Strategy to Arrest and Reverse Coronary Artery Disease: A 5-Year Longitudinal Study of a Single Physician's Practice." *Journal of Family Practice* 41 (1995): 560–8.

41. Campbell and Campbell. *The China Study.* Pg. 126–7.

42. "Position of American Dietetic Association on Vegetarian Diets." *Journal of the American Dietetic Association* 97 (1997): 1317–21.

43. Campbell and Campbell. *The China Study.* Pg. 79.

44. Ibid. Pg. 48.

45. Ibid. Pg. 48–9.

46. Ibid. Pg. 50.

47. Doll, Richard, and Richard Peto. "The Causes of Cancer: Quantitative Estimates of Avoidable Risks of Cancer in the United States Today." *Journal of the National Cancer Institute* 66 (1981): 1192–1265.

48. "Colleen Patrick-Goudreau: Debunking the Myths of Veganism." YouTube video; "Colleen Patrick-Goudreau: Author, Speaker, Joyful Vegan." Joyful Vegan website. Accessed April 2015. www.joyfulvegan.com.

49. Howley, E. T., and Dixie L. Thompson. *Fitness Professional's Handbook, Sixth Edition.* Knoxville, TN: Human Kinetics, 2012. Pg. 94.

50. Davis and Melina. *Becoming Vegan.* Pg. 41.

51. Ibid. Pg. 40.

52. Ibid. Pg. 42.

53. Fuhrman. *Eat to Live.* Pg. 92.

54. Davis and Melina. *Becoming Vegan.* Pg. 48.

55. Ibid. Pg. 46–7.

56. O'Connor, Anahad. "Fish Oil Claims not Supported by Research." The New York Times website. March 30, 2015. Accessed April 2015. http://well.blogs.nytimes.com/2015/03/30/fish-oil-claims-not-supported-by -research/?_r=0.

57. Ibid.

58. Ibid.

59. Tuttle, Will. *The World Peace Diet*. New York: Lantern Books, 2005. Pg. 98–9.

60. "Think Fish Is a Health Food? Think Again." Accessed April 2015. PETA website. http://www.peta.org/living/food/think-fish-health-food/.

61. Novick, Jeff. "The Myth of Complementary Protein." Jeff Novick website. March 28, 2012. Accessed April 2015. http://www.jeffnovick.com/RD/Articles/Entries/2012/3/28_The_Myth_Of_Complimenting_Proteins.html.

62. Lappé, Frances Moore. *Diet for a Small Planet*. New York: Ballantine Books, 1981. Pg. 162.

63. Campbell and Campbell. *The China Study*. Pg. 30.

64. Davis and Melina. *Becoming Vegan*. Pg. 121.

65. Ibid. Pg. 123.

66. Ibid. Pg. 122.

67. Ibid. Pg. 121.

68. McBride, Judy. "B12 Deficiency May Be More Widespread Than Thought." United States Department of Agriculture website. August 2, 2000. Accessed April 2015. http://www.ars.usda.gov/is/pr/2000/000802.htm.

69. Davis and Melina. *Becoming Vegan*. Pg. 130.

70. Ibid. Pg. 108–10.

71. Ibid. Pg. 106.

72. Ibid. Pg. 113.

73. Brown, Elizabeth Nolan. "Omega 3's: 8 Vegetarian Ways to Sneak More into Your Diet." The Huffington Post website. February 26, 2012. http://www.huffingtonpost.com/2012/02/26/omega-3-vegetarian-vegan_n_1299283.html.

74. Holick, Michael, and Tai Chen. "Vitamin D Deficiency: A Worldwide Problem with Health Consequences." The American Journal of Clinical Nutrition website. April 2008. http://ajcn.nutrition.org/content/87/4/1080S.long.

75. Davis and Melina. *Becoming Vegan*. Pg. 138.

76. "Top 10 Foods Highest in Vitamin D." HealthAliciousNess.com website. Accessed April 2015. http://www.healthaliciousness.com/articles/high-vitamin-D-foods.php.

77. Davis and Melina. *Becoming Vegan*. Pg. 134.

78. Ibid. Pg. 133.

79. Ibid. Pg. 134.

80. Barnard, Neal. "Breaking the Food Seduction." Physicians Committee for Responsible Medicine website. Accessed April 2015. http://www.pcrm.org/shop/byNealBarnard/breaking-the-food-seduction.

81. "Position of the America Dietetic Association and Dietitians of Canada: Vegetarian Diets." American Dietetic Association. 2003. http://www.ncbi.nlm.nih.gov/pubmed/12826028.

82. "Colleen Patrick-Goudreau: Debunking the Myths of Veganism." YouTube video.

CHAPTER TEN

1. "Earthworks Passive Solar Greenhouse." Wayne State University website. Accessed April 2015. http://clas.wayne.edu/seedwayne/Earthworks-Passive-Solar-Greenhouse.

2. "Mission." Earthworks Urban Farm website. Accessed April 2015. http://www.cskdetroit.org/EWG/about_us/mission.

3. Dabovich, Melanie. "Veganic Farmers Work Without Animal Fertilizers." USA Today website. June 18, 2008. Accessed April 2015. http://usatoday30.usatoday.com/money/economy/2008-06-18-678220175_x.htm; "Veganic Farming and Gardening." Woodstock Farm Sanctuary website. Accessed April 2015. http://woodstocksanctuary.org/learn-3/global-environment-issues/veganic-farming-and-gardening/.

4. "Veganic Farming and Gardening." Woodstock Farm Sanctuary website.

5. Dabovich. "Veganic Farmers Work Without Animal Fertilizers." USA Today website.

6. "Food-Veganic Agriculture." Huguenot Street Farm website. Accessed April 2015. http://www.huguenotfarm.com/food.php#veganic.

7. "Veganic Farming and Gardening." Woodstock Farm Sanctuary website.

8. "Beetle Banks." Game & Wildlife Conservation Trust website. Accessed April 2015. http://www.gwct.org.uk/farming/advice/sustainable-farming/beetle-banks/.

9. "Making t/ Connection Chp 5 Farming." YouTube video. Posted by the Vegan Society. November 3, 1010. Accessed April 2015. https://www.youtube.com/watch?v=-bp2-bsRaow.

10. Dabovich. "Veganic Farmers Work Without Animal Fertilizers." USA Today website.

11. Bohanec, Hope. *The Ultimate Betrayal: Is There Happy Meat?* iUniverse, 2013. Pg. 190.

12. Pieters, Adrian. "Green Manuring: Principles and Practice." U.S. Department of Agriculture report, Sustainable Farmer website. 1927. Accessed April 2015. http://sustainablefarmer.net/pdflibrary/library -greenmanuring.pdf.

13. "Frequently Asked Questions." World Population Balance website. Accessed April 2015. http://www.worldpopulationbalance.org/faq.

14. "Benefits of Soy." National Soybean Research Laboratory website. Accessed April 2015. http://nsrl.illinois.edu /content/benefits-soy.

15. "Human Numbers Through Time." NOVA Science Programming on Air and Online website. Accessed April 2015. http://www.pbs.org/wgbh/nova/worldbalance/numb-nf.html.

16. Based on a rough average of 0.75 gallons of water and 3 pounds of food per day.

17. Based on a rough average of 30 gallons of water and 90 pounds of feed per day.

18. Holt-Gimenez, Eric. "We Already Grow Enough Food for 10 Billion People . . . And Still Can't End Hunger." Common Dreams website. May 8, 2012. Accessed April 2015. http://commondreams.org/views/2012/05/08 /we-already-grow-enough-food-10-billion-people-and-still-cant-end-hunger; Tuttle, Will. "Plants Feel Pain Too? What's a Vegan to Do?" The World Peace Diet website. October 26, 2014. Accessed April 2015. http://www.worldpeacediet.com/2014/10/plants-feel-pain-too-whats-a-vegan-to-do/.

19. Shah, Anup. "Beef." Global Issues website. Accessed April 2015. http://www.globalissues.org/article/240/beef.

20. "Did You Know?" Wisconsin Soybean website. Accessed April 2015. http://www.wisoybean.org/news/soybean _facts.php.

21. Oppenlander, Richard. "Blog: The World Hunger-Food Choice Connection: A Summary." Comfortably Unaware website. April 22, 2012. Accessed April 2015. http://comfortablyunaware.com/blog/the-world -hunger-food-choice-connection-a-summary/.

22. Pimental, D., and M. Pimental. "Sustainability of Meat-Based and Plant-Based Diets and the Environment." *American Journal of Clinical Nutrition* 78, no. 3 (2003): pp. 660S–663S; Reijnders, L., and S. Soret. "Quantification of the Environmental Impact of Different Dietary Protein Choices." *American Journal of Clinical Nutrition* 78, no. 3 (2003): pp. 664–8.

23. Oppenlander. "Blog: The World Hunger-Food Choice Connection." Comfortably Unaware website.

24. Robbins, John. *The Food Revolution.* San Francisco: Conari Press, 2010. Pg. 285.

25. Rudarakanchana, Nat. "China Absorbs Wheat: Imports Skyrocket 5000% For December 2013." International Business Times website. February 4, 2014. Accessed April 2015. http://www.ibtimes.com/china-absorbs-wheat -imports-skyrocket-5000-december-2013-1553185.

26. Lucas, Jake. "Chinese Grain Imports to Strain World Food Supply-Expert." Thomson Reuters Foundation website. October 18, 2013. Accessed April 2015. http://www.trust.org/item/20131018112455-p601w.

27. "Biography of Lester Brown." Earth Policy Institute website. Accessed Aprl 2015. http://www.earth-policy.org /about_epi/C32.

28. Lucas, Jake. "Chinese Grain Imports to Strain World Food Supply-Expert." Thomson Reuters Foundation website. October 18, 2013. Accessed April 2015.

29. Brown, L. "China's Water Shortage Could Shake World Grain Markets." Worldwatch Press Release. April 22, 1998; "Falling Water Tables in China May Soon Raise Food Prices Everywhere." Worldwatch. May 2, 2000.

30. Robbins, John. *The Food Revolution.* San Francisco: Conari Press. 2010. Pg. 286–8.

31. "Global Hunger-News." Bread for the World website. Accessed April 2015. http://blog.bread.org/global -hunger/.

32. Halweil, Brian. "United States Leads World Meat Stampede." Worldwatch Issues Paper. July 2, 1998.

33. Cohen, Joel E. *How Many People Can the Earth Support?* New York: WW Norton. 1995. Pg. 54.

34. Block, Ben. "UN Raises 'Low' Population Projections for 2050." WorldWatch Institute website. 2013. Accessed April 2015. http://www.worldwatch.org/node/6038.

35. "Population of the Entire World, Yearly, 1950-2100." Geohive website. 2012. Accessed April 2015. http://www.geohive.com/earth/his_history3.aspx.

36. Motavelli, Jim. "Paul and Anne Ehrlich: The Countdown Continues on the Population Bomb." *E—The Environmental Magazine.* Nov/Dec 1996. Pg. 10–12.

37. Marcus, Erik. *Vegan: The New Ethics of Eating.* Ithaca, NY: McBooks Press. 2001. Pg. 164.

38. Kendall, Henry W., and David Pimental. "Constraints on the Expansion of the Global Food Supply." *Ambio* 23, no. 3 (May 1994): p198–205.

39. Ibid.

40. "Meatonomics: The Bizarre Economics of Meat and Dairy." Meatonomics website. Accessed April 2015. www.meatonomics.com.

41. Anderson, Will. *This Is Hope: Green Vegans and the New Human Ecology.* Winchester, U.K.: Earth Books. 2012. Pg. 43.

42. Harper, A. Breeze. *Sistah Vegan: Black Female Vegans Speak on Food Identity, Health, and Society.* New York: Lantern Books. 2010. Pg. 21.

43. "About." Beyond Meat website. Accessed April 2015. http://beyondmeat.com/about.

44. Bessante, Chanelle. "10 Questions: Ethan Brown, CEO, Beyond Meat." Fortune.com website. January 31, 2014. Accessed April 2015. http://fortune.com/2014/01/31/10-questions-ethan-brown-ceo-beyond-meat/.

45. Ibid.

CHAPTER ELEVEN

1. "Myth vs. Reality." EarthSave website. Accessed April 2015. http://earthsave.org/pdf/ofof2006.pdf.

2. "Crop Yield Verification." Gardens of Eden website. Accessed April 2015. http://www.gardensofeden.org/04%20Crop%20Yield%20Verification.htm; Aldridge, Tom, and Herb Schluback. "Water Requirements for Food Production." *Soil and Water* 38 (Fall 1978). University of California Cooperative Extension. 13017; Ehrlich, Paul, and Anne Ehrlich. *Population, Resources, Environment.* San Francisco: Freemna, 1972. Pg. 75–6.

3. "Dietary Greenhouse Gas Emissions of Meat-Eaters, Fish-Eaters, Vegetarians and Vegans in the UK." Climatic Change. 2014. http://link.springer.com/article/10.1007%2Fs10584-014-1169-1/fulltext.html.

4. "Sustainability of Meat-Based and Plant-Based Diets and the Environment." *The American Journal of Clinical Nutrition.* 2003. http://ajcn.nutrition.org/content/78/3/660S.full.

5. Ibid.

6. "Myth vs. Reality." EarthSave website.

7. "Water Footprint Assessment." University of Twente, the Netherlands. http://waterfootprint.org/en/water-footprint/; "Measuring the daily destruction of the world's rainforests." *Scientific America.* 2009; http://www.scientificamerican.com/article/earth-talks-daily-destruction/; "Dietary Greenhouse Gas Emissions of Meat-Eaters, Fish-Eaters, Vegetarians and Vegans in the UK." Climatic Change. 2014; Oppenlander, Richard A. *Food Choice and Sustainability.* Minneapolis, MN: Langdon Street, 2013; "Meat-Eater's Guide to Climate Change and Health." The Environmental Working Group. http://static.ewg.org/reports/2011/meateaters/pdf/methodology_ewg_meat_eaters_guide_to_health_and_climate_2011.pdf.

8. Chang, Elliot. "Infographic: How Much It Would Cost for the Entire Planet to Switch to Renewable Energy." Inhabitat website. September 24, 2013. Accessed April 2015. http://inhabitat.com/infographic-how-much-would-it-cost-for-the-entire-planet-to-switch-to-renewable-energy/.

9. "The Role of Livestock in Climate Change." Food and Agriculture Organization of the United Nations. Accessed April 2015. http://www.fao.org/agriculture/lead/themes0/climate/en/.

10. Bauer, Susanne, et al. "Improved Attribution of Climate Forcing to Emissions." Science Magazine website. October 30, 2009. Accessed April 2015. http://www.sciencemag.org/content/326/5953/716.figures-only.

SELECTED BIBLIOGRAPHY

Anderson, Will. *This Is Hope: Green Vegans and the New Human Ecology.* Winchester, UK: Earth Books, 2012.

Bohanec, Hope. *The Ultimate Betrayal: Is There Happy Meat?* iUniverse, 2013.

Campbell, Colin T., and Thomas M. Campbell II. *The China Study: The Most Comprehensive Study of Nutrition Ever Conducted.* Dallas, TX. Benbella Books, 2006.

Cohen, Joel E. *How Many People Can the Earth Support?* New York: WW Norton, 1995.

Colb, Sherry F. *Mind If I Order the Cheeseburger? And Other Questions People Ask Vegans.* New York: Lantern Books, 2013.

Davis, Brenda and Vesanto Melina. *Becoming Vegan: The Complete Guide to Adopting a Healthy Plant-based Diet.* Summertown, TN: Book Publishing Company, 2000.

Eisnitz, Gail. *Slaughterhouse.* Amherst, NY: Prometheus Books, 2007.

Foer, Jonathan Safran. *Eating Animals.* New York: Back Bay Books, 2009.

Francione, Gary L., and Anna Charlton. *Eat Like You Care: An Examination of the Morality of Eating Animals.* Charleston, SC: Exempla Press, 2013.

Fuhrman, Joel. *Eat to Live: The Amazing Nutrient-Rich Program for Fast and Sustained Weight Loss.* New York: Little, Brown, 2011.

Goodall, Jane. *Harvest for Hope.* New York: Warner Wellness, 2005.

Harper, A. Breeze. *Sistah Vegan: Black Female Vegans Speak on Food, Identity, Health, and Society.* New York: Lantern Books, 2010.

Howley, E. T., and Dixie L. Thompson. *Fitness Professional's Handbook, Sixth Edition.* Knoxville, TN: Human Kinetics, 2012.

Imhoff, Daniel, ed. *CAFO.* San Rafael: Earth Aware, 2010.

Kolbert, Elizabeth. *The Sixth Extinction: An Unnatural History*. New York: Henry Holt, 2014.

Lappé, Frances Moore. *Diet for a Small Planet*. New York: Ballantine Books, 1981.

Lyman, Howard. *Mad Cowboy: Plain Truth from the Cattle Rancher Who Won't Eat Meat*. New York: Touchstone, 1998.

Marcus, Erik. *Vegan: The New Ethics of Eating*. Ithaca, NY: McBooks Press, 2001.

Oppenlander, Richard A. *Comfortably Unaware: What We Choose to Eat Is Killing Us and Our Planet*. New York: Beaufort Books, 2012.

———. *Food Choice and Sustainability: Why Buying Local, Eating Less Meat, and Taking Baby Steps Won't Work*. Minneapolis, MN: Langdon Street Press, 2013.

Pachirat, Timothy. *Every Twelve Seconds: Industrialized Slaughter and the Politics of Sight*. New Haven, CT: Yale University Press, 2011.

Potter, Will. *Green Is the New Red: An Insider's Account of a Social Movement Under Siege*. San Francisco: City Lights Books, 2011.

Ridgen, Bob. *The Economics of Pig Production*. Ipswich, UK: Farming Press Books, 1993.

Robbins, John. *The Food Revolution: How Your Diet Can Help Save Your Life and Our World*. San Francisco: Conari Press, 2010.

Schlosser, Eric. *Fast Food Nation*. New York: Perennial Books, 2002.

Taylor, L. *The Healing Power of Rainforest Herbs*. Garden City Park, NY: Square One Publishers, Inc, 2004.

Tuttle, Will. *The World Peace Diet: Eating for Spiritual Health and Social Harmony*. New York: Lantern Books, 2005.

INDEX